MENZIES TO KEATING

Menzies to Keating

The Development of the Australian Prime Ministership

GLYN DAVIS
JOHN HART
COLIN HUGHES
CLEM LLOYD
RUSSELL TROOD
JOHN UHR
JAMES WALTER
PATRICK WELLER *(editor)*

MELBOURNE UNIVERSITY PRESS
1992

First published 1992

Printed in Hong Kong
by Hing Yip Printing Co. Ltd.
for Melbourne University Press, Carlton, Victoria 3053

National Library of Australia Cataloguing-in-Publication entry

Menzies to Keating: the development of the Australian prime ministership

Bibliography.
Includes index.
ISBN 0 522 84498 7

1. Prime ministers — Australia. 2. Politicians — Australia. 3. Australia — Politics and government — 1945–. I. Weller, Patrick, 1944–.

354.940313

PREFACE

The idea and plan for this book had their origin with a similar work on the American Presidency, *Roosevelt to Reagan*, conceived and edited by Malcolm Shaw of Exeter University, England, and published in 1987. The publisher of that work, Christopher Hurst, thought the idea sufficiently good to extend to other polities, including Australia, and Professor Tom Millar, then director of the Menzies Centre for Australian Studies at London University, put him in touch with the authors. We appreciate the constructive facilitating role played by both of them.

Most of the chapters of the book, when in draft, were presented at a seminar organised by the Centre for Australian Public Sector Management, Griffith University, on 6 April 1991. The authors thank all the participants at that seminar for their comments on the draft chapters and their participation.

The book was typeset in the office of the Centre for Australian Public Sector Management. Marie Gehde and Patricia Gauvin set the text and coped with later amendments. Genevieve Essa and Emma Craswell assisted in proofreading the manuscript and preparing the bibliography and index. To them all I owe thanks for their patience and support.

Griffith University
Nathan, Queensland
April 1992

PATRICK WELLER

CONTENTS

Preface v

Notes on the Contributors ix

Introduction *Patrick Weller* 1

Chapter

1. Prime Ministers and Cabinet *Patrick Weller* 5

2. Prime Ministers and their Staff *James Walter* 28

3. Prime Ministers and Parties *Glyn Davis* 64

4. Prime Ministers and Parliament *John Uhr* 81

5. Prime Ministers and the Media *Clem Lloyd* 109

6. Prime Ministers and the Electorate *Colin A. Hughes* 138

7. Prime Ministers and Foreign Policy *Russell Trood* 156

8. An Australian President? A Comparative Perspective *John Hart* 183

9. The Development of the Australian Prime Ministership *Patrick Weller* 202

Select Bibliography 212

Index 220

CONTRIBUTORS

GLYN DAVIS is senior lecturer in politics and public policy at Griffith University. In 1989-92 he was a commissioner of the Public Sector Management Commission in Queensland. He is author of *Breaking Up the ABC* (1988) and co-author of *Public Policy in Australia* (1988).

JOHN HART is senior lecturer and head of the Department of Political Science at the Australian National University. He is author of *The Presidential Branch* (1987) and many articles on the American presidency.

COLIN HUGHES is professor of government at the University of Queensland. He is a commissioner of the Electoral and Administrative Review Commission and a former Australian Electoral Commissioner. He is the author of many works and articles on Queensland politics, most recently as co-editor of *Political Crossroads: the Queensland Election of 1989* (1991).

CLEM LLOYD is professor of journalism at the University of Wollongong. His books include *Out of the Wilderness: The Return of Labor* (1974) and *Press and Parliament* (1988).

RUSSELL TROOD is senior lecturer in international relations at Griffith University. He is director of the Centre for Asian-Australian Relations and the author of articles on Australian foreign policy.

JOHN UHR is senior lecturer in the Public Policy Program at the Australian National University. He has written widely on the Australian parliament, ethics in public life and the senior executive service.

JAMES WALTER is director of the Menzies Centre for Australian Studies at London University. He is on secondment from Griffith University where he is professor of Australian Studies. He is author of *The Leader: A Political Biography of Gough Whitlam* (1980) and *The Minister's Minders: Personal Advisers in National Government* (1986).

PATRICK WELLER is professor of politics and public policy at Griffith University. He is director of the Centre for Australian Public Sector Management and author of *First Among Equals: Prime Ministers in Westminster Systems* (1985) and *Malcolm Fraser PM* (1989).

INTRODUCTION

Patrick Weller

Ben Chifley, Labor prime minister from 1946 to 1949, was a skilled politician, an effective leader of a difficult team and an expert at drawing the best out of the bureaucrats who served him. If somehow he were to return to Canberra in 1991, over 40 years after he resigned, and to sit at the desk of Bob Hawke, a more recent Labor prime minister, would he instinctively still know how to do the job? Or has it changed beyond recognition, so that the skills required in 1949 and the challenges faced then are no preparation for the 1990s?

To put it another way, if John Hewson, as leader of the opposition, wants to prepare for the position of prime minister, could he draw lessons from the practices and experience of Robert Menzies in 1939, when he was sworn in as prime minister for the first time? Or is the task too different?

These essentially are the questions that this book seeks to answer. Of course there have been substantial physical and technological changes. Chifley would not recognise many of his physical surroundings. Canberra is now a larger city, the new Parliament House is a grander, more luxurious building, the range of government activities has expanded, the employees of the Commonwealth public sector have increased.

The technological changes would be even more noticeable — television, computers, telecommunications, satellites and rapid air travel have all altered the pace of political life. The constant media concentration on the position of the prime minister through 1991 and the speculation about, and reporting of, Hawke's decline and fall would be strange to a prime minister whose actions were reported primarily in the press, and who never had to face a television interview.

Other aspects of the job would appear familiar. Hawke's Labor Party is the same party as the one that Chifley led; its formal institutions have partially changed their representative structure, but the history remains constant. The Australian constitution, so restrictive it prevented Chifley's policy of bank nationalisation, has remained unchanged in all its essential features, even though a broader interpretation and developments in international law have extended the scope for federal action. The language of the Westminster system, however poorly that concept defines the workings of the political system, remains intact. Australian government remains cabinet government, collective in its wisdom; departments are headed by ministers who require parliamentary positions in the Senate or House of Representatives. Prime ministers must still face question time in the House. In terms of political institutions change may appear minimal.

But do changes in the ways those institutions work have an impact on the job of prime minister? Each author in this study was invited to address a set of questions similar to those in a study of the US presidency. All contributors were asked:

> What has been the nature of the change that has occurred in relation to their aspect of prime ministerial activities? Was change modest or rapid? Was it linear or oscillatory? Was there a watershed after which things were different? How did each of the prime ministers who served during the period contribute to such change as occurred?[1]

The emphasis is thus on the change and development of the *prime ministership*, rather than the activities of the individuals who held that position.

Within those general directions, authors were able to pursue the topic in their own way. The picture that emerges is one that mingles continuity and change. Some authors see the fundamental position as unaltered, even if the means to achieve those ends is different. In other areas there may be dramatic changes that have given prime ministers greater capacity to control political forces, that have allowed them to dominate the political agenda, or perhaps perversely, that have made them more vulnerable to removal by their own party. Thus the changes in relations with cabinet, party and parliament may appear small, while the capacity of the bureaucracy, access to the media and the ability to run foreign affairs more individually may have strengthened the hand of a prime minister.

The people who held the position of prime minister provide the raw data on which this analysis is based. Although it is not the purpose of the book to provide a series of sketches or condensed biographies, it is still worth giving a reminder of who the prime ministers were, what experience they had and how long they survived. If the two caretaker prime ministers (Frank Forde and John McEwen) who held office for a few days after the death of the incumbents in 1945 and 1967 are excluded, 11 people have held the position of prime minister since Menzies was first sworn into office in 1939. Their records are set out in Table 0.1.

Some very general comments can be made. The prime ministers are all men and, except for Fadden, drawn from the two major parties. For most of the period substantial parliamentary experience was a prerequisite for office. Menzies had been in the Victorian upper house before he was elected to federal parliament. Hawke is the obvious exception, although his 11 years as president of the Australian Council of Trade Unions and

1. These questions were drawn from those asked in Malcolm Shaw (ed.), *From Roosevelt to Reagan*, London: C. Hurst, 1987, p. 3.

his term as federal president of the ALP meant that he had a long record at the highest level of political life before he became a member of parliament. Of the 11 prime ministers who left office, only one did so at a time of his choosing — Menzies in 1966. Two died in office — Curtin in 1945 and Holt in 1967. Three were rejected by their own parties — Menzies in 1941, Gorton in 1971 and Hawke in 1991. Fadden was defeated on the floor of the House of Representatives. The other four — Chifley in 1949, McMahon in 1972, Whitlam in 1975 and Fraser in 1983 — were rejected by the electorate. Prime ministers, it seems, rarely give up office willingly; nor are they often able to survive for too long the vicissitudes of electoral fortunes and party faith. Defeat comes eventually in some guise.

Table 0.1. AUSTRALIAN PRIME MINISTERS

	Party	*Date of becoming PM*	*Age when sworn in*	*Years in federal parliament when became PM*	*Period in office (years/months)*
Robert Menzies (1)	UAP	1939	45	5	2/4
Arthur Fadden	CP	1941	46	5	-/1
John Curtin	ALP	1941	56	10	3/9
Ben Chifley	ALP	1945	60	8	4/5
Robert Menzies (2)	Lib	1949	55	15	16/1
Harold Holt	Lib	1966	58	31	1/11
John Gorton	Lib	1968	57	19	3/2
William McMahon	Lib	1971	63	22	1/9
Gough Whitlam	ALP	1972	56	20	2/11
Malcolm Fraser	Lib	1975	45	20	7/4
Robert Hawke	ALP	1983	54	3	8/9
Paul Keating	ALP	1991	47	22	

Seven years in an office as demanding and onerous as that of prime minister is a lengthy time. And three of the prime ministers survived at least that long. Even though history — or at least recent history — tends to remember the final image of defeated leaders, political analysts need to ask rather what use they made of their position, how they pulled the levers of power, what restrained them and what made them more or less effective.

This book therefore examines the position of prime ministers by exploring their relationships with the most important institutions of government: the cabinet that sits at the heart of government and which they chair; the party that elects and maintains prime ministers; the parliament to which prime ministers are accountable; the bureaucracy which aids and advises them; the electorate to whom prime ministers must appeal; the media which delivers and interprets their messages; and the world outside Australia which prime ministers must meet in their capacity as head of government. Then the position is put into a comparative perspective. The media have tended to emphasise the role of prime ministers, to give the leaders the aura of presidents. As a way of emphasising the power of prime ministers the comparison of prime ministers with presidents may be attractive; as an analytic tool it can be deceptive. Yet it is worth asking how the Australian prime ministership differs from the position of the US presidency, if only to appreciate better its strengths and weaknesses. Finally a concluding chapter draws out briefly those indications of continuity and change in an assessment of the development of the Australian prime ministership.

1

PRIME MINISTERS AND CABINET

Patrick Weller

Prime ministers must work with their ministerial colleagues and through the institution of cabinet. In Australia executive government is collective in its form and its expectations. The influence of the prime ministers and their impact on policy will depend on their capacity to cajole, persuade or bully cabinet colleagues — either individually or collectively — into accepting their approach or their solutions. To trace the impact of cabinet government on the position of the prime minister it is necessary to develop two lines of inquiry:

- how have the procedures of cabinet changed?
- what impact have those changes had on the relative positions of prime ministers and ministers?

The nature of cabinet government changed substantially in the last 40 years. That change is an alteration in the balance of influences, not in the status of cabinet. The formal position remains the same; cabinet is the forum in which the senior ministers, under the chairmanship of the prime minister, determine many of the crucial issues of the day — and others of less significance. Cabinet is a committee of politicians unrecognised by the constitution, but attributed by convention with the final authority of government. The distribution of power within cabinet depends in part on the personalities involved; that is inevitable in a forum where a group of the powerful mixes and debates.[1] The chemistry between individuals can never be forecast or interpreted as part of some trend.

But changes to the structure and workings of cabinet, and thus to the environment within which ministers have had to work, have also had a substantial impact on the balance of power. The workload of cabinet has increased; the complexity and interrelatedness of government functions have become more marked; the bureaucracy supporting the cabinet has become more substantial and sophisticated (even if in different forms); the use of committees has become more systematic; the rules that direct the behaviour of cabinet and the formulation of

1. For a summary of the debate, see Patrick Weller, *First Among Equals: Prime Ministers in Westminster Systems*, Sydney: Allen & Unwin, 1985, ch.1.

submissions have become more precise and more demanding. Consequently the controls over the proceedings and arrangements of cabinet have developed. The expectations and formal position remain massive. As more is expected of government, so the task of cabinet becomes more difficult.

In these changes prime ministers have been both architect and beneficiary. Some changes were deliberate attempts by prime ministers to change the machinery; in other cases they were the result of diligent and effective bureaucrats who wanted to streamline cabinet processes and make cabinet more orderly and manageable. But it needs to be stated that, from the available evidence, no Australian prime minister has shown a fascination with the processes of cabinet for their own sake; they are naturally more interested in the policy outcomes. Cabinet government is a means to an end. An effective system of cabinet government that functions smoothly is a necessary, if not sufficient, condition for political success. To that extent all prime ministers need to be interested in cabinet.

The Changing Workload

One means by which the impact of cabinet government can be judged is by an analysis of the workload. How far, under different prime ministers, has the nature of cabinet government changed? The figures in Table 1.1 (p.25) show some significant trends: a fairly regular increase in the number of meetings, business and decisions up to 1981 and then a decline that is almost as consistent. These figures are important in so far as they illustrate the degree to which prime ministers may want cabinet approval or support for decisions, rather than making them individually or, more frequently, in consultation with the relevant minister.

The growth in the total number of meetings and in business before 1983 is at times startling. But it is evident that it is not an *irreversible* trend. By the late 1980s the number of meetings and the sheer volume of business had returned to the level of the mid-1960s, even though the number of decisions remained more substantial. The contrast is particularly marked if the high point of cabinet activity, 1979, is contrasted with the July 1989–June 1990 figures: 436 meetings compared to 121; 2534 items of business compared to 560; 3037 decisions compared to 1110. In other words, the apparent activity had fallen by two-thirds. There were some cosmetic reasons for the changes; for instance, ministers were required to submit one budget submission covering all their programs, rather than individual submissions for each program. There is a danger in too easily assuming that statistics indicate a substantial change in style, rather

Table 1.1 CABINET AND COMMITTEES

		Meetings			Business				Decisions/Minutes					
Govt[1]		Cabinet	C'tees	Total[3]	Submissions	Memos	Items Without Submission[4]	Total	Total[5]	With Submission[6]	Without Submission[7]	Appointments	Endorse of C'tee Decisions[8]	Budget
Menzies	1950	50	108	158	237		5	242	456	451	5			
	1955	47	62	109	342		119	461	705	586	119			
	1960	57	81	138	463		165	28	589	424	165			
	1965	67	92	159	622		213	835	785	572	213			
	1970	68	73	141	615	114	285	1014	786	501	285			
McMahon	1971	56	106	162	561	130	304	995	747	443	304			
	1972	47	129	176	431	115	357	903	805	448	357			
Whitlam	1973	58	133	191	858	203	680	1741	1896	1143	753	73	394	220
	1974	39	92	131	661	162	502	1325	1327	761	566	64	240	131
	1975	37	110	147	548	160	548	1256	1216	548	668	120	188	80
Fraser	1976	76	122	198	971	236	725	1932	2244	1355	889	164		378
	1977	112	182	294	865	195	800	1860	2478	1556	922	122		426
	1978	164	265	429	966	618	1043	2627	3141	1911	1230	187		557
	1979	97	339	436.	809	801	924	2534	3037	1917	1120	196		579
	1980	70	257	327	757	753	674	2184	2655	1577	868	194		561
	1981	112	320	432	762	952	930	2644	3856	2702	1154	224		701
	1982	104	201	305	642	649	575	1866	2123	1368	755	180		468
Hawke	1983	63	283	346	709	494	438	1641	2964	2298	666	228	953	535
	1984	56	160	216	478	401	260	1139	1817	1444	373	113	540	354
	1985	58	156	214	601	900	218	1719	2459	2048	411	193	900	636
	1986	60	184	244	441	590	148	1179	1802	1455	347	199	822	441
	1987	41	148	189	439	468	153	1060	1699	1372	327	174	515	565
	1988	44	156	200	366	336	143	845	1509	1159	350	207	415	353
	1989[2]	47	117	164	327	370	110	807	1130	830	300	190	294	313

Notes:
1. Figures cover full calendar year incorporating:
   - In 1971 end Gorton/beginning McMahon (10-03-1971)
   - In 1972 end McMahon/beginning Whitlam (05-12-1972)
   - In 1975 end Whitlam/beginning Fraser (11-11-1975)
   - In 1983 end Fraser/beginning Hawke (11-03-1983).
2. Actual figures for the first nine months of 1989 adjusted on the assumption that the workload pattern in 1989 is typical of the last two years.
3. Includes ministry.
4. Excludes appointments from 1973.
5. Includes budget, appointment and endorsement (Whitlam and Hawke) figures from 1973 only.
6. Includes endorsements by the Whitlam and Hawke governments.
7. Includes appointments from 1973.
8. Endorsement figures include some estimates.

than a different procedure or new ways of counting; nevertheless the reduction in activity remains substantial.

The reasons for this reversal of the trend may be varied: the delegation of business to ministers, the consolidated decision-making in amalgamated departments. Yet one substantial reason is likely to be the degree to which prime ministers are concerned that they should be conscious of what was being done within the government. There was thus a substantial jump from the business and number of decisions under McMahon to those that occurred under Whitlam, while cabinet activity reached its peak under Fraser. If there is not a continuing trend, the interaction between the prime ministers and cabinet needs to be further explored.

The Bureaucratisation of Cabinet Procedures

The trend in the bureaucratisation of cabinet procedures was more consistent. In December 1949

> Menzies approved a two page statement of Cabinet procedures. This statement was incorporated along with some material in a *Handbook of Cabinet and Cabinet Committees* which was circulated the following year to Ministers' secretaries and some departmental leaders. The new procedures represented not so much a radical departure from existing arrangements as a consolidation and development of them.[2]

It was the first attempt to specify the rules for the presentation of submissions, to require consultation and to establish the role of the Cabinet Secretariat (later the Cabinet Office).

But, as was often the case, the rules were not always followed. Early in 1950 there were complaints that submissions were inadequately prepared, that the four-day rule (as it was then) was too often ignored. There were, as a consequence, frequent instructions by prime ministers to tighten up the application of the rules.

Advice to new ministers, explaining how the system worked, was fairly rudimentary, as the briefing for a new minister in 1955 illustrates:

> (a) Cabinet meetings are usually held about once a week of about 2 1/2 hours duration plus Cabinet Committee meetings during the week when required. The usual meeting time is Tuesday at 10.30 am. Meetings occur out of [the Parliamentary] session but less regularly.
> (b) Seating – He should sit between Mr. McMahon and Mr. Townley – this is roughly across the table from the Prime Minister.

2. 'Development of Cabinet Procedures' in *Annual Report: Department of Prime Minister and Cabinet 1984*, Canberra: AGPS, 1985, p. 13.

(c) The general procedure at a meeting is as follows: – An agenda is, where possible, available to Ministers at the start of the meetings, but the Prime Minister decides on the order of business which rarely coincides with the order on the business list. Ministers wishing to raise matters for discussion do so by means of written submissions, copies of which are sent to the Cabinet Secretariat beforehand (at least 4 days before a meeting) and the Secretariat has these circulated to Ministers for their study and to enable them to seek advice from their Departments. The Prime Minister then asks the Minister responsible for the item to explain its various aspects and implications and to recommend an appropriate line of policy. After this the matter is open for frank discussion by any Minister who can add anything of value so that a good decision can be reached.

(d) The only other person in Cabinet room besides Ministers is the Secretary of Cabinet. Officials do not attend Cabinet meetings except on very rare occasions when Cabinet wishes to consult a senior official.

(e) The Cabinet Secretariat is a section of Prime Minister's Department responsible for servicing Cabinet, i.e. transmitting the submissions to Ministers, arranging meetings, providing the Secretary, writing and circulating the decisions.[3]

All these processes gradually became more detailed and explicit. In 1969, for instance, Sir John Bunting, the secretary of the Cabinet Office, wrote a detailed letter to all ministers explaining the implications of the first decision on procedures taken by the new government.[4] By 1980 the *Cabinet Handbook* had become a lengthy document.[5] In 1983, the handbook was published for the first time. By 1988 a second and expanded edition, now covering over 60 pages, explained what should be done.[6] It included nine chapters:

- Organisation of Cabinet
- Cabinet Conventions and Principles
- Cabinet Program
- Cabinet Business
- Consultation
- Preparation of Cabinet Documents
- Handling of Business without Submission
- Cabinet Minutes
- Security and Handling of Cabinet Documents

Appendices listed the membership of cabinet committees, explained the functions of cabinet liaison officers in departments, detailed the

3. *Ibid.*, p. 23–4.
4. Reproduced in P. Weller and M. Grattan, *Can Ministers Cope? Australian Ministers at Work*, Melbourne: Hutchinson, 1981, pp. 215–19.
5. Reproduced in *Politics*, 17(1), May, 1982, pp. 146–63.
6. *Cabinet Handbook* (Revised edition 1988), Canberra: AGPS, 1983.

forecasting requirement and the forms for cabinet documents and provided a guide to drafters of cabinet submissions.

Who was responsible for these changes? As far as can be ascertained, most of the initiatives came from the officers of the Cabinet Office. They were concerned to ensure that ministers received proper notice of agenda, carefully argued and intelligible submissions, timely circulation of submissions to allow them to be absorbed and reasonably speedy advice of cabinet's decisions. The better the procedures, the less likely ministers were to be 'sandbagged' in cabinet by unexpected submissions suddenly brought in. When ministers or officials complained about the inadequacies of the system, or tried to bypass the rules, a note was made of the problems and they were then rectified in the next edition of the *Handbook*. Sometimes political opportunities were taken to make changes that would, in their view, improve cabinet's ability to concentrate on most substantial issues. In the Fraser government 'under-the-line items', that is, items for discussion but without any written submission, were often taken first and sometimes took up a disproportionate amount of the time. When the Hawke government was elected, the Cabinet Office proposed that those items be taken after the formal business. It made the submissions more important and ensured their progress.

Prime ministers were at times concerned that the rules were not being adequately obeyed and required that they be more rigorously followed — they would ask, for instance, that the Cabinet Office tighten the adherence to the seven-day rule.[7] Occasionally reviews were politically initiated. Fraser held two such reviews of cabinet procedures — in 1978 and 1982 — to try to reduce the workload, while the Labor Party's task force on government, reporting in 1979 and 1982, proposed several plans for the organisation of cabinet. The *Cabinet Handbook* took account of political sensitivities; the description of collective responsibility was redesigned to reflect the practice of the Hawke government after one minister resigned on principle from cabinet because of a policy disagreement but wanted to stay in the ministry! The result of course made a mockery of any traditional definition of collective responsibility, but neatly made the point that convention followed practice.[8]

In their basic form, the cabinet procedures have become more bureaucratised. Departments are now required to forecast likely submissions, fulfil stringent criteria in the form and conditions that submissions must meet, formally consult with other departments and reflect the outcomes of those discussions in the submissions, and then lodge them with the Cabinet Office seven days in advance to give time

7. See, for example, Fraser's request in P. Weller, *Malcolm Fraser PM: A Study in Prime Ministerial Power in Australia*, Ringwood: Penguin, 1989, p. 115.
8. *Cabinet Handbook*, 1983, paragraph 2.1, p. 3.

for circulation. That process of development has been continuous. A similar trend for dealing with cabinet business can be seen in the development of a structured and predictable system of cabinet committees.

Cabinet Committees

Controlling the structure and use of cabinet committees has always been the prerogative of the prime ministers. They choose which minister will serve on which committee, what the terms of reference are, and whether the committee will have the authority to make final decisions. Yet there has been a constant search for effective sets of committees that can both reduce the workload of the full cabinet and effectively settle politically or administratively sensitive issues.

Prior to 1949 governments created systems of cabinet committees, but none had a sustained impact or lengthy existence. Chifley, for instance, used a combination of ministers and officials in a way that has not been copied since.[9] In 1950 Menzies established 17 standing committees to sift the relevant facts and sometimes make decisions. However, items were not directed to them and the business kept reverting to the full cabinet. *Ad hoc* committees were common; by 1955 Menzies had created almost 140 different committees. In the hope of introducing a better system for dealing with business, Menzies formed a Prime Minister's Committee and a Vice-President's Committee. The former was the forerunner of the inner cabinet created in 1956; the latter became the vehicle for shifting work to 'deal with submissions on matters of administration and matters which require the application of principles which have already been adopted'.[10] In 1956 an inner cabinet was created and six standing committees were appointed. *Ad hoc* committees were still used as required. Submissions were directed either to full cabinet or to committees. This system was continued in general principles until 1972.

The Whitlam government came to power with a blueprint for effective government. Eleven standing committees were created with the intention that all business be directed initially to them, with recommendations then sent to cabinet for endorsement. Although the membership of cabinet committees was fixed by the prime minister, any minister could attend (but not vote on) any committee. By the May 1974 election the committee system had become largely redundant,

9. L.F. Crisp, 'Central Coordination of Commonwealth Policy-Making: Roles and Dilemmas of the Prime Minister's Department,' *Public Administration*, Sydney, 26 (1), 1967.
10. 'Development of Cabinet Procedures', *loc. cit.*, p. 18.

with too little time for meetings or for their recommendations to be digested before being considered or approved by the full cabinet.

As a consequence far more weight was given to *ad hoc* committees, particularly the Expenditure Review Committee that analysed the budget submissions before the 1975 election. Their membership was limited and attendance restricted. The ERC was the most lasting legacy of the Whitlam government to cabinet procedures; in one form or other it has been re-established consistently since. The Expenditure Review Committees (often called the razor gangs) comprise a group of senior ministers appointed to review the budgetary proposals of ministers. Fraser appointed such a committee, usually under Lynch's chairmanship, every year. In other respects too Fraser's system of standing committees was similar, both in its creation and in the problems it met. The first Economic Committee was abolished because most of the possible business was discussed by the full cabinet, but Monetary Policy and Wages Policy Committees dealt in a specialised way with economic issues. Other committees, such as the Public Information Committee, reflected the prime minister's frustration with the presentation of government decisions; it was later abolished, but its history illustrates the point that committees are often appointed to meet transient political perceptions.

If economic questions were sometimes discussed in the specialised committees, political management was potentially discussed in the Coordination Committee that contained the five parliamentary leaders and other ministers whom the prime minister chose to co-opt. The agenda was varied, but depended on the prime minister's interests and the political sensitivities at the time. It was often seen as a *de facto* inner cabinet.

The Hawke government had developed, prior to coming to office, a further structure of committees; its procedures required that issues were considered by the relevant committee before a recommendation was authorised by cabinet. Although, unlike the Whitlam government, Hawke followed the coalition precedent of creating a cabinet of 'inner' ministers, the committee system ensured wide involvement of all ministers in decision-making. The ministers outside cabinet were members of those committees in which their departments had a policy interest. Cabinet was generally required to endorse all committee decisions. Issues of great sensitivity were directed straight to cabinet.

The system worked fairly well in the first four years. It was altered in 1987 after the reorganisation of the machinery of government created 16 departments, each of which was headed by a cabinet minister. The cabinet ministers were then 'assisted' by junior ministers. With every department therefore assured of representation in cabinet, a different set of priorities was set. It was no longer necessary to use the cabinet committees to ensure involvement. The new 1987 committee structures had three co-ordinating committees (Legislation, Parliamentary Business, Expenditure Review), three policy development committees (Public Service Reform, Social Justice and Structural Adjustment) and two functional committees (Security and General Administrative). The last named was effectively the second team, including a majority of non-cabinet ministers; minor items were directed to it for settlement.

There is a growing reliance on, and formalisation of, the committee structures. Getting the cabinet system 'right' is a constant challenge; constellations of committees have been created and withered. Under Menzies, according to Crisp,[11] the Liberal cabinet played the major roles. As the workload increased, so substantive issues were both considered there and in committee. Because of the absence of available records, it is often difficult to place the precise location of all decisions, but in the Fraser government a range of important decisions — on South Africa, taxation and monetary prices — were taken in committee.

To what effect? Prime ministers could decide who was involved and when. Whitlam's use of the ERC was a break from the earlier practices of his government because access was *not* open to all ministers. Fraser's Monetary Policy Committee was limited in access but important in its outcomes because it ensured that economic policy was discussed in cabinet committee, instead of being fixed by the treasurer, sometimes in consultation with the prime minister. At a time when the Treasury was reluctant to share information — even with the prime minister — the committee broadened ministerial involvement and allowed counterweights to the Treasury to develop. Gorton had preferred to argue his budget on a one-to-one basis with his treasurer, McMahon.[12] Fraser's Coordination Committee could be an important forum, with outsiders complaining that its use was part of a system of widening circles of commitment by which Fraser extended his views. The ever-present search for better committee systems showed their importance; the prime minister's capacity, and increased willingness, to develop committees indicated their authority.

Perhaps most important, prime ministers could decide which issues were or were not decided as part of the cabinet system. Chifley, for instance, used a mixture of ministers and officials in committees; the trusted public servants who attended were part of the 'official family'. Gorton by contrast was accused of relying on 'cronies'. The labelling reflected in part the standing of the two, but in practice it goes further. All prime ministers are advised by a group of senior and trusted ministers and officials. How they use that group is likely to be

11. Crisp, *op. cit.*
12. Alan Reid, *The Gorton Experiment*, Sydney: Shakespeare Head Press, 1981, pp. 198–9.

important. Gorton's unpopularity with his colleagues was partly caused by his tendency to announce conclusions to cabinet without allowing discussion. That led one senior minister to comment: 'If Gorton wants to work as leader of a team, he'll get all the loyalty in the world; if he goes it alone, both he and us will have had it.'[13] Ministers are more prepared to support a leader if cabinet government is maintained, even if only in appearance. Whatever the result, if decisions are announced as a consequence of meetings of kitchen cabinets or groups of cronies, rather than being sent to cabinet even for cursory discussion, resentment will grow.

One option available to prime ministers is to give that inner group a formal status by making it part of the cabinet system and, more significantly, giving its decisions the weight of cabinet authority. Fraser's Coordination Committee was regarded in those terms; a senior official explained:

> Coordination committee was a testing group for her to discuss a good range of political issues and tactics. Not every item in Coordination needed a decision. Most prime ministers have that sort of sounding board. Few have often given it the designation of a cabinet committee.[14]

The formal use of committees and the circulation (however limited) of their decisions was thus a significant change — for those issues that were actually brought to cabinet. It was a logical extension of the bureaucratisation of cabinet and the extension of official support into further activities of the prime ministers.

The Effect of Bureaucratisation on the Prime Ministers

The supporting structure provides the instruments for control; prime ministers determine how, and indeed whether, they will be used. Prime ministers, for instance, are reputed to manipulate the cabinet agenda to suit their own political purposes, refusing to list issues if they want to avoid discussion. As the forecasting of submissions was developed, so obviously the potential scope for the use of that power was increased. But there is little evidence it was widely used. Sir John Bunting, secretary to cabinet for 17 years, denied that claim:

> Before each meeting the Cabinet secretary conferred with the Prime Minister about the business list, but always on the basis of presenting the full list of available and prospective papers. If there were any special urgencies known to the Cabinet Secretary, he mentioned then. The upshot was always that

13. *Ibid*, p. 163. For other unilaterial decisions, see pp. 158–63, 384–5.
14. Weller (1989), *op. cit.*, p. 139.

the Prime Minister, having looked at the list, having heard whatever the Cabinet Secretary had to say about urgency, made his own assessment and decided on the list. It was rarely that any paper was held back very far out of its list, and that was only because others had to have priority.[15]

When the system became more routine, the proposed agenda for the forthcoming week for both cabinet and cabinet committees would be presented to Fraser and Hawke. But, if the minister was keen to have an item discussed, it was generally allowed fairly readily. Fraser commented:

If a minister wanted the submission before cabinet, in my view he had a right to have it before cabinet and not some months or even weeks after the submission was in the list.[16]

Several sets of interviews with ministers in later governments endorse that general view. Ministers do not recall (with the possible exception of the McMahon ministry) difficulty in getting items listed.

Nor did the process of recording and circulating decisions change. Prime ministers still summed up. Menzies, according to Bunting:

made no formal or detailed summing up at the end of the discussion, or rather it was by no means his habit to do so. Occasionally yes, but for the most part he would indicate by a sentence or two the essence of the decision or where it lay. He might simply say 'Well, we'll proceed on the lines that X suggested'. He would in all those instances be relying on the Secretary to the Cabinet to have made a note or at any rate to have understood the points and be in a position to put them on paper.[17]

That system was continued, occasionally to the frustration of ministers who believed that the consensus proclaimed by prime ministers did not always reflect the opinions in the room. From all accounts prime ministers did not require votes. Bunting recalls only one, recorded amid hilarity on an insignificant question, during Menzies's long reign.

A determination not to hold votes was common to all prime ministers except Whitlam, who accepted the long tradition of the Labor Party that regarded votes as a means of settling disputes. Nevertheless prime ministers often kept a note of which ministers and which numbers were on each side of a debate — hence the comment that Fraser gave 'eight-six' decisions, when he was one of the six and summed up in their favour. But prime ministers have all tended to weigh votes as much as count them. Menzies would give particular

15. Sir John Bunting, *R.G. Menzies: A Portrait*, Sydney: Allen & Unwin, 1988, pp. 90–1.
16. Quoted in Weller (1989), *op. cit.*, p. 47.
17. Bunting, *op. cit.*, pp. 88–9.

weight to the opinions of McEwen, Fadden, McBride, Paltridge and Townley, while Fraser listened to Anthony and Nixon because of the political nous they would bring to a debate. Menzies, according to Bunting,

> looked to getting the right solution — to conviction rather than consensus. This, I believe, was one of the reasons behind his objection to voting in Cabinet. Not all votes or opinions were equal. He hardly ever heard an opinion in Cabinet from any minister without multiplying it out by some factor of his own to establish the value to be put on it.[18]

In the later coalition cabinet, Fraser went to great lengths to ensure there was widespread support for the proposals. He thought that if several ministers were strongly opposed, an issue probably warranted more attention. Votes might end debate; they would not end divisions of opinion.

The circulation of cabinet decisions gradually expanded. Before 1956 they were sent only to those ministers required to take action or who had a special interest. After the division of cabinet into an inner group distinct from the full ministry, it was decided that all ministers, including those not in cabinet, should receive copies of all cabinet minutes, although they were only given to permanent heads if departments were required to act. By March 1957 all but a few submissions were circulated to ministers; in August 1962 they received all business lists, even for the meetings they were not nominated to attend.[19]

That was the formal practice. But there were many exceptions. Sometimes committee decisions were circulated only to committee members; on other occasions prime ministers would require a more limited circulation to maintain confidentiality. Decisions of the Defence and Foreign Affairs Committee and the Monetary Policy Committee under Fraser were often limited to members; Coordination Committee business lists and decisions were not always circulated — at the prime minister's request.[20] Ministers sometimes made complaints about too limited circulation, but to little avail. The responsibility was the prime minister's, and that was exercised.

The procedure for under-the-line items appears to have been fairly consistent throughout the period. Ministers were always required to write to the prime minister to ask if an issue of high urgency or political sensitivity could be raised in cabinet. The Cabinet Office would provide a recommendation and the prime minister would make a decision, agreeing to its being raised, asking for the issue to be

18. *Ibid.*, p. 89.
19. 'Development of Cabinet Procedures', *loc. cit*, p. 23.
20. For discussion of circulation, see Weller (1989), *op. cit.*, pp. 143–4.

incorporated in a written submission, or refusing the request. Under the Hawke government, under-the-line items became even more formalised, with written lists of items to be raised and circulated before the meeting.

Prime ministers used some evolving procedures to maintain control of the proceedings of cabinet: the agenda, the summary at the end of discussion, the circulation of decisions. As the procedures became more formalised, so it was easier to use those powers, even if it was now more obvious.

Prime Ministers and Cabinet Involvement

While the rules surrounding cabinet may have changed, the degree to which prime ministers have intervened has remained a matter of choice from personality to personality, from year to year, from issue to issue. It can not be prescribed by any established set of procedures. But it can be *assisted* by extensive briefing and it is in that area that the changes have occurred.

As individuals, prime ministers followed different strategies. Menzies always made some contribution, Bunting recalls;[21] Whitlam was a dominant questioning figure on issues that concerned him. Fraser had a concern to ensure that all decisions were suitable and wanted assurances from ministers of the likely consequences; he would often cross-examine ministers in a way that terrified them. Hawke was concerned that the solutions were saleable; his personal interest was said to be limited to a few central issues where his influence was considerable. In every case involvement depended both on specific interest and on the chair's powers to run the meeting.

Those powers were of course extensive. As long as ministers collectively do not object, prime ministers can determine how long a debate will last, who will speak, when enough views have been expressed; they can establish the terms of a discussion, stating that a debate is, for instance, not about whether public sector cuts will be made but where they will be found: the principle is settled, the debate is about details. Menzies gave ministers plenty of latitude, but ensured that he got a contribution from at least one of the cabinet heavies. Fraser sometimes had to draw out opinions from reluctant ministers: he was prepared to continue the cabinet debates until widespread agreement was reached, leading to claims that cabinet was in session for so long it developed a bunker mentality; exhausted ministers were prepared to acquiesce, even if they did not agree. Hawke was prepared to allow debate to continue until satisfied that a consensus existed on many

21. Bunting, *op. cit.*

issues, leading to extensive meetings. The powers of the prime minister in the chair are substantial, but not absolute.

Issues not settled to prime ministers' satisfaction could be put off; one minister claimed Fraser

would get ministers to withdraw submissions on the most curious pretexts; and ministers would do so rather than have the submissions rejected substantially. The ministers would talk to the prime minister after the meeting and the submission would come back in a different form — and with a greater chance of success.[22]

There is nothing new in prime ministers using the opportunities given to them by their chairmanship. Bruce's colourful and frustrated account of Billy Hughes' chaotic cabinet style — unique, because it took available powers to their absolute limit — provides a detailed illustration of the opportunities prime ministers have:

When I joined the Government in December 1921, I discovered that Cabinet Meetings were the most strange and mysterious affairs, where really nothing was seriously discussed. I think this was felt by all other members of the Cabinet other than the Prime Minister but no-one had moved in the matter. I accordingly went into the ring and as a result I obtained Cabinet's agreement to there being a formal Agenda for Cabinet Meetings, every Minister who had put an item on the Agenda having to circulate a paper to all members of the Cabinet outlining the proposals and what he had in mind before the item would be discussed by Cabinet.

When these proposals were put to the Prime Minister he cordially accepted them — with, I am quite sure, the mental reservation that he had not the slightest intention of allowing anything of the sort to happen.

An attempt was made to put the new proposals into operation but the Prime Minister completely defeated them. He continued his usual practice of arriving at Cabinet Meetings anything up to half an hour late and producing some new and generally wild scheme. As a result, Cabinet proceeded to discuss his new scheme before going anywhere near the Agenda and generally speaking what took place was that the whole of the Cabinet meeting was devoted to the attempt to dissuade the Prime Minister from his latest idea.

To overcome this it was suggested to the Prime Minister that when it was impossible for him to be on time for a Cabinet Meeting the Cabinet should proceed with the Agenda under the chairmanship of the next senior Minister. This also the Prime Minister agreed to.

We then made an attempt to carry out this idea and on two or three occasions it worked quite well. Decisions were reached on a number of matters that were listed for consideration. The Prime Minister however also managed to defeat this move. His method was on his arrival at a Cabinet Meeting to ask what had been decided. He thereupon set about asking whether the decision

22. Weller (1989), *op. cit.*, p. 139.

was a wise or an unwise one, in order to get it upset. In this generally speaking, owing to his extraordinary influence over Cabinet members, he was successful.

After having tried to get a proper Agenda and subsequently trying to get the Agenda considered even before the Prime Minister arrived, I came to the conclusion that with an eccentric genius like Billy Hughes it was imposible to have any well regulated procedure for the Cabinet. As a result I ceased putting items on the Cabinet Agenda with regard to Treasury matters and simply went ahead and did whatever I thought was necessary.[23]

No other prime minister presided over such a chaotic cabinet — and Hughes was eventually overthrown — but the description shows how the power can be used.

But why did they win so often? Institutional and procedural factors may have helped, but they were the symbols, not the real cause of authority. Prime ministers usually won because of their sheer weight and quality. According to Hasluck, Menzies dominated for one reason:

The simple explanation and the one nearest to the truth is that Menzies was the best man there. His authority came primarily from the recognition of his bigness . . . In cabinet the authority he had because he was perceptibly the best man around the table was reinforced by the respect he gave to cabinet responsibility.[24]

Whitlam could dominate a cabinet by his personality and Fraser was dogged, well-briefed, on top of all the issues. Hawke's skills of chairmanship were recognised by his colleagues.

Sometimes prime ministers are given their way because as party leaders they have weight and often goodwill; the government's future depends so much on their performance. As one Fraser minister said:

A prime minister has got a certain amount of room to move. He can take an unpopular stance on a limited number of issues. If he does it too much, he will exhaust his political capital.[25]

But the capital is substantial. In the preparation for Hawke's 14 March 1991 economic statement, one senior minister commented: 'The prime minister won because this is Hawke's statement. He gets what he wants.' It might be added that he did not always win, but was too skilled to demand support too often. Indeed it is the desire to over-use that capital, or even stating too bluntly that prime ministers do not need to consult cabinet, that can lead to problems. When Gorton was

23. Quoted in 'Development of Cabinet Procedures', p. 6.
24. Paul Hasluck, *Sir Robert Menzies*, Melbourne University Press, 1980, p. 16.
25. Quoted in Weller (1989), *op. cit.*, p. 142.

asked if prime ministers had the constitutional powers to make decisions individually, he responded:

Oh, they are there. You can make a decision and say that's it. Then if the rest of your cabinet doesn't like it they can say: 'Well, we won't go along with it'. So that is just too bad for the prime minister, so he can get out, I suppose.[26]

He identified the danger clearly. Cabinet will not try to force a withdrawal unless its collective patience is at an end. Gorton's downfall illustrated the lack of patience with his unorthodox ways. Consulting cabinet more — however often he had already determined the outcome — might have allowed him to survive.

Prime ministers may have strong views, or merely choose to direct the discussion. They will always have the strongest voice because of their position. As one senior Liberal put it:

In the Liberal party there is no equality. If the prime minister and the deputy leader of the Liberal party are agreeable and the rest are against it, the opinion of the two . . . Well, the rest wouldn't be against it.[27]

Every cabinet has some ministers who will always support the prime minister. When the prime ministers speak, even if against the consensus, most ministers will let them have their way.

Nevertheless, prime ministers are required to be consistent if they are to retain support. Alan Reid contrasts the approach of Gorton and Menzies:

Menzies's ministers knew that Menzies would consult his own self-interest, and the government's and the Liberal party's long term political well-being before he indulged his personal prejudices and moved against any of them, and would not stir up needless strife. Provided they operated within this known context, their position was secure and the only thing they had to fear was Menzies's personal displeasure. But Gorton consulted only his whims and even the most powerful among ministers was not safe.[28]

Fraser and Hawke may have consulted widely before cabinet, but ministers were at least more certain that the processes would be pursued and opportunities for debate were there, if the minister was tough enough to insist. Cabinet government should not be whimsical and prime ministers appreciate the need to maintain the support of ministers at the same time as hard decisions may be made.

26. Quoted in Reid, *op. cit.*, p. 129.
27. Weller and Grattan, *op. cit.*, p. 191.
28. Reid, *op. cit.*, p. 192.

In these involvements in cabinet debates, the position of prime ministers has been further strengthened by the development of personal briefs. The system of prime minister's briefs was initiated under Chifley and became more established under Menzies. The intention of the brief was to provide the prime ministers with chairman's notes, explaining what the issues were, whether the submission was urgent, who was involved. It also included some substantive views on policy, a new departure for the department. Under Menzies they were 'written in relaxed but thought-provoking terms, made available only to the prime minister and treated privately by him'. Menzies regarded them as useful challenges to thought, and maintained their privacy. But, to the embarrassment of the department, under his successors these private notes became more routine, with some prime ministers even reading out to cabinet the 'Prime Minister's Department's views'.[29]

The process of briefing has become more sophisticated and wide-ranging, particularly under Fraser where the department developed great skill in drawing out the essence of issues. Each brief followed a standard format. It started with the department's recommendation. It then provided a brief summary of the background, a review of the issues and an assessment of the options — almost always in two pages or less. The prime minister never had to go into a cabinet without a brief on every issue to be discussed. Occasionally, the department became an active policy participant as well as honest broker between other departments. Its activities reflected the demands of the prime minister. When Fraser wanted to be briefed on everything involved in government, the department became hyperactive; under Hawke it was much quieter. Yet the system and potential remain, a potential that can make the prime minister not only the most feared member of cabinet because of political weight, but also the best informed. Where knowledge and power are combined, the authority of the prime minister is enhanced. Briefing makes that combination easier to achieve.

Prime Ministers and their Ministers

While prime ministers worked with ministers collectively in cabinet, they also had to deal with them individually. Although to an obvious extent the nature of that relationship depended on political and personal links, it could also depend on the importance of the prime minister's patronage and the interest of the leader — as a matter of choice or necessity — in the minister's portfolio.

The significance of patronage varies from party to party, although not to the extent that might appear at first sight. Liberal prime

29. Bunting, *op. cit.*, p. 79.

ministers select their ministers; the Labor parliamentary caucus elects its ministry. However the Liberal leader must take account of the coalition demands of the National Party, and the need for Senate and state representation in choosing the ministry. By contrast, while the Labor ministry has, since 1983, been settled by negotiation between the left, right and centre left factions, Hawke was able to lay down some conditions he wanted fulfilled — as he did after the 1987 election when he sent the factions back to reconsider their list of names.

The power of patronage is persuasive with those outside the ministry who want selection and with those inside who want promotion. Prime ministers have the final decision about which portfolio ministers receive and, even if they consult with senior colleagues, they have the final choice about who will be in cabinet and who will be left in the outer ministry. Whether that has an impact on the behaviour of ministers will depend in part on their confidence, in part on their portfolios and, in a coalition government where National Party ministers do not depend on the prime minister for their ministries, in part on their parties. In every cabinet there are some people who can be seen as the prime ministers' votes as they will not oppose any policy clearly supported by them.

Subservience depends on sanctions and on need. Sanctions include dismissal, but that is rare. In the last 25 years only one cabinet minister has been removed by a prime minister simply because he was not up to the job. (Other Labor ministers were dumped by their factions.) One or two others have been offered demotion to the outer ministry. Some have resigned or been stood down because of their *personal* involvement in some error. Leading challengers to the prime minister — Fraser in 1971, Peacock in 1982, for example — have retired to the backbench. But it has been rare for the prime minister to *initiate* such actions. There is a preference to remove such challengers from parliament or to create vacancies in cabinet by offering comfortable diplomatic or government positions. Most cabinet ministers do not feel their places are constantly at risk, even when a newly elected or re-elected prime minister is in the ascendent. No leader can afford to have too many alternative centres of power on the backbench, particularly as in Australia it is so easy to mount a challenge at any time.

Of course when a prime minister is in a weak position, ministers need not fear for their jobs. After Peacock's challenge in 1982 and the farce of the TV affair that led to two resignations, it would have been difficult for Fraser to lose many more senior ministers. After Keating's first push in 1991, Hawke was unable to remove leading Keating supporters, even when they publicly challenged government directions. Sanctions require strength to be meaningful. That has never changed.

However, there have been moves for prime ministers to be consistently more involved in some policy areas. If Chifley left the development of foreign affairs to Evatt, and Menzies gave Spender a fairly free hand, the links between Fraser and Peacock, or Hawke and Evans, are much closer. This is partly a consequence of changed communications, so prime ministers are kept closely informed of any developments. This also is a result of rapid transport that allows prime ministers to make state visits or attend summits while still keeping in touch with domestic developments. Whitlam, Fraser and Hawke have taken a greater interest and involvement than their immediate predecessors, although Menzies' longevity ensured his presence was notable. Further, it seems that more issues concerning foreign affairs are now dealt with by cabinet committee than happened before.

So too in budget development and economic policy. Whereas formerly the budget was developed by the treasurer in occasional consultation with the prime minister, the last 15 years have seen that process put into commission. More departments are involved. The cabinet committees widen ministerial participation. Prime ministers can receive more detailed briefings on the economic issues and proposed program cuts if they choose; the decisions have cabinet authority. Whereas once economic and financial policy was the primary prerogative of the treasurer, cabinet's involvement in the detail of economic policy, and prime ministers with an ability to comment and express opinions whenever they desire, have changed that process.

A Changing Balance?

How can the impact of these changes be explained? There are three alternative explanations that relate to the nature of cabinet government in Australia. The first concerns the balance between individual ministers and the cabinet as a collectivity; what might be regarded as part of the 'collective problem'. That problem is determining the extent to which the individual minister rather than the cabinet is decisive, and the degree to which the latter can be properly briefed to make clear and informed decisions. Thus, it can be asked to what degree those changes have assisted the cabinet ministers as a collectivity, so strengthening the processes of cabinet government. A second interpretation is that the development of the cabinet structures has primarily assisted the prime ministers, by giving them greater control over the proceedings of cabinet. A third, less often stated hypothesis, asks whether the changes have assisted the officials of central agencies in controlling the proceedings of cabinet and of other departments; as the complex government fragments, so bureaucratic rules allow some coherence and direction to be maintained.

The first two propositions are of course related and follow the traditional British debate about prime ministerial power that argues that cabinet government has been replaced by prime ministerial government. They ask whether cabinet is — or ever was — the real centre of decision-making authority or whether the locus of power has shifted elsewhere. For over 20 years little progress has been made in that debate, often because it has become a semantic argument about when collective government actually exists. Dunleavy and Rhodes have sought to approach this question more systematically by proposing that authority may be exercised by:

- the prime minister individually
- prime ministerial cliques
- cabinet government
- ministerial government
- segmented decision-making
- bureaucratic co-ordination.[30]

Of course these categories are not mutually exclusive or self-contained. Different types of decision may be made in different arenas; any prime minister may shift from one arena to another. Nomenclature may be misleading; one prime minister's cabinet committee may be another's kitchen cabinet and a third's personal clique. Nevertheless the categories provide some interesting analytic tools with which to examine the interaction between prime ministers and their cabinets and they may assist in interpreting the way in which the Australian cabinet is organised.

Who then has gained from the changing rules and practices in the Australian political system? The traditional answer is that the prime minister uses the cabinet rules, committee structures and the additional briefing as a means of dominating cabinet outcomes. Coupled with the other advantages derived from his office, the prime minister dictates the form and content of cabinet decisions. The general diagnosis may be correct: prime ministers are able to dominate much of the debate and the records suggest they generally have their way when they are concerned to push a policy.

Yet that is no newly emergent truth, as any study of strong leaders such as Hughes or Chifley illustrates. The power of personality, the aura of authority, the dependence on effective leadership were all as crucial as the use of the rules, usually far more so. Better briefing has consolidated the position.

30. P. Dunleavy and R. Rhodes, 'Core Executives Studies in Britain', *Public Administration,* 68 (1), Spring 1990.

Bunting agrees that the development of cabinet procedures has led to a changing balance, but argues it has not led to a loss of power from ministers to the prime minister; rather, ministers have lost authority to the collectivity of cabinet. He believes that whereas once the term 'ministerial government' would have been accurate, it has now been supplanted by 'cabinet government'. Once ministers came to cabinet with individual standing, regarded as masters of their portfolios with a strong presumption that their proposals would be approved. Ninety per cent of the submissions were accepted. Later far more items were taken to cabinet, which was in its turn more critical and likely to reject the submissions. Bunting concludes:

> By a variety of means, and imperceptibly, Cabinet has inflated itself and ministers reduced themselves. The doctrine that each minister runs his own department is still the doctrine, it is not any more so much the practice. There is much more than in Menzies' time a sharing arrangement . . . That did not prevent [the minister] talking to colleagues, talking to the Prime Minister, going to Cabinet. All those things were available and were used, but they were used as adjuncts and not as controls or discipline over the minister. In other words the minister used Cabinet. Now, when a minister announces that he has a policy initiative in mind and will be taking it to cabinet, he is forgetting that in his field he is the authority, the highest authority. He yields that to Cabinet. He puts himself in the part of applicant or supplicant. The Cabinet is using him.[31]

It is an arresting thesis because it fits rather better with the empirical evidence than notions that prime ministerial government has replaced cabinet.

It also need not be an irreversible trend. Under Fraser, nervous ministers brought a wide range of issues to cabinet seeking prime ministerial approval and collegial support. Under Hawke the establishment of the larger amalgamated 'mega-departments' allowed the senior ministers greater freedom to make independent decisions within their larger departments, thus decreasing the pressure on cabinet to consider less central issues. Cabinet remained the body for the issues of substantial or economic significance. But Hawke was still able to make independent policy announcements — on the economic trilogy or involvement in the Gulf war — that required endorsement; though not too often, in order to retain cabinet support.

Even so, if Bunting's argument is followed to its logical conclusion, then who is best able to use the processes of cabinet to advantage?

More and more items came to cabinet, partly as a consequence of the desire for involvement by the cabinet leadership, partly due to

31. Bunting, *op. cit.*, p. 83-4.

nervousness on the part of ministers. So the importance of many submissions declined. Ministers were prepared to accept decisions they did not fully accept but were not prepared to argue with. Acquiescence replaced agreement. Some issues — the central ones — would still be debated at length. On those the prime ministers' authority might be imposed. But as defeats from ministers became more common, so they became less serious. Prime ministers, and particularly Fraser, were able to direct government as much *through* the process of cabinet consultation as by bypassing it. And all in the name of collective authority.

Hawke reduced the numbers of submissions and perhaps pushed some decisions back to the ministerial heads of the larger departments. Yet the expectation that cabinet would make the central decisions remained. Whereas in earlier times ministers may have made an individual decision, perhaps after consultation with the prime minister, more now went to cabinet where the prime ministers could, if they cared, be master. Cabinet involvement could be turned into a requirement for prime ministerial approval.

This procedure was accentuated when the use of committees was enlarged. Budgetary policy could be shifted from the treasurer in consultation with the prime minister, to a committee when the prime minister and other colleagues debated and decided the issue. Fraser's Monetary Policy Committee reduced the Treasury's monopoly on economic information and forced it to become part of the advisory system. The arenas for debate were determined by the prime minister; the decisions were put into commission.

Cabinet committees — at times perhaps a version of government by prime ministerial clique — may have grown in importance, although it is necessary to note that the term 'cabinet system' must be regarded broadly to refer to all the official meetings of the cabinet and its committees. In terms expressed by Dunleavy and Rhodes, the formal style of authority shifted from ministerial government to cabinet government.

There is less evidence for the proposition that prime ministers made decisions outside the cabinet on a regular and unchallenged basis than there is for the view that much of the time they worked through cabinet. Where independent action was tried, trouble for the prime minister could follow. But prime ministers were often vastly influential within cabinet, and that was acceptable to ministers.

Indeed that insistence on working through the procedures and practices of cabinet makes sense. If prime ministers can dominate decision-making through cabinet and its committees, why try to make it explicitly individual and ask for trouble? If the changes of the past 40 years have seen a growing sophistication in the procedures of cabinet, then through that process the prime minister too has been strengthened. Cabinet government may be flourishing; but the prime minister can still determine where decisions are made. The development of cabinet government to a higher level of activity and authority has, paradoxically, been a crucial factor in extending the prime minister's authority and span of control.

2

PRIME MINISTERS AND THEIR STAFF

James Walter

A prime minister's department has existed in Australia for 80 years, but its growth into a significant entity has been a feature of the post-World War II period. The growth and elaboration of the prime minister's private office has been even more recent, a development of the 1970s and 1980s. How did each phase of growth in the prime minister's staff relate to the political context of its time and what impelled it? What particular services did the department and the private office provide? How did each of these entities regard the other, and how did they interrelate in their common objective of serving the prime minister? In what ways did the demands of successive prime ministers influence what happened? In what ways have the capacities of the prime minister been extended and shaped by these developments?

The overarching answer is that such institutional changes are linked to the general tendency in Western democracies to accentuate the role of the head of government in both the symbolic and the policy aspects of politics. As a prime minister increasingly becomes the focus of such expectations, there will be a practical demand for more information, greater administrative support and direct policy advice. The extent to which these are provided, and the ways in which they are provided, will affect prime ministers' capacities to manage relations with cabinet, public service, parliament, party and constituency. In Australia, attention to the specifics of this process is essential to understanding the prime minister's power over the political agenda.

The Prime Minister's Department

The Prime Minister's Department (PMs) was established in Australia in 1911, on the instructions of Andrew Fisher. It grew from Fisher's sense that the business accruing to the prime minister was expanding, and that the administrative support given to that point through External Affairs (by virtue of the convention that the prime minister should also be minister for external affairs) did not serve the purpose of a head of government. The ambitions of Fisher's private secretary, Malcolm Shepherd (who had also served Deakin, Watson and Reid), were also said to be influential: he became first secretary of the Prime Minister's

Department. Yet it also paralleled developments in the states: Victoria, Tasmania, Western Australia and New South Wales all had premiers' departments by 1910.[1]

In its first incarnation, the functions of the prime minister's department were those of co-ordination and communication. Its major responsibilities were to provide liaison between the government and the Governor General's Office, a link with parliament on legislation, a formal channel for communication with the British government, and a conduit to the state governments. Between the abolition of the Department of External Affairs in 1916 and its re-emergence in 1935, PMs also assumed the specific external relations functions. At various times it accumulated a range of other minor administrative responsibilities, but 'its functions ordinarily rose little above the significance or dignity of post office, records office and guardian of protocol'.[2] A cabinet secretariat evolved within PMs from the late 1920s, becoming progressively more formalised through the 1930s. In 1940 the secretary of PMs, Frank Strahan, was admitted to cabinet to record decisions, yet continued to see his role as very circumscribed, restricted to circulating submissions, recording decisions and distributing these to relevant ministers.[3] It seems that all the department's secretaries up to and including Strahan saw, and may have been encouraged to see,

> the department primarily as an administrative and only in some areas a coordinating apparatus . . . because they were reluctant to modify this conception, no systematic policy advice . . . [was] tendered . . . nor did [the department] seek a general coordinating role.[4]

The transition of the department, from a post-box into an important feature of central government machinery, must then be understood in the context of post-World War II politics.

If, despite the attendance of its secretary to cabinet meetings, the department's co-ordinating role remained vestigial after the war, this may have been partly because the then prime minister, Ben Chifley, was himself central to policy co-ordination, and relied for support on both the Treasury — since he was treasurer as well — and his 'official family' in the Department of Post-War Reconstruction.[5] Yet thought was being

1. L.F. Crisp, 'Central Coordination of Commonwealth Policy-Making: Roles and Dilemmas of the Prime Minister's Department', *Public Administration*, 26 (1), 1967, pp. 30-1; PMC, *History of the Department of Prime Minister and Cabinet: Extract from the Department of Prime Minister and Cabinet Annual Report 1978-79*, Canberra, 1979, pp. 3–6.
2. Crisp, *op. cit.*, p. 31.
3. *Ibid.*
4. PMC, *op. cit.*, p. 7.
5. L.F. Crisp, *Ben Chifley: A biography*, London: Angus & Robertson, 1960, p. 257.

given to what was to happen with the winding down of war-time agencies, not least by senior staff in the Department of Post-War Reconstruction who looked forward to an influential future elsewhere. At the same time, it was recognised in Australia, as in the other Western democracies, that the role of head of government was of increasing importance in the central machinery of government. Thus, Chifley's minister for Post-World War Reconstruction, John Dedman, argued in March 1949:

> The basic consideration seems to me to be that the office of prime minister is becoming more and more the pivot around which the whole governmental machine turns. In carrying out his tasks the prime minister needs a group of well qualified officers who can take hold of different issues as they arise and develop them in cooperation with the officers of the administrative departments to the stage where the policy decision that is involved is clearly presented.[6]

By coincidence, Frank Strahan, who had operated very much according to the limiting conventions of his predecessors, was due to retire in mid-1949. The way was thus open for a fresh approach and he was replaced as secretary of the Prime Minister's Department by Allen Brown, formerly director-general of Post-War Reconstruction and very much in tune with the views Dedman was urging on Chifley. Brown's intellectual strength and administrative skills were to be integral to the changes to come.

This was the setting for significant reorganisation. At its centre was the recommendation that the Economic Policy Division of the Department of Post-War Reconstruction be transferred to PMs. The pragmatic purpose was to persuade Chifley to relinquish the Treasury and to wean him from Treasury as his primary source of advice, but more broadly it was intended that the former Economic Policy Division should be the core of an expanded cabinet secretariat. Brown also fought for additional positions for an expanded range of functions, arguing to the Public Service Board in November 1949 that 'the time had passed when the department should be regarded as merely a channel of communications'.[7] While there was debate between the Public Service Board and PMs over the principle of whether the department should have branches appearing to duplicate functions of other departments, the Board agreed to the establishment of an Economic Policy and Research Section as the first specialised policy area in the department. This acceptance of arguments for policy expertise as the basis for a broader co-ordinating and overseeing role was the foundation for the increasing centrality of PMs in policy formulation in later years.

6. Crisp (1967), *op. cit.* p. 34.
7. PMC, *op. cit.*, p. 13.

Neither the reorganisation nor the transition of the Economic Policy Division from Post-War Reconstruction to PMs were complete when the ALP lost the 1949 federal election, and Menzies succeeded to the prime ministership. However, the principles and the decisions which had been foreshadowed up to that point were accepted by Menzies's cabinet: the determination to wind-up the Department of Post-War Reconstruction and to transfer to PMs the Economic Policy Division, Office of Education, Universities Commission and the Commonwealth Scientific and Industrial Research Organisation (CSIRO) was confirmed within two days of the installation of Menzies's first ministry. Thereupon some 30 officers from the Department of Post-War Reconstruction joined PMs — including three who were to become future permanent heads of that department: E.J. Bunting, C.L.S. Hewitt and G.J. Yeend. The transfer was to have lasting effects: the department had acquired a group which presumably shared some of the lofty ambitions of post-war reconstruction and with experience in policy formulation. The new prime minister, lacking Chifley's bases in the broader public service, yet keen to exert his authority, was ready to encourage its advising role, and — working under the reflection of his authority — it was able to develop its function as a central co-ordinating agency. The process was marked by intense competition and manoeuvring for the prime minister's ear.[8] Brown and the department tended later to minimise the ramifications of this change and to emphasise the separation of the secretarial and co-ordinating and advising functions,[9] yet the basis for PMs to become a policy player had been established.

The reorganisation settled what were to remain the parameters of departmental operations until the 1960s, bar one important innovation. In 1955, Menzies gave a formal direction (at Brown's request) that the department was to give him advice on all cabinet submissions. This put paid to the resistance from the Public Service Board (PSB) to the department staffing itself for all-round capability, though the PSB and others maintained the challenge for some time afterwards. Specific functions fluctuated: some responsibilities were accumulated because of prime ministerial interest (for instance, Menzies's interest in education enhanced the role of the Office of Education) or because the department served as a catch-all for new and difficult functions, but equally, in time, functions could be reallocated to new departments. This flexibility in adding and shedding functions was to be a recurrent feature of the department. The economic policy role may never have flourished in quite the way its progenitors hoped, partly because Menzies wished to range widely and was not much interested in economic management as such, but also because Menzies had and used direct access to key Treasury

8. G.J. Yeend, 'The Department of Prime Minister and Cabinet in Perspective', *Australian Journal of Public Administration*, 38 (2), 1979, p. 134.
9. PMC, *op. cit.*, p. 15.

officials, especially while Arthur Fadden was treasurer.[10] But the primary function of the department, that of providing advice and guidance to the prime minister and the government on the whole range of Commonwealth activities, developed, and integral to this was the relationship between the prime minister and his departmental secretary. Allen Brown established the pattern, but it was brought to full flower by his successor, John Bunting, appointed secretary of the Prime Minister's Department in January 1959.

Bunting has given a useful account of his and the department's work with Menzies. Bunting stressed his own role as cabinet secretary and the department's function as cabinet secretariat. In the early phase after reorganisation, the practice was to provide the prime minister with a chairman's notes on submissions: background, relationship to other portfolios and other matters and any urgent factors for consideration. Initially advice came largely from the Economic Policy and Research Section, but eventually, after the experimental phase, all submissions came to be (or potentially could be) subjects of such anticipatory briefing. In part, this indicated, too, the strengthening and diversification of PMs. The practice came to be that officers were expected to write, in Bunting's terms, 'not as experts but as inexperts': Menzies did not want technical advice (which was available elsewhere) so much as his officers' own views, a 'cerebral reaction'. There was no concealment in the preparation of briefs since PMs officers inevitably consulted with their equivalents in other departments. There was nonetheless debate about the involvement of officers who, given the nature of Menzies's requirements, had neither technical nor professional links with the specific matter on which they were commenting. To some extent this was defused by the understanding that the briefs were private: Menzies took what he wanted and discarded as he chose; whatever he used was used on his own responsibility and without attribution. The strategy depended for its success on the tact and sense of the prime minister, and Bunting's assessment of its success, at least with Menzies, is unqualified.[11]

Menzies commented himself on the value of these briefs to him:

> The Prime Minister's Department . . . had become in effect the cabinet secretariat. Individual submissions had to be put in three days before the cabinet meeting. Brown, who had assembled some officers of great talent . . . fed out to two or three of them the submissions for comment or added information. They consulted the department or departments concerned, and provided Brown with notes to which he attached some shrewd observations of his own. The day before cabinet, greatly aided by these labours, I studied all

10. Crisp (1967), *op. cit.*, p. 38; Donald Horne, *The Lucky Country: Australia in the Sixties*, Ringwood: Penguin, 1964, p. 8.
11. Sir John Bunting, *R.G. Menzies: A Portrait*, Sydney: Allen & Unwin, 1988, pp. 77–82.

of these submissions and formed some tentative views or questions of my own.

This meant that when cabinet met I was extremely well informed . . . probably the only one who had been furnished with comprehensive notes on all the submissions and had studied them . . . the function of the prime minister, as I understood it, was to be as well informed as he could be, to encourage exposition and debate, to question ministers on their submissions, sometimes very closely, and to come in at the appropriate time . . . with some proposition which would embody the general view.[12]

Brown, and later Bunting, derived authority for PMs not only from their briefing role but, through the power of the secretary's access to cabinet, the privilege of direct knowledge, the secretary's responsibility for translating general decisions into operational terms and relating these to individual departments, and the corollary function of mediating between departments. One account of this argues that Bunting, above all, developed this approach to co-ordination, and that the co-ordinating role of the department was thus translated into the authority of the umpire.[13] Bunting focused on process rather than policy, and emphasised the habits of informal consultation, networking and serving as the prime minister's eyes and ears throughout the bureaucracy.[14] He was 'a source of guidance on sensitive political issues and a balancing factor within the bureaucracy seeking compromise and consensus; [his] style was circumspect and its substance conservative, as was the government of the day.'[15]

Bunting worked best with Menzies, who shared his view of co-ordination as the essence of central administration. Though he served Liberal governments for 13 years, it is clear that later Liberal prime ministers failed, in his view, to appreciate the indirect means which allowed the department effectively to mediate. For one thing, they failed to understand the benefits of informality and of personal communication, and began to treat the department's notes not as private, to be used on their own responsibility, but as ammunition to be publicly quoted. The department's advice thus could be seen as confronting the authority of ministers within their own portfolios, emphasising cabinet rather than ministerial government. PM's views 'were given place above their station. We were responsible, now and again inspired contributors, but essentially we were there to help the prime minister in his chairmanship and not as universal advisers.'[16]

12. Robert G. Menzies, *The Measure of the Years*, Melbourne: Cassell, 1970, p. 34.
13. F.A. Mediansky and J.A. Nockels, 'The Prime Ministers' Bureaucracy,' *Public Administration*, 34 (3), 1975, p.. 206.
14. *Ibid.*, pp. 206–7.
15. *The Australian*, 18 October 1974.
16. Bunting, *op. cit.*, p. 83.

The co-operative pattern so smoothly worked out between Brown, Bunting and Menzies, and by virtue of which PMs consolidated its influential role in central government in the 1940s and 1950s, was disrupted when John Gorton became prime minister in 1968. Gorton faced new demands: the Liberal Party was no longer so dominant; the easy mastery Menzies had displayed in his later years had not been matched by Holt; the political and electoral context was more volatile and the old verities that had governed post-war politics were under challenge. Gorton's own position in his party, and his relations with his coalition partners, were less secure than those of either of his predecessors. His response was to play up the populist and activist aspects of his style. As a consequence, he demanded a different kind of support from his department. He wished to stress positive advice and policy initiation, and hence Bunting's emphasis on co-ordination and influence through mediation was not to his taste. His solution was to appoint a new secretary to PMs, C.L.S. Hewitt, whose reputation as a forceful activist seemed to meet his needs. When he met widespread resistance to this replacement of John Bunting, his compromise was to create a separate department of the Cabinet Office with Bunting as its head.[17]

This situation, which Bunting himself described as 'not exactly rehearsed',[18] may have appeared to constitute a radical break, or a new evolution, in the department's affairs. Lenox Hewitt, working to Gorton's brief, made appointments of several key officers who were his own men, involving substantial promotions and some controversy. The department was reshaped to meet the monitoring as well as initiating function Gorton demanded, and in consequence it increased in size and in its range of capabilities. Hewitt worked directly with the prime minister's office in a way probably unmatched since Shepherd and Deane in the early years of the department (1912–28). In consequence, he accrued authority not so much as umpire or mediator but because his relations with Gorton were so direct and he was taken as the interpreter of the prime minister's wishes.[19]

Yet the new direction did not succeed, in part of course because Gorton himself was not a successful leader. In part, too, it was because Gorton did not recognise the hidden constraints of such a division of labour. Hewitt may have had greater access to the prime minister, but he did not attend cabinet, so he could not have an overview of all that was going on, and this served as a constraint on his advice. No longer able to claim inside knowledge of the workings of cabinet, the department lost weight in its interdepartmental negotiations. On the other hand, Bunting continued to attend cabinet but was no longer so involved in the working

17. Mediansky and Nockels (1975), *op. cit.*, pp. 207–8.
18. Prime Minister's Department file: 76/2341: E.J. Bunting to A.S. Cooley, Chairman, Public Service Board, 13 October 1972.
19. Mediansky and Nockels (1975), *op. cit.*, pp. 208–9.

up of policy or the briefing role. Further, even with expanded capabilities, there were practical limits on the department's capacity to initiate policy since at best it could acquire expertise only in limited areas.[20] With Gorton's political demise in 1971 the experiment ended. While William McMahon's replacement of Gorton as prime minister did not lead to the dismantling of the enlarged departmental organisation, within days of his accession it was announced that the two departments — Prime Minister's and the Cabinet Office — would be amalgamated to form the Department of Prime Minister and Cabinet (PMC) under John Bunting. McMahon, it was said, was 'unable or unwilling to use his department',[21] yet it was early in 1972, under McMahon, that approval was given for a substantial staff increase in PMC. If McMahon did not take advantage of this in the remainder of his indecisive premiership, his government's provision of the means for the prime minister to have a greater impress on policy was the platform on which Whitlam would build.

The role of the PMC in the policy process surged ahead under the Whitlam Labor government (1972–5). Under Whitlam there was great pressure once more for overall co-ordination and for the capacity to support prime ministerial initiatives. The department had won a case for substantial staffing increases earlier in 1972, and this was the resource for meeting the challenges of the new ALP administration. There was an immediate increase in the level of legislative activity, and associated demands on PMC for guidance on ministerial and cabinet practices.[22]

The new government, however, at first placed limits on the role of PMC. It came to power with the suspicion that the public service had been so accustomed to the conventions and practices of conservative rule over 23 years that it might not be a suitable instrument for effecting Labor's purposes. Initially, therefore, Whitlam attempted to maintain his initiative by supplementing his department with advice from special task forces, committees of enquiry and a significant augmentation of his private office (of which more below). Indeed, there was an early attempt to make the prime minister's private office into a driving force in government.[23] Another organisational change was the establishment in 1973 of the Priorities Review Staff (PRS), attached to the Department of the Special Minister of State (SMOS) and intended to play a significant role in policy co-ordination by establishing government priorities, undertaking specific studies and reviewing the implementation of

20. Yeend, *op. cit.*, p. 137; Patrick Weller, 'Do Prime Minister's Departments Really Create Problems?' *Public Administration*, 1983, 61, p. 63; PMC, *op. cit.*, p. 18; Mediansky and Nockels (1975), *op. cit.*, pp. 208–9.
21. *Ibid.*, p. 210.
22. PMC, *op. cit*, p. 18; Yeend, *op. cit.*, p. 141.
23. Peter Wilenski, 'Ministers, Public Servants and Public Policy', *Australian Quarterly*, 51 (2), 1979, pp. 37–8.

programs. Whitlam (like Chifley) also established a broader base for himself within the public service by taking on the foreign affairs portfolio as well as the prime ministership; his view being that the prime minister is, anyway, the *de facto* minister for External Affairs. His intense interest in foreign affairs and wish to play a role on the international stage made him turn instinctively to the Foreign Affairs Department (its head, J.K. Waller, was involved, along with Bunting, in the first planning meeting Whitlam held after his election).[24]

If PMC was initially limited by Whitlam's other sources of advice, this did not last. The year 1973 was a time of furious work and somewhat awkward negotiation: Whitlam's private office staff were suspicious of the motives and abilities of public servants who tended to reciprocate; the department took time to adjust to the lessening of contact with the prime minister.[25] Nonetheless, Whitlam had inherited, as a result of the Gorton initiatives, a larger and more complex department than his predecessors had enjoyed, and in time its capabilities became evident. Then began an upgrading of existing branches and a gradual movement of departmental interests into policy areas of special interest to the Labor government. After a year, Whitlam was persuaded to relinquish the foreign affairs portfolio because of the pressure of the prime ministerial role. In 1974, the PRS was moved from SMOS into the ambit of the deputy prime minister, and then to PMC, bringing the tools of policy co-ordination entirely within the departmental sphere once more. Most significantly, the attempt to make Whitlam's private office the policy dynamo failed:

> . . . as the implementation of policy became increasingly complex, a small group of people simply could not keep track of a government's entire policies and programs. Since it was thought . . . undesirable to expand the size of the . . . office, the other alternative was taken, and it was decided, in the words of one of the participants, 'to turn the Prime Minister's Department into a Prime Minister's Department', with a change in personnel and style and in outlook. What was intended . . . was that [PMC] would play less of an information-gathering and neutral-umpire-for-the-settlement-of-interdepartmental-disputes role and (shades of Gorton and Hewitt) more vigorously assert the prime minister's views and priorities to other departments.[26]

One indication of the new intention was the establishment within PMC in early 1975 of a Policy Coordination Unit to identify policy areas in need of special attention and to ensure that new proposals were consistent with broader government strategy. Another was the appointment at

24. Graham Freudenberg, *A Certain Grandeur: Gough Whitlam in Politics,* Melbourne: Sun Books, 1978, pp. 239-40.
25. Yeend, *op. cit.*, p. 142.
26. Wilenski, *op. cit.*, p. 38.

around the same time of John Menadue as secretary of PMC, to succeed John Bunting (who moved to London as Australian high commissioner). Menadue had been a former private secretary to Whitlam, a one-time ALP candidate for federal election and the general manager of Mirror Newspapers Ltd. His appointment generated some controversy, but in a sense his role was to re-establish PMC in the role that had been intended in the late 1940s, as the government's key co-ordinator. One of the tasks on which he began was to regulate and channel the advice of the extra-bureaucratic groups: the Policy Coordination Unit was a means to this end. By serving as the conduit to bring advice together into a single strand, PMC once more established itself at the centre of government. By responding to the prime minister's wish to intercede on a wider range of policy issues, the department further expanded its capacities.[27]

The dismissal and then electoral defeat of the Whitlam government in December 1975 might have been expected to be a setback to an agenda that had begun to enhance the role of PMC in central government. On the contrary, the aspirations and style of the Liberal prime minister, Malcolm Fraser, provided a further fillip for the department. Menadue, to the surprise of some, survived the transition and continued to work as attentively for Fraser as he had for Whitlam, in the process continuing the departmental development begun in 1975. Fraser's own driving interest in all the activities of government, and desire to understand all the implications of cabinet decisions while trying to integrate them into government priorities, demanded a powerful PMC with a capacity to attend to a broad range of detail.[28] He was, like Gorton and Whitlam, an activist who needed a support structure that would serve to keep the policy initiative in his hands. It was said that with Fraser, policy co-ordination expanded so far as to become policy control, an instrument for the prime minister's power over other ministers.[29]

In early 1976 the PRS and the Policy Coordination Unit within PMC were amalgamated into the Projects Division, to be concerned with major policy reviews. This signalled recognition that overall policy co-ordination was a function of the department as a whole. Fraser's demands were the catalyst for a reorganisation that saw PMC's ability for across-the-board co-ordination achieved, and the long-standing resistance from other departments to that co-ordination (on the grounds that such enhanced capacity was an inefficient duplication of their functions) defeated. At the same time, PMC's attempts to maintain fruitful links with line departments were sustained, for instance through marked

27. Mediansky and Nockels (1975), *op. cit.*, p. 217.
28. Patrick Weller, *Malcolm Fraser PM: A Study in Prime Ministerial Power*, Ringwood: Penguin, 1989, p. 57.
29. Wilenski, *op. cit.*, p. 38; F.A. Mediansky and J.A. Nockels, 'Malcolm Fraser's Bureaucracy', *Australian Quarterly*, 53 (4), 1981, p. 395.

expansions in the number of officers from other departments seconded to PMC under Menadue and his successors.

In 18 months Menadue managed to bring together and institutionalise diverse sources of advice in an organisation capable of covering the range of major government activities. Officers were familiar with their fields, well connected to appropriate departments and able to assemble information quickly into digestible briefs. When Menadue left, to become Australian ambassador to Tokyo in September 1976, he was replaced by Alan Carmody, brash, aggressive and demanding but an experienced public servant, former secretary of the Department of Business and Consumer Affairs and a man acutely sensitive to the prime minister's requirements. Carmody set to work not to expand but to improve and reorganise PMC. An extra division was established, the unique position of under-secretary was created, and the second division structure was upgraded (while being numerically reduced) to give PMC the status and prestige of one of the 'big' line departments (such as Treasury). The Public Service Board noted that the new structure

> reflected the changing role which had emerged for the department since the previous reorganisation in 1973 and which was evidenced by significantly increased responsibility for policy coordination and development, forward planning, priority setting, strategy advice and program evaluation and review.[30]

Fraser's concern to direct government activity on key issues directed Carmody's reorganisation, and Fraser himself justified that reorganisation by commenting on the onerous burdens on his officers, while denying that other areas of the public service faced such increased responsibility. Carmody died suddenly, perhaps succumbing to the pressure of two years of dynamic activity and relentless demands, in 1978. The then under-secretary, Geoffrey Yeend, was quickly appointed to replace him.[31]

Yeend was the antithesis of Carmody: calm, unflappable, conscious of what was needed and what was possible, with a tendency to play down the role of PMC.[32] He was the last of the group of people (which had included Bunting and Hewitt) which had moved to PMs in 1950 from the Economic Policy Division of the Department of Post-War Reconstruction. He was thus perhaps the most experienced senior officer in PMC and had represented continuity, and knowledge of the ways of the bureaucracy, for both Menadue and Carmody.[33] Constrained by staff ceilings, Yeend proved adept at shedding some responsibilities and

30. PSB, *Annual Report,* Canberra, 1978, p. 22.
31. Mediansky and Nockels (1981), *op. cit.*, pp. 407-10; Weller (1989), *op. cit.*, pp. 34–43.
32. Weller (1989), *op. cit.*, p. 39.
33. Mediansky and Nockels (1981), *op. cit.* p. 410.

modifying others to respond to the prime minister's interests. Under Yeend, PMC did not increase in size, but proved able to maintain its influence by astutely shifting resources to problem areas and expecting more of its staff.[34] This demonstrated the extent to which, because it has no programs to run or legislation to implement, PMC is relatively unconstrained by a logic of form related to functions.[35] Yet despite intense activity, dictated by Fraser's demands, Yeend was able to claim with justification that there had been stability and continuity in the department's role, and that it retained its non-partisan function as adviser, co-ordinator and facilitator.[36] Yeend's work in strengthening the machinery of cabinet co-ordination under Menadue and Carmody came to fruition with Fraser's demand for adherence to detailed and codified rules of procedure for cabinet business; as secretary, Yeend could administer these rules, imposing discipline on the policy departments.

The permanent heads of PMC were among Fraser's closest advisers. There was in consequence some tension between its collective role of cabinet service and its support for the prime minister. Yeend has accepted that the department sometimes offered alternative advice:

> We do not feel inhibited in what some might interpret as the role of second opinion. Our branches have built up an understanding of policy issues and an expertise in coordination; our officers are sought out for their advice and assistance. We have scope for probing and proposing.[37]

But he balanced that by arguing its concern for the whole:

> It is not our business to have ministers surprised in the cabinet room with questions they have not anticipated, or be faced . . . with propositions they have not considered.[38]

On the whole, PMC broadened its range because the prime minister wanted advice on everything, and became a strong department because the prime minister wanted a strong department.[39]

There was doubt about whether PMC would retain the authority it had achieved under Fraser after the election of the Hawke ALP government in 1983. Public service reform was on the agenda, and one of the suggestions was that PMC be restructured to differentiate between the

34. *Ibid.*, pp. 410–15.
35. Weller (1989), *op. cit.*, p. 35.
36. Yeend (1979), *op. cit.*; G. J. Yeend, 'The Co-ordinating Role of the Department of Prime Minister and Cabinet', in Michael Wood, Christopher Williams & Campbell Sharman (eds), *Governing Federations: Constitution, Politics, Resources*, Sydney: Hale & Iremonger, 1989, pp. 84–96.
37. Yeend (1979), *op. cit.*, p. 143.
38. *Ibid.*, p. 143.
39. Weller (1989), *op. cit.*, pp. 39–43.

policy-advising and cabinet secretariat functions, with two officers of permanent head status.[40] Yeend, however, was involved in the discussions with Hawke about managing the transition, and in the event — at least with respect to PMC — the least disruptive options were preferred. But Hawke's style was the obverse of Fraser's: he was a political manager and consensus chairman, more interested in monitoring his ministers than in questioning their policies. The demand for alternative assessments of policy, therefore, was less.[41] In consequence, it was suggested initially that Labor ministers had greater freedom than their Liberal predecessors, that power was decentralised and that PMC reverted to being essentially a co-ordinating body in the Menzies mould.[42] On the other hand, such things as the early decision to hold a National Economic Summit (which would establish the Economic Planning Advisory Council — EPAC) required a lot of groundwork which gave PMC ample scope on the policy side, and those within the department saw no diminution in PMC's policy role in this period. It was noted that Yeend established an easy relationship with Hawke and that PMC still provided comprehensive briefs on how every submission fitted in with government policy.

Yeend retired early in 1986 and was replaced by Mike Codd. Codd had joined PMs in 1969 and by the late 1970s had risen to the position of under-secretary, where he was reckoned to be notably effective and not afraid to stand up to Fraser. Between 1981 and 1986 he had experience at permanent head level in a number of more junior departments — Employment and Industrial Relations, the Industries Assistance Commission and the Department of Community Services. By the time he returned to PMC as secretary, the Hawke government was in its second term, economic and managerial problems were looming, and the stress on managerialism, efficiency and economic rationalism was decidedly to the fore. Codd proved to be attuned to these new demands. PMC was closely involved in the planning that was to lead to the significant machinery of government changes Hawke announced immediately after the 1987 elections; parts of the private sector consultant, David Block's, report which was said to have generated these changes were published in the PMC Annual Report (1986–7); and Codd himself played a prominent role in explaining the intentions of those changes thereafter.[43]

40. Patrick Weller, 'Transition: Taking Over Power in 1983', *Australian Journal of Public Administration*, 42, (3), 1983, p. 305.
41. Weller (1989), *op. cit.*, p. 57.
42. Richard Farmer, 'Hawke defuses an old Fraser power source', *The Bulletin*, 29 November 1983, p. 29.
43. See, for instance, Mike Codd, 'Inside the Government Changes', *GO: Government Officers Magazine of Administration and Purchasing*, March 1988, pp. 8-10; Michael Codd, 'Cabinet operations of the Australian government', in

The intention of the machinery of government changes was to produce a leaner, more flexible and more cost-effective public service, with more devolved responsibilities for program development, personnel planning and financial management. The proposed measures, following Block's Efficiency Scrutiny Review, were said to be derived from best private sector practice (though Block's report was strongly criticised when it became public).[44] The resulting *Administrative Arrangements Act* (1987) '. . . changed the ministry into a two-tier structure and amalgamated departments to achieve economies of scale by removing perceived overlap and duplication. The Prime Minister . . . argued that these measures "increased the government's capacity to impose functional and strategic direction on government activity as part of economic reform" . . .'[45] It is not to the point here to analyse these administrative changes in detail, but to note that they had significant ramifications for PMC.

It was said at the time that the decisions behind these reforms represented a triumph for PMC and for Codd, who had spoken to every department to assess views and then arranged for PMC to draft the blueprint before the election.[46] Hawke certainly spoke later of a 'comprehensive review of the structure of government' undertaken by PMC.[47] The influence of PMC was demonstrated and enhanced by its role in orchestrating the process and implementation of reorganisation.[48] While PMC itself remained essentially unchanged, its centrality to the government machine was augmented by the abolition of the Public Service Board. This was announced as one of the measures to eliminate duplication of functions. There was to be a public service commissioner and an Australian Public Service Management Advisory Board (chaired by PMC). A further consequence was that the secretary of PMC took over the role formerly played by the chairman of the Public Service Board in advising on the appointment of departmental secretaries (except for the post of secretary, PMC). Thus, a statutory officer had been replaced by a

---

Brian Galligan, John Nethercote and Cliff Walsh (eds), *The Cabinet and Budget Processes*, Canberra: The Federalism Centre, 1990, pp. 14–15; Mike Codd, *The Role of Secretaries of Departments in the APS*, PSC Occasional Papers, No. 8, Canberra: 1990; M. H. Codd, *Federal Public Sector Management Reform: Recent History and Current Priorities*, PSC Occasional Papers, No. 11, Canberra: 1991.

44. See, for instance, S.R. Kelleher, 'Scrutinizing a Scrutiny', *Canberra Bulletin of Public Administration*, 52, 1987, pp. 72–6; Marion McInnes, 'Public sector reform under the Hawke government: Reconstruction or deconstruction?' *The Australian Quarterly*, 62 (2), 1990, pp. 117–18.
45. *Ibid.*, p. 111.
46. Paul Kelly, *The Weekend Australian*, 25–26 July 1987.
47. *Commonwealth Parliamentary Debates (CPD)* (House of Representatives), 15 September 1987, pp. 43–6.
48. John Halligan, 'Reorganizing Australian Government Departments', *Canberra Bulletin of Public Administration*, 52, 1987, p. 41.

departmental secretary, and the secretary of PMC in effect became head of the public service.

Whatever the particular criticisms mounted against these changes,[49] it is clear that control of appointments (formerly distanced through a statutory officer) has become more clearly the preserve of the prime minister and his department. Yet this may have been no more than the formalisation of a pattern that had prevailed for some years (pre-dating Hawke), giving the head of PMC no more than the authority that has traditionally resided with the British and Canadian equivalents.[50] Despite devolution and streamlining, the public service reforms under Hawke produced an even more centralised government machine, with PMC integral to its operation. The effect of the 1987 reforms, though, in making the bureaucracy more responsive to the ministry and the prime minister, can be seen as a continuation of the trend traced here since the 1940s. A measure of the extent of PMC's indirect influence throughout the service is that it appears increasingly to be becoming the unofficial training ground for secretary-level appointments: by 1989, 50 per cent of departmental secretaries were former senior officers of PMC — in 1985 it had been 30 per cent and in 1974, 15 per cent.[51] This is hardly surprising: given the other trends augmenting prime ministers' centrality, their opinion on departmental secretary appointments will be crucial, and those who have worked closely with them are likely to be advantaged.[52] The inference that a leaner, more centralised service, more responsive to ministerial control, is by extension more politicised, should not be drawn. PMC may now take political factors into account more explicitly in tendering advice than once seemed customary. But to insist that PMC and the public service generally be aware of political contexts in the advice given is not at odds with the conventions of neutrality and impartiality as between parties: it is quite different to giving political advice as that is commonly understood.[53]

Prime ministers do have resources other than PMC, not only the private office but also the ability to resort to other elements of the public service. Chifley and Menzies had direct relations with certain Treasury officials, Whitlam with Foreign Affairs, and Fraser would approach whomever he chose in the quest for information. Bodies established in the 1970s and 1980s as attachments to the prime minister's portfolio, like the Office of National Assessments (ONA) and the Economic Policy

49. See for instance, S.R. Kelleher, 'The Apotheosis of the Department of Prime Minister and Cabinet', *Canberra Bulletin of Public Administation*, 54, 1988, pp. 9–12.
50. Patrick Weller, 'Politicisation and the Australian Public Service', *Australian Journal of Public Administration*, 48 (4), 1989, p. 375.
51. S.R. Kelleher (1989), 'Departmental Secretary Appointments Observed', *Canberra Bulletin of Public Administration*, 58, 1989.
52. Weller, 'Politicisation' (1989), p. 376.
53. Compare Weller's arguments, *ibid.*

Advisory Council (EPAC), feed material directly to prime ministers, contribute an important professional aspect to their briefings, and are frequently significant in the determination of new policy positions. And PMC itself is dependent on the other departments: specific expertise is always in the relevant line department and where the prime minister calls for this, PMC must draw it in. For all its centrality, PMC continues to mediate rather than originate.

One means of reviewing this history is to look at the changing size, organisational structure and division of work in PMC, alongside the level of cabinet business, since the 1940s. Measures of the level of cabinet business are provided in chapter 1, where it is noted that the growth in the number of meetings is startling. The trend in the bureaucratisation of cabinet business, under the aegis of PMC, is also discussed there. Alongside this, we can survey the growth of the department from four divisions in 1949 [54] — only one of which (Economic Policy and Research) had a specific policy rationale — to nine divisions in 1989[55] — six of which might be described as policy-oriented. Within those nine divisions were 23 branches, some as big as a division had been in 1949. Flowing from this, a considerable elaboration in the department's functions between 1949 and 1989 can be traced.[56] The current state of play can be seen in the departmental organisation chart in Table 2.1.

The Prime Minister's Office

There have always been loyal operatives at the side of the chief executive in Australia, though the source from which such personnel have been drawn has changed. In the early years of the Commonwealth there seemed little distinction between advice to government and personal support to the executive — and prime ministers commonly relied on the nascent bureaucracy for both. However, as the bureaucracy settled into an administrative service role, a new breed of personally appointed press secretaries emerged to specialise in the role of sympathetic political adviser. Lloyd Dumas, appointed by Billy Hughes in 1916, may have been the start of the line. Still, little emerged to disturb the assumption of complementary roles between politicians and bureaucracy. Indeed, the 'classical phase' arguably reached its high point with World War II when, despite a bureaucratic explosion and departmental innovation, circumstances facilitated a congruence of approach between political and bureaucratic leaders — instanced in Chifley's 'official family'. The post-war period, however, saw the emergence of a sophisticated career

54. PMC, *op. cit.*, p. 13.
55 PMC, *Annual Report 1988-89*, Canberra, 1989, pp. 6–7.
56. The 1949 and 1979 functions are detailed in Yeend (1979), *op. cit.*, pp. 148-9, and can be compared with PMC (1989), *op. cit.*, pp. 1–5.

bureaucracy. This body began to be perceived as limited in political responsiveness, and conservative ministers began to experiment with personal appointees. In turn, Whitlam's determinedly reformist government took office with the expectation that the bureaucracy would impede its aims, and so commenced the institutionalisation of personally appointed ministerial staff.[57]

In the period between Chifley's innovative use of his 'official family', and the election of the Whitlam Labor government in 1972, L-CP governments largely relied on traditional patterns of staffing ministerial offices. Elements of an 'official family' remained, for instance, in Menzies's friendly relations with key PMs officials such as Bunting, ready interaction with Wilson and Randell in Treasury and resort to Liberal Party figures such as J.R. Willoughby and Edgar Holt; in Harold Holt's appointment of journalist Keith Sinclair (to PMs rather than his office) as speech writer and extra intellect; in Gorton's reliance on Hewitt to create a new network of advice within the public service; in McMahon's turning to H.C. Coombs (though with PMs knowledge) as personal 'guru' and the use of party employee John Howard in the run-up to the 1972 election. But, formally, the practice was to follow the British model, where (until the Wilson government's 1964–70 innovations) the private office was virtually an annex of the department, staffed by departmental officers. In the Australian case, however, these officers were rarely the 'high fliers' seconded to ministers in Britain, though there were exceptions.[58]

The Labor Party determined to change this on coming to power. The initiative has been said to have come from Whitlam himself, but if this was so, almost certainly the detailed preparatory planning was carried forward by others.[59] With a general concern for strengthening the hands of ministers in their dealings with their departments, the idea of ministerial 'cabinets' along French lines was toyed with,[60] before it was decided to expand and upgrade the role of ministerial staff. Allied to the concern with enhancing ministerial power was the conviction that Labor's program of reform and change would impose quite different demands upon the bureaucracy than those that had stemmed from the L-CP government's preoccupation with managing the status quo. Under such general heads, a series of specific reasons for staff changes have commonly been adduced:

57. For a comprehesive history of the growth in ministerial (including prime minister's) private office staff to the mid-1980s, see James Walter, *The Ministers' Minders: personal advisers in national government*, Melbourne: Oxford University Press, 1986.
58. Geoffrey Yeend, for instance, served a stint in Menzies's private office as the prime minister's private secretary.
59. C.J. Lloyd and G.S. Reid, *Out of the Wilderness: the Return of Labor*, Melbourne: Cassell, 1974, pp. 149–50.
60. Wilenski, *op. cit.*, p. 36.

Table 2.1. DEPARTMENT OF PRIME MINISTER AND CABINET; ORGANISATION CHART, AS AT 30 JUNE 1989*

Secretary and Secretary to Cabinet

Executive Assistant

Deputy Secretary			Deputy Secretary			Deputy Secretary		
Economic Division *First Asst Secretary*	Industries Trade & Resources Division *First Asst Secretary*	Social Policy Division *First Asst Secretary*	Cabinet Office *Director*	Parliamentary & Government Division *First Asst Secretary*	International Division *First Asst Secretary*	Office of the Status Women *First Asst Secretary*	Corporate Services Division *First Asst Secretary*	Office of Multi-cultural Affairs *First Asst Secretary*
Education & Labor Markets Branch	Trade & Industry Group	Income Support & Health Branch	Cabinet Business & Programming	Parliamentary Branch	Foreign Affairs Branch	Community & Social Policy Branch	Corporate Support Branch	Liaison & Equity Branch
Economic Assessments Branch	Infrastructure Branch	Cultural & Welfare Services Branch	Cabinet Services	Government & Legal Branch	North America & Defence Branch	Employ-ment & Education Policy Branch	Ceremonial & Hospital-ity Branch	Co-ordina-tion & Information Branch
Fiscal & Taxation Policy Branch	Primary Industry & Environment Branch	Social Justice Secretariat			Office of Security & Intelligence Coordination			
	Resource Assessment Commission							

* Adapted from PMC (1989), *op. cit.*, pp. 6–7.

- there was strong suspicion of the public service elite, which was felt to have been conditioned in a policy sense by 23 years of working with the L-CP coalition.
- there was a wariness of entrenched bureaucratic and departmental interests which might be expected to conflict with government interests, and which had seemingly triumphed in the recent past.
- Labor had commitments to new departments in areas where no public service expertise existed; it was essential for ministers in these departments to be able to call on expertise and support from elsewhere.
- Labor's shadow ministers in opposition had drawn heavily on voluntary unpaid advisers. It was natural to repay that debt by the appointment of such people to positions in ministers' own offices, and would ensure the continued availability of their advice.
- the ALP came to office with specific policy commitments articulated in the party platform, and it was desirable for ministers to have around them people who understood and supported that platform, and who were familiar with the institutions and machinery of the ALP.
- there was a belief that wisdom need not reside solely in conventional institutions, and that it would therefore be desirable to multiply the government's sources of advice.
- prime ministers led the ministry in pointing out the necessity of having politically sensitive staff in their private offices in order to minimise the involvement of public service officers in the party political work those offices would inevitably have to handle.[61]

After considerable debate, and a deal of wrangling with the Public Service Board which found it difficult to move away from the traditional pattern, a new format for the private office was agreed. Essential to this was a new staff category of ministerial officer, which would cover all private secretaries, advisers and research officers in ministerial offices. The gradings given to these ministerial officers were more senior than those that had applied to ministerial staff in the traditional system, indicating the enhanced significance that was intended to attach to the private office. The prime minister was entitled to a much larger staff (21 as opposed to eight in the average ministerial office) and could appoint ministerial officers at two grades above those fixed for the rest of the ministry.

61. G.T. Briot and C.J. Lloyd, 'Ministerial Staff Members', Submission no. 466, *Royal Commission on Australian Government Administration*, Canberra: RCAGA, 1976, pp. 3–4; Lloyd and Reid, *op. cit.*, pp. 265–6; M. Roberts, 'Ministerial Advisers: A Background Paper', Research Paper no. 6, Canberra: *RCAGA*, 1976, pp 2–3; R.F.I. Smith, 'Ministerial Advisers: The Experience of the Whitlam Government', *Australian Journal of Public Administration*, 36, 1977, pp. 133–58.

The prime minister's office, not only larger than those of his colleagues but also with a more pronounced policy capacity, might be taken as prototypical of the intentions behind these innovations. Before the election, thought had been given to the structure of the office and to its role, and a paper had been prepared at Whitlam's request by Dr Peter Wilenski, a public servant then on leave who was to become Whitlam's first principal private secretary after the election.[62] Whitlam, therefore, was prepared to swing his personal staff into office and into action immediately, whereas the arrangements for staffing the other ministerial offices were not agreed until June 1973. Wilenski himself describes how, in 1973 and 1974, there was an attempt to make the prime minister's office into a driving force in government, not only supporting and advising the prime minister but also overseeing and co-ordinating the implementation of Labor's platform across the board. After some early success, the task of keeping track of increasingly complex programs became too large for such a small group, and it was decided instead to transform PMC so that it might more vigorously assert the prime minister's policies and priorities. Thereafter the influence of the office declined.[63]

If the prime minister's office itself experienced declining influence, how successful was the scheme at large? Many commentators (including Wilenski) have rated it only a modest success; indeed a study commissioned by the Royal Commission on Australian Government Administration concluded: 'The work done by ministerial advisers varies considerably, but their part in the policy process has been essentially limited and confined'.[64] It is commonly pointed out that advisers were essentially dependants, not only appointed and disposable at a minister's whim but serving only in the manner he or she allowed: they had limited scope for entering the political process in their own right. It has been argued that such staff were eventually neutralised, circumvented, or co-opted by the public service.[65]

Against these limiting views, however, other material can be cited. In a long article on the erosion of Treasury influence over economic decision-making in 1974, Robert Haupt argued that the Treasury 'believed itself to be done in by the new style of administrative arrangements adopted by the Labor government'. The ministerial advisers in particular are cited as having a decided advantage over the department — control over what finally goes to a minister. It was felt that Treasury had lost its pre-eminence 'in the vital information game':

62. Lloyd and Reid, *op. cit.*, pp. 265–6.
63. Wilenski, *op. cit.*, pp. 37–8.
64. Smith, *op. cit.*, pp. 157–8.
65. Smith, *op. cit.*; Wilenski, *op. cit.*

now the Treasury's up-to-the-minute submissions have had to meet the view of ministerial advisers who have . . . been overwhelmingly hostile witnesses. There is a feeling within the Treasury that the balance has been rather lop-sided: that ministerial advisers get to make comments to ministers entering cabinet, but that the Treasury does not get anything like a fair chance to reply.[66]

Indeed, in another dispute about the role and influence of advisers late in the term of the Fraser Liberal-National Country Party government, the head of Treasury referred back to the allegedly adverse outcome of these 1974 events as a warning.[67] Beside this instance of advantage in bureaucratic in-fighting might be placed some evidence of political effectiveness within the parliamentary party. In correspondence with this author, one Labor cabinet minister of the period has argued:

at the prime ministerial level . . . staffers regard themselves as being more powerful than ministers or private members of parliament. Indeed, they almost invariably do have more influence with their prime minister than do the ministers . . . in all cases, the staff can, and do, influence a minister's relationships with his peers and senior public servants. This is crucial in the case of the prime minister. It is my firm belief that Crean, Cairns, Cass, Connor and Cameron were demoted or dismissed at the prompting of Whitlam's ministerial staff together with the influence of senior public servants. I believe the reports that Gough's disastrous decision to recall parliament for a one day sitting on 9 July 1975, germinated in the mind of a staffer; and that Hawke's . . . decision to hold a Royal Commission into certain aspects of his own government was made without the approval of cabinet.

The limitations of this experiment are easier to see in retrospect. One newspaper of the time expressed what was undoubtedly a common view in speaking of '. . . an influx of rough-haired young 'ideas' men — more than 100 of them at latest count, many of them graduates — who have been hired as ministers' private advisers beyond the control of the monolithic Public Service Board'.[68] Not only did the ALP government's change in established staffing practices attract attention, but also some of the appointments created controversy, and some of the advisers were outspoken about their views of their roles, so this became a visible group, the most prominent members of which readily gained media attention. This was especially the case with the prime minister's staff.[69]

66. Robert Haupt, 'Treasury Opts Out', *Australian Financial Review*, 27 August 1974.
67. Michelle Grattan, 'Stone letter hits "meretricious players of the advisory stage" ', *The Age*, 25 November 1982.
68. *The Age*, 28 August 1973.
69. Roy Forward, 'Ministerial Staff Under Whitlam and Fraser', *Australian Journal of Public Administration*, 36 (2), 1977, p. 159.

It is also the case that these innovations provided the means by which a politically engaged group with strong network ties was drawn into the parliamentary political process. One commentator, John Edwards, gives expression to this:

I suppose when I walked into Parliament House earlier this year [1973], I would have known half the personal staffs who had already arrived, through nothing more conspiratorial than a left-liberal history in the local Labor party, the Sydney and NSW Fabian Societies, the anti-Vietnam movement and three years on the *Financial Review*. It was as though a part of a whole generation had marched through Kings Hall and filtered through to the various ministers' offices. It's in the discovery of so many connections that one realises just what a small country this is, and how important face-to-face groups are.[70]

In part, the networks allowed advisers to reach out into the party, academia, the media and politically active parts of the community in a way never open to the public service, and this outreach activity was to remain an important potential of the private office under succeeding prime ministers. The network relationships also made for swift communication and promoted like-minded attitudes and responses to events. These people were activists, wanting to play a part in what one of them described to me as 'a great reform government'. Like their predecessors who in the 1940s had sought a similar end through the bureaucracy, their hopes were to be confounded by the unprecedented fall of the Whitlam government in 1975.

To the extent that the 'smooth' functioning that had prevailed under the L-CP coalition was disrupted, the inner workings of the public service were opened up to ministerial scrutiny and challenge. The public service was gingered-up, forced to argue for and justify its case in an unprecedented way. While staffers were dependent upon their ministers, many of them were left free to define their own roles and did this in ways that gave them considerable scope for action.

Malcolm Fraser built in opposition the skeleton of a staff group which he was to take into government with him. In 1973 he had engaged a public relations firm to advise on his image; the operative they assigned to him, Alistair Drysdale, went on to assist him in policy development relating to his shadow portfolio of industrial relations, and in the challenge by which Fraser was to topple the then opposition leader, Billy Snedden. In 1974, Fraser began to call on the services of a Melbourne academic, Dr David Kemp, as a speech writer. Kemp had clearly defined views on liberal philosophy and leadership, expounded in what was to

70. John Edwards, 'Political Scientists in Politics', Paper delivered at the Australasian Political Studies Association Conference, August 1973, p. 3.

become an influential article, 'A leader and a philosophy',[71] written after the defeat of the L-CP in 1972, and clearly serviceable to Fraser in his bid for power. Kemp had been brought to Fraser's attention by Liberal MP Tony Staley, a former academic who had worked with Kemp in the University of Melbourne Politics Department and had been Fraser's lieutenant in the challenges to Snedden. After Fraser became Liberal Party leader in March 1975, he brought in Dale Budd as his principal private secretary to run his office of leader of the opposition. Budd had worked for him once before, as private secretary, when Fraser had been minister for defence in Gorton's administration. Similarly, in 1975 Fraser's office had engaged the then director of the Australian Associated Press's Canberra bureau, David Barnett, as press secretary. Barnett had expressed his sympathy for Fraser's cause to Tony Staley after the first challenge to Snedden, then offered his services — via party director Tony Eggleton — to the office of the new leader when Snedden was toppled. These four were integrally involved in Fraser's 1975 campaign and were to form the nucleus of his private office when he became prime minister.

Not only did Fraser bring into office with him the nucleus of a staff developed in opposition, as had Whitlam, but his staff entitlement as prime minister was not cut from the level enjoyed by Whitlam, despite pressure from PMC for a reduction and despite his government's cuts elsewhere in the public service (including other ministers' staffs). His rhetoric of suspicion of reformist initiatives, of trust in the permanent bureaucracy, and of responsibility requiring cut-backs, is belied by the importance attached to his own advisers. As the only minister to retain an extensive staff, Fraser enjoyed an even greater measure of policy dominance over his colleagues than had Whitlam.

There were other means by which Fraser ensured his pre-eminence, but the retention of an extensive staff was also based on quite clear views developed within the private office of what its purpose should be, and on Fraser's own growing conviction of the value of ministerial staff. By the end of 1977, in the Garran Oration, Fraser was arguing in terms of:

> the valuable role being played by ministerial staff in strengthening ministerial control. The ministerial staff provide an important support to the minister in carrying out those functions which cannot be delegated to departments without handing over responsibilities which must be his alone. The ministerial staff have become an important increment to the resources available to the elected government in carrying out the task for which it was elected.
>
> The experience of the present government shows that it is possible for the ministerial staff and departments to work harmoniously together in carrying out their respective functions. Provided it is recognised that the functions of

71. David Kemp, 'A leader and a philosophy', in H. Mayer (ed), *Labor to Power*, Sydney: Angus & Robertson, 1973, pp. 48–59.

> these two groups of staff are distinct, it is possible to avoid the damaging competition which arose in the past. I have no doubt that the system can continue to develop in a way which strengthens the principle of ministerial responsibility in our system of government.

These views, however, were not to give rise to significant changes in his office structure until 1981, after what may be regarded as a period of prolonged fencing with the bureaucracy.

When Fraser was elected, PMC urged ministerial staff cutbacks and further development of its own policy role.[72] By and large Fraser accepted that advice, except in one particular instance: the reduction of his own private office was resisted. Nonetheless, the advice was taken to the extent that Fraser's office was initially set up in a fairly conventional manner — albeit with his successful staff from opposition, Budd (principal private secretary), Kemp (senior adviser), Barnett (press secretary), and Drysdale (press officer), at its core — while Fraser worked closely with PMC on policy and co-ordination.[73] There was no attempt, then, to make the private office a policy dynamo in the manner that had been first attempted by the Whitlam office in 1973.

In 1976, David Kemp left Fraser's staff to resume his academic career; his role as senior adviser was taken up by another Melbourne political scientist, Petro Georgiou. Then, in 1978, Dale Budd left the office to establish a consultancy business. At that point, there was an attempt, influenced by the federal director of the Liberal Party, Tony Eggleton, to make the office more politically attuned and closely in touch with the party organisation. Eggleton's personal assistant from the national secretariat, Darcy Tronson, took Budd's place as principal private secretary. The office may have gained in political sensitivity but at the cost of administrative effectiveness: the move was not a success. And it was strongly resisted from the first by the secretary of PMC, Geoffrey Yeend. Hence, when Tronson left the staff in late 1979 to return to a job at Liberal Party headquarters, a new phase was ushered in with the appointment of a permanent public servant and career diplomat, Michael Cook, to the newly titled position of chief executive.

If at this point Fraser had been successfully persuaded of the centrality of the bureaucratic element to the private office, before the year was out he was to be profoundly dissatisfied. Cook provided competent administration of the office, but tried to preserve a public servant's 'neutrality' when it came to the inevitable political decisions and actions the private office had to take. The problem came to a head with the October 1980 election campaign. Cook's resistance to any involvement

72. Russell Schneider, *War Without Blood: Malcolm Fraser in Power*, Sydnen: Angus & Robertson, 1980, p. 5; Mediansky and Nockels (1981), *op. cit.*, pp. 395–400.
73. G. Hawker, R.F.I. Smith and P. Weller, *Politics and Policy in Australia*, St Lucia: University of Queensland Press, 1979, pp. 120–2.

in the political aspects of the private office's work in effect precluded him from participation in the campaign. So Fraser's office lacked leadership and co-ordination at a crucial time, and Fraser was forced to campaign without an effective personal staff. Although Fraser retained power, for the first time since 1975 the L-NCP government looked seriously threatened. The difficulty of the campaign, and the abundant criticism of the way in which the campaign had been conducted, compounded his conviction that the private office had seriously let him down. Determined not to face future difficulties of this sort, Fraser instigated the moves which were to lead to significant revamping of the private office, developing it beyond the structure that had been inherited from his Labor predecessor.

His first move was to turn back to the personnel who had served him well in 1975 and 1976. Dr David Kemp, now a professor of politics at Monash University, was invited to return to the staff. Kemp had begun to argue for a more far-reaching policy and political role for the private office during his earlier period of service with Fraser, and the invitation to return was tantamount to a recognition of the force of that argument. On Kemp's acceptance of this invitation, Michael Cook resigned to return to the public service, as director-general of the Office of National Assessments. With Kemp's return, the office was both expanded and upgraded.

At the senior level, the office was strengthened by moving away from the ministerial officer gradings initiated by Labor and bringing in advisers paid as consultants. Kemp was appointed director of the private office and was paid on a consultancy basis, at a level significantly above that which would have been accommodated under any of the previous ministerial officer gradings. By bringing the salary of the director of the prime minister's office within the public service permanent head range, the importance of the position and the calibre of its occupant would be signalled clearly. Further, the director's position was now to be the apex of the whole ministerial staff structure, the point of direction and co-ordination, and the fulcrum for a stronger and more independent structure. With the emphasis on policy overview and co-ordination now attached to the director's role, the work of office administration passed to another new position, that of senior administrator (somewhat akin to the former position of principal private secretary) and Dale Budd was invited to return to the office temporarily in that capacity and charged with tightening up office functions and helping to find and train his successor. Budd, too, was paid as a consultant, as were some high-level part-time academic advisers: Professor John Rose, an economist from the University of Melbourne, and Professor Cliff Walsh, an economist from the University of Adelaide. (At the same time, the treasurer, John Howard, had another academic economist, Professor John Hewson of the University of New South Wales, on his staff on a consultancy basis.)

The prime minister also called on the advice of a foreign affairs specialist, Professor Owen Harries of the University of New South Wales, who had initially been brought into government service at the instigation of the then foreign minister Andrew Peacock in 1977 and was situated in the Department of Foreign Affairs. However, he had gradually been taken up by the prime minister, and now moved into PMC to work at Fraser's behest.

These initiatives were popularly represented as 'a triumph of academia over bureaucracy', or hailed as the 'return of the eggheads',[74] and (more significantly) one newspaper headed its report 'Private team moves into PM's realm'.[75] By late 1981, the prime minister's private office under Fraser had become a more powerful policy resource than any enjoyed by his predecessors. Table 2.2 gives a comparison of senior prime ministerial staff under Whitlam (in 1974) and Fraser (in 1981) and underlines the structural and qualitative changes.

By late 1981 the prime minister's private office was a body of senior status and impressive credentials. Within the government, the partisan, political and policy role of the office (and by extension of other ministerial staffs) was now recognised. The bureaucratic element was subordinate, as the value of a politically attuned staff was asserted. It was accepted that any advice entailed certain values and assumptions, that the values of the public service might not necessarily complement those of the government, and that it was therefore essential to have a mechanism for evaluation staffed by those who clearly shared the government's aims and philosophy. Indeed, the prime minister's office laid considerable stress on its concern with the philosophical consistency of the government's actions, evaluating in these terms both the advice it was receiving and the initiatives put forward by different ministers. The object was to encourage the government's unity of purpose as well as broader party unity. The intention was not for the office to use its own expertise to generate alternative policy advice, but rather to call on its resources of technical competence combined with political sensitivity, to evaluate the advice that was being put forward. The aim, therefore, was not to compete with the public service, but rather, by commentary and consultation, to stimulate it to work along lines that took cognisance of the government's political purposes. In other words, the private office was not designed primarily as a source of policy initiatives but to extend the prime minister's directive and controlling capacities with respect to the public service and the generation of policy. Coincidentally, of course, it gave Fraser a considerable capacity to overview the work of his ministerial colleagues.

74. *The Age*, 21 February 1981; *The News*, 11 April 1981.
75. *Sydney Morning Herald*, 17 February 1981.

Table 2.2 PRIME MINISTER'S STAFF 1974: MR WHITLAM

Designation	*Name*	*Salary (1981 level)*
Ministerial Officer 5	Mr J. Spigelman	$32,250
Ministerial Officer 3	Mr G. Blunden	$24,954–25,821
Clerk Class 11	Ms E. Reid	$29,096
Ministerial Officer 3	Mr M. Delaney	$24,954–25,821
Ministerial Officer 1	Ms C. Summerhayes	$17,718–18,879
Press Secretary	Mr E. Williams	$29,792
Public Relations Officer	Mr D. Solomon	(no 1981 equivalent)
Public Relations Officer	Mr E. Walsh	(no 1981 equivalent)
Media Secretary	Ms P. Warn	(no 1981 equivalent)

(*Total staff of PM's private office:* 21)

PRIME MINISTER'S STAFF, 1981: MR FRASER

Designation	*Name*	*Salary/Consultancy*
Director	Professor D. Kemp	$50,000
Senior Administrator	Mr D. Budd	$46,950
Senior Adviser (part-time)	Professor C. Walsh	$ 8,183
Consultant to PM (part-time)	Professor P.J. Rose	$ 9,900
Senior Adviser (MO 4)	Dr D.N. White	$32,228
Senior Private Secretary (MO 4)	Dr D. Rosalky	$32,228
Press Secretary (JA 4)	Mr D.F.S. Barrett	$29,792
Press Officer (JA l)	Mr O. Lloyd	$23,694–24,581
Ministerial Officer/cabinet (Clerk Class 9)	Mr R. Bagley	$23,224–24,083

(*Total staff of PM's private office*: 23)

After the experiences of 1980, it was also felt that the office must play a more direct role in liaising with the party more generally, and in facilitating contact between cabinet and backbench, and communication with the party secretariat, state branches and organisations such as the Young Liberals.

Arguably, Fraser's private office might have been expected to take up a role akin to that originally intended for Whitlam's priorities review staff. Unlike that ill-fated body, it could not be shunted aside as a peripheral oddity — located in parliament with the prime minister, the private office was the strategic point where the flow of information from both party and public service institutions came together, and for the first time it had the personnel and facilities to take advantage of this. Yet events were to prevent the new structure realising its potential.

The evolution of the prime minister's private office was a late development in Fraser's term, impelled by 'the smell of defeat'[76] around the 1980 campaign and Fraser's conviction that a more effective office was essential to his resurgence. The L-NCP coalition remained embattled throughout 1981–2: Fraser's office had neither the time nor sufficiently settled circumstances to reach top gear. Changes of key personnel played their part. Speech writer Alan Jones left the staff in early 1981, commenting 'it's no career being speech writer to a prime minister'. Special adviser on foreign affairs, Owen Harries, left Fraser's service late in 1981 to take up the plum appointment of ambassador to UNESCO. David Kemp, out of whose discussions with Fraser the new office structure had emerged, and a key figure in its implementation, returned to his academic post at the end of 1981 following a family tragedy. He was succeeded by Dr Denis White, a political scientist and colleague of Kemp's from Monash University who had been brought into the office as an adviser by Kemp early in 1981, but who had neither the political nor the intellectual gifts of his colleague. Dale Budd's chosen successor as senior administrator, Keith Witney, an economist from the ANZ Bank, stayed with the office less than a year and was in turn succeeded by Ron Harvey, a public servant from PMC who reverted to the title of principal private secretary. After seven years heading the prime minister's press staff, David Barnett resigned to join a consulting business in 1982. A senior staffer was moved to remark in retrospect: 'These things tend to be built around personalities, and if a personality is removed and is not adequately replaced . . . the system changes'. Indeed, by the end of 1982, the urgency of 'restocking' the prime minister's private office, and the possibility of new procedures as a result of this, was a matter of public comment: one report referred to 'the power vacuum behind the throne'.[77] The experiment came to an end early in 1983 when Fraser gambled on calling an early election and lost.

If the prime minister's private office was not as effective as had been hoped in realising the intentions that had impelled its restructuring, it was nonetheless a significant advance on the groundwork established by the Whitlam government. What is more, the potential for policy influence of 'the private team' began to be recognised, and their names began to appear in the press, just as had those of Whitlam's team when these operations were more novel. The controversy surrounding the level of Kemp's reappointment to the office sparked speculation about the 'power' that would attach to his position. As the new office settled down, the names of economic advisers Rose, Walsh, and Hewson (the latter attached not to the prime minister but to the treasurer) began to figure frequently in commentary on economic policy. Indeed, when a business

76. *Australian Financial Review*, 2 January 1981.
77. *The Australian*, 1 January 1983.

magazine commenting on the making of the 1982 budget referred to the 'troika' of Walsh, Hewson, and Ed Visbord (a deputy secretary in PMC) as the government's most influential economic think-tank, the secretary of Treasury was provoked to a stinging reply, attacking 'meretricious players of the advisory stage', and warning of 'what happened to [the Whitlam] . . . government' in 1974 when it 'stopped listening' to Treasury.[78] Walsh later explained this response as a defence against Treasury's loss of power over a budget the strategy of which it found unpalatable, but asserted in unabashed terms 'that advisory staff will very much have the role of trying to educate the bureaucrats . . . to the direction the government wants to go in'.[79] It is evident that Fraser's advisers did not, finally, cast themselves in the low profile, service role that many commentators had predicted for them in the early months of the L-NCP government. Indeed, seized with the importance of their work, they might be argued to have pushed the limits of the adviser role further than any of their Labor counterparts in 1972–5. The legacy of the Fraser years was a prime ministerial office system that could serve as a significant political and policy resource for subsequent governments.

While Hawke maintained a prime ministerial staff exactly the size of Fraser's, reproducing the advantage Fraser had enjoyed over his colleagues, he gave pre-eminence to different sorts of skills and organised his office differently. There is some evidence that overall co-ordination of ministerial staff was intended to flow from the senior levels of Hawke's private office, a recognition of the doctrine Kemp had articulated under Fraser. Initially the political and party elements were accentuated in the organisation of the office: a public service officer, Graham Evans, with extensive experience in Foreign Affairs and Treasury, took the principal private secretary role; Hawke's principal adviser, Peter Barron, had been a key figure on NSW premier Neville Wran's team; and his senior adviser Bob Hogg, had served successfully for six years in the difficult position of state secretary of the Victorian Labor Party. Hawke also drew in people of academic expertise and used the consultancy system much as Fraser had. But while academics and experts had a role, they were far more subsidiary than such intellectuals as Wilenski under Whitlam or — more importantly — Kemp, Rose and Walsh under Fraser. Hawke was less interested in ideas than Whitlam and, while sharing Fraser's drive to win at all costs, less interested in philosophical justification than Fraser. 'Hawke saw politics as a contest of men rather than a battle of ideas . . . he made too few concessions to the idealism of the ALP . . .'[80] The staffing of his private office reflected this: Barron, a ruthless and intelligent pragmatist tutored by the distinctively hard-nosed NSW

78. Michelle Grattan, *The Age*, 25 November 1982
79. ABC Radio, *PM*, 21 June 1983.
80. Paul Kelly, *The Hawke Ascendancy*, Sydney: Angus & Robertson, 1984, p. 214.

machine, assumed the central role that Kemp had been called on to play under Fraser.

With the emphasis on the practical, Hawke's office showed more functional rationalisation than had Fraser's. It was divided into three groups: the administrative and secretariat group, the advising group, and the media relations group, with staff roles specifically designated within each group. Hawke's office perhaps appeared an administratively more effective unit than Fraser's. Nonetheless, it remained, like its predecessors, a sprawling political unit where there was little attempt at effective co-ordination, perhaps as a result of the individualistic working practices of ministerial staffers. It is important to note here that Hawke's office at first was clearly developed on the basis of arrangements introduced by Kemp under Fraser, and arguably represented a more pointed recognition of the argument which motivated Kemp's modification: namely, the importance of the elevation of the partisan and political elements (as opposed to the purely administrative and functional roles) of the private office.

A further modification to staffing patterns in ministerial offices by the Hawke government was the legislative provision in 1984 for ministers to appoint consultants on top of their established staff entitlement. Previously it had been possible to appoint consultants for specific tasks within departments, through departmental machinery, but this did not satisfy demands for consultants to work directly for ministers. Fraser had introduced consultants into the office of prime minister and treasurer, but the 1984 legislation gave a statutory basis for the entire ministry to take up this practice. This initiative came under recurrent attack as a covert means of awarding rewards to party loyalists and an augmentation of political resources to the ministry that was difficult to vet.[81] But resort to such consultancies was spread across cabinet and Hawke's own usage was not particularly marked, suggesting it was not a facility he especially needed.

Over time, however, there were changes in Hawke's office which indicated a move away from initial intentions, and indeed a move away from the pattern introduced under Whitlam and developed under Fraser. There was a reversion to the practice of drawing key private office staff from the public service, and in particular from PMC, rather than from partisan sources. When the Hogg/Barron duo broke down (Hogg left first, allegedly unhappy that he had been relatively less influential than Barron; Barron left in 1986), it was not replicated. Hogg was not replaced in the same sense: the two roles became one. Although other political advisers were appointed after Barron — such as Bob Sorby, and Geoff Walsh (who was regarded as particularly competent) — none of

81. See, for instance, heated debates in the Senate, *CPD* (Senate), 23 November 1989, pp. 3125–8; and 28 November 1989, pp. 3447–8.

these achieved the profile or the influence that had been attributed to Barron. More significant was the continuity of able public servants at the organisational hub of the office in the principal private secretary's role — Evans first, then Chris Conybeare, Sandy Holloway and Dennis Richardson, all from PMC. And this in turn reflected what was most important — the effective relations established with Hawke by the heads of PMC, Yeend and then Codd, and the department's view that there should be 'a fully co-operative working relationship between the department and staff working in ministers' private offices. That task is made easier the more that administrative and advising staff in the ministers' private offices are drawn from the portfolio department.'[82]

Whitlam, and Fraser in particular, did not necessarily want such smooth co-operation, seeking instead the sort of friction that would ginger-up both sets of players and produce competing options, from which they could choose. They each had a philosophy and an agenda that demanded both intellectual and political input from the loyalists at their sides. Hawke was of a different nature, concerned not with grand vision but with the solution of immediate problems. And PMC, in concert with his office, gave him what he wanted. As early as 1986, therefore, press observers noted:

> When he first came to power . . . the public service was distrusted — as a newcomer to parliamentary politics Hawke didn't understand how it worked. He has since discovered that there is efficiency in the public service: he has learnt what they have to offer and they have learnt how to work with him. The influence of his office staff has decreased because he has found a circle of public servants whose advice he trusts. He does not, as did Whitlam, look for alternatives to bureaucratic advice.[83]

Emblematic of the differences were the briefings each prime minister sought. Every prime minister had taken advantage of PMC briefing notes, such as those described by Bunting and Menzies earlier. But, on matters of policy, Whitlam and Fraser drew on other sources as well — extra-parliamentary and party contacts, and private office advisers in particular. Fraser instituted daily oral briefings before parliament in which PMC officers and his private office staff participated. There was no such pattern of oral briefings with Hawke. This is not to say that he sought no advice from friends, party contacts or personal staff, but his preference was for briefing notes and so the process of producing a paper relating to each decision dominated. PMC was adept at producing these papers. Hawke sometimes took wider soundings after reading them, but often simply accepted them. They appeared to serve his needs.

82. Codd (1990), *op. cit.*, p. 24.
83. *Sydney Morning Herald*, 26 April 1986, p. 37.

Not surprisingly, the structure and the size of the private office scarcely changed under Hawke: there was no further pressure to extend or transform this resource, and in outline the office looked much the same in 1988[84] as it had in 1983 — with the difference that individuals in specific roles were now more likely departmental than political. The departmental view was that close communication with the prime minister's office had been encouraged by bringing in able officers from the public service, and indeed that offices dominated by political appointees were prone to become decreasingly relevant in the policy process over the long term. In contrast, one line of public commentary stressed that the politicised private office became less necessary as the public service — and especially PMC — underwent changes that made it increasingly politicised and attuned to giving the government what it wanted.[85]

At the time of writing, the received view, at least among those involved, was of the complementarity of PMC and the private office, as this passage attests:

> The Prime Minister's Office under Mr. Hawke never saw itself as being in competition with the Department for influence over the policy process. On the contrary, it was the accepted doctrine in the Office that the two had complementary capabilities and that a close working relationship was very much in the Prime Minister's interest.
>
> The relevant capabilities of the Prime Minister's office included automatic access of staff to the Prime Minister himself, the closeness and informality of their contact with the Prime Minister, the multi-disciplinary skills (policy, politics, media, speech-writing and so on) brought together in the Office and sensitive antenna attuned to the political and parliamentary milieu. The capabilities of the Department, as seen from the Office, included a capacity to provide high quality advice quickly across virtually the whole range of Government policy, the outreach of the Department into the Public Service generally, the Department's capacity to energise the Government system to get decisions implemented effectively, its ability to stand back from day to day events and to propose creative longer term initiatives and its commitment and discretion.
>
> Staff in the Office and officials in the Department each regarded contact with the other as amongst the most important of their day to day working relationships in Canberra.
>
> Differences of view did occur. On occasions, one side might criticise the other. But there was always the wider context of a mutual interest, clearly recognised, in working together. And this was strengthened in many cases

84. See *CPD* (Senate), 13 December 1988, p. 4129, and compare the table outlining Fraser's private office staff, on p. 52.
85. See, for instance, 'Chairman Bob of Australia Limited', *Sydney Morning Herald*, 26 April 1986; special issue of the *Canberra Bulletin of Public Administration*, 52, 1987; 'Life's not peachy for mandarins', *Australian Financial Review*, 29 April 1988; 'The fade-out of the Humphreys', *The Bulletin*, 16 April 1991.

by close personal connections which built up over the years and the quite extensive rotation of Departmental staff through the Office.[86]

Whatever the long-term assessment of these processes, it is clear that under Hawke the political and personal edge that both Whitlam and Fraser demanded in the private office was tempered: Hawke's expectations of and use of the private office more nearly approached Menzies's practice than that of his immediate predecessors. Yet the office — in size and structure — remained a significant resource and one which a dissatisfied prime minister could readily turn into a political and personal tool once more. Fraser, after all, swiftly adopted that resort when he became dissatisfied with the quality of political advice he was getting towards the end of his term. And as the Hawke government became increasingly embattled, the perception that the prime minister was not receiving the right quality of political advice was frequently voiced in party circles. What could be more natural, then, than that attention should turn once more to enhancing the political calibre of the private office? Equally, to the extent that the public perception that the public service has been politicised by Labor holds, then, if there is a change of government, there will be an incentive for the new prime minister to reinforce the partisan and loyalist element in the private office as his weapon against the bureaucracy (just as Whitlam did). But, for the moment, the dominant role of PMC is not in question.

Conclusion

We can review these developments both to assess the flux of influence and power of the prime minister's staff, and to assess their effects upon the capacities of prime ministers. In relation to the first point, it is clear that the entity that becomes the strategic point for the flow of information in the public service *and* has the prime ministers' ear is potentially the most influential body in government. In relation to the second, the prime ministers' enhanced ability to monitor, question and command alternatives from ministerial colleagues — because of better support and greater variety of information — can allow dominance in the policy process. Yet the potential for policy supremacy may not be matched by an enhanced capacity to attract appropriate political advice: prime ministers for all their resources can still find themselves divorced from party and electoral expectations, as Fraser found in 1983 and Hawke in 1991.

Dedman's perception, in 1949, that prime ministers would be the pivot of post-war government, was our starting point. Prime ministers

86. Sandy Hollway, Deputy Secretary, PMC, and former principal private secretary in Hawke's office, personal communication.

would need support; the supporting body — their department — would have to mediate and co-ordinate. From the first, the question that followed was: to what extent would the co-ordinating body need policy expertise (in some sense, duplicating line departments) to enable it effectively to co-ordinate? Despite Bunting's profession in 1988 that PMs officers worked 'not as experts but as inexperts', the struggle over this issue began with the wrangle over the Economic Policy and Research Section in 1949. It was not resolved until 1976, when Fraser's demand that PMC should have the capacity to attend to the full range of policy detail finally overcame departmental resistance. The steps that had paved the way for this, however, were the demands of his predecessors, Gorton and Whitlam, that PMC should respond on a wide range of issues and act not simply as umpire and mediator but as a vigorous agent of their initiatives in the policy process.

The *de facto* influence of the secretary of PMC, because of privileged access to knowledge of what went on in cabinet, and its translation to the other departments, by the mid-1970s was formalised in such bodies as the Policy Coordination Unit and the Projects Division within PMC, charged with bringing the flow of advice together (and reinforcing PMC's centrality). The strategic location of PMC was not, however, uncontested as, at various times, the prime minister's office itself became the focal point in the flow of information. The intention that it become the policy dynamo was most evident in the early years of Whitlam's government; its failure to achieve this was the incentive for reinvigorating PMC. Yet the sense that the private office staff were 'hostile witnesses' in the interaction with PMC did not entirely evaporate, and when Fraser felt his department could not adequately serve his political needs the private office was revamped again, with the explicit intention that it be the strategic point for the flow of information. That impetus faded under Hawke, partly because the public service underwent reform designed to make it more sensitive to government needs. In that process of reform a more streamlined and centralised public service placed PMC even more firmly at the centre of government. For most of the Hawke period, the relations between PMC and the private office were smooth and co-operative.

Each step in the process has been influenced by a complex interplay of demands generated by the broad political context, the needs of the individual prime ministers and the capacity of individuals in the support infrastructure to respond. Chifley and Menzies needed the tool with which to fashion 'the new order' in the post-war reconstruction era, H.C. Coombs and A.S. Brown provided the blueprints for a PMs department. Gorton faced a volatile political climate in which the old verities were under challenge. He also had to prove himself. He sought, therefore, to fashion a vigorous department with the capacity to initiate and with like-minded men (recruited by Hewitt) in key roles. Whitlam wanted people of ideas to match his grand visions and needed structures to draw them in. His government, distrusting the public service, experimented with alternatives — a private office fashioned to Wilenski's design — before reinvigorating the department. Fraser, too, pursued a philosophical vision. Moreover, he was pressed by the demand to address economic decline and his own drive to be central to and control everything. So he expanded the policy capacity of the department and the role of the private office, further still. But Menadue's capacity to manage the transition from Whitlam to Fraser at PMC was crucial, and the elaboration of the private office probably depended on Kemp. Hawke, caught even more than Fraser by Australia's economic predicament, and personally inclined to management and consensus rather than an ideological agenda, was preoccupied with streamlined, cost-effective government and with solving economic problems first. Yeend and Codd were attuned to his needs and adept at refashioning the department to serve them. As the partisan element was increasingly less emphasised in the private office, the department and the office co-operated; PMC was ascendant but, in the public perception, increasingly prone to the attack of being itself political.

Underlying networks are of interest. Chifley's 'official family' was fashioned within the public service and not solely from his own department — but these were people recruited to an expanding service with the explicit aim of fashioning a new order, so can be assumed to have been like-minded. Menzies and his Liberal successors maintained varieties of an official family — and Menzies certainly called on officers of departments other than his own — but all were from the public service pool. It was with the creation, instead, of a 'private office' family, under Whitlam and Fraser, that different networks were brought directly into the policy process at the prime minister's side. Their constituents were party loyalists but also organic intellectuals[87] — that is, bearers of ideas and expertise charged with articulating a vision appropriate to their ideological project and period: the apogee was 'the triumph of academia' noted under Fraser. The perspectives of private office academics and public servants were sometimes notably at odds. Hawke drew less on academics and experts than had Whitlam and Fraser. And the networks were brought together again — partly by bringing consultants into the public service far more widely, partly by changing the means of recruitment for senior levels of the public service itself, partly by the practice of encouraging high fliers within the public service to serve a term in ministerial offices (including that of the prime minister). Arguably, the congruence of approach between prime ministers and their

87. For more extended discussion of this borrowing of Antonio Gramsci's concept, the organic intellectual, see James Walter, 'Intellectuals and the political culture', in Brian Head and James Walter (eds), *Intellectual Movements and Australian Society*, Melbourne: Oxford University Press, 1988, pp. 237–73.

public service advisers noted under Chifley was achieved again under Hawke. Yet whether the directly political work of outreach to party and constituency, and the directly political advice flowing from this, can ever be handled by means other than the partisan loyalist in the private office is a moot point. To the extent that this is downplayed, prime ministers may risk losing touch with the opinion that will keep them in office.

In summary, the post-war period has seen a significant augmentation of the resources available to a prime minister. The ability of prime ministers to monitor, probe and generate alternative policy options has been enhanced. They are, simply, better armed than any of their colleagues. This gives prime ministers the capacity to dominate the management of government. Whether a significant infrastructure, attuned to responding to their demands and to translating them to the public service, also generates the quality of political advice appropriate to a volatile context is a much more ambiguous question.

3

PRIME MINISTERS AND PARTIES

Glyn Davis

> No matter how great the leader, however, his tenure of power is never certain. Some change in the personnel of his gang or in the situation complex may bring his rule to a speedy end. He makes mistakes; the gang loses confidence in him, and he is 'down and out'. If he becomes conceited and bossy, he is sure to find himself summarily deposed, although he may for a time retain his power through sheer physical force. A new boy may appear, moreover, to contest the old leader's power through fighting him or in some other test of skill. The democracy of the gang, primitive though it may be, is a very sensitive mechanism, and, as a result, changes in leadership are frequent and 'lost leaders', many.[1]

The great era of street gang studies appears to have passed. Gone are those researchers happy to spend years in some poor American urban neighbourhood, ducking through a twilight zone of railway yards and factories to observe gangs in their natural 'ecology'. Frederic M. Thrasher counted 1313 gangs in Chicago, each with its own patch and characteristic social patterns. These street urchins briefly appeared in some realist Hollywood films of the late 1930s, a gaggle of boys roaming together until reform school, war, marriage or worse left a new clan to claim their mark. Though these groups shared much in the way of background and structure, Thrasher could find little pattern in gang leadership. Some gangs valued prize fighters, others dare-devils, brains or those firm of decision. Indeed, concluded Thrasher, the leader 'grows out of the gang', providing the qualities it requires at a particular time. Leaders then rule absolutely, but tenuously.

Where Thrasher began, William Foote Whyte[2] followed with a classic study of a street-corner society. Whyte investigated the social structure of an Italian slum in a place he called 'Cornerville' but others knew as inner Boston. Amid his rich data, Whyte observed a surprising regularity: the leader of a street gang 'always gave out more money and favours than he received'.[3] In the shifting and transitory social

1. F.M. Thrasher, *The Gang*, University of Chicago Press, 1927, p. 355.
2. W.F. Whyte, *Street Corner Society*, University of Chicago Press, 1943.
3. G. Easthope, *A History of Social Research Methods*, London: Longman, 1974, p. 96.

organisation of the street-corner gang, with membership voluntary, association fluid and rivalry rife, leadership is hard won and held. This is not the mere domination of the fittest but a more subtle relationship between leaders and led. Leaders may give more than they take, but loyalty is always provisional. Groups held together by one charismatic individual are susceptible to the charms of another. Like the streets themselves, gangs provide a domain across which leadership is contested.

Studies of this genre express a common finding of the social sciences: leadership is a function of organisation. Depending on context, only particular types of authority are considered legitimate. And legitimacy, as Blau reminds us, is the only basis of stable, organising power; unless the exercise of authority is within the bounds of accepted norms, the group has no incentive to co-operate.[4] Though an organisation may accept a range of leadership styles, it will not submit lightly to one outside its values. As Thrasher concluded:

> The leader of the gang is what he is because in one way or another he is what the boys want. The function of leadership is an inevitable growth out of the conflicts and other activities of the gang. The natural leader is the boy who comes nearest to fitting the requirements of this function: he 'fills the bill.'[5]

To fill the bill, mirror the membership, personify dreams and aspirations — these are the hopes of most aspiring leaders. Those who govern may emerge from limited choices and a lack of available alternatives. They may be elevated by a single bold action — a daring theft, a brazen robbery or an audacious leadership challenge. But they require the right values to carry the group. Some leaders benefit from the clearly defined role offered by their organisations; we have expectations of bishops and generals shaped by long-established patterns. When the organisation is diffuse, though, new leaders must find their own course or end, like Thrasher's former gang bosses, deposed and lost.

Though street gangs are fascinating there is a danger in making too much of the simile. They cannot literally stand for something else. Only street gangs are quite like street gangs. Yet a good analogy can help guide us through the essential feature of an issue. In examining a topic such as the relationship between prime ministers and parties, for example, it would be simple to produce a long list of attributes. Prime ministers typically perform the following 27 functions . . . parties respond in these enumerated ways . . . While analytically entirely valid, lists give no sense of dynamics, no feel for how the system operates in practice. Lists are listless, lifeless and desiccated descriptions of a rich and interesting reality. Metaphor and simile, on the other hand, give the

4. P.M. Blau, *Exchange and Power in Social Life*, New York: John Wiley & Sons, 1964, p. 200.
5. Thrasher, *op. cit.*, p. 357.

flavour of actuality.

It can be argued that mainstream Australian political parties resemble a street gang. Simms has described the Liberal Party as 'terrain across which conflict occurs',[6] where leaders have authority but not tenure. They preside at the pleasure of their colleagues, over organisations which have formal rules but in practice comprise several overlapping domains loosely bound by a national title; parliamentary wings, a national secretariat, state and territory branches and a standing soviet of members, committees and factions contend as centres of power. The federal organisation may shade into major sectional interest groups and, in the case of the Liberals, into a near-permanent alliance with the Nationals. Members share a common ambition to see their party in office, but the structures they work through are voluntary, complex and often lacking neat boundaries. As Aitkin, Jinks and Warhurst note, there is 'no such *thing* as the ALP. The Australian Labor Party is a label which applies to many sets of relationships between people.'[7]

The leader is expected to flourish in all the potential assemblies offered by an Australian political party — the local meeting, the electoral council barbecue, the state council gathering, the parliament and the cabinet. To be plausible the leader must embody the values of the party; to be successful he or she must win the support of a small, individually ambitious but collectively nervous and risk-averse collective known as the parliamentary caucus. The art is finding a leadership style which draws together this broad group of people, focuses their hopes and — by offering the prospect of spoils, unity or direction — keeps their support. In such an exchange, party leaders may indeed have to give more than they take. A leader must nurture support and offer rewards since the party can withdraw support, and with it office, at any time.

In the 1920s social scientists found authority in a street gang provisional and contingent. Several generations later we might conclude the same of a different set of leaders. As Weller[8] has observed, the relationship between leader and party is 'essentially transactional'. In the language of those earlier social scientists, authority is based on 'social exchange' which, unlike economic bargaining, involves future obligations and so trusting others to keep their end of the deal.[9] It requires ability, guile and the right attributes at the time for a leader to stay on top in a structure where power is held only through continuously shifting alliances.

6. M. Simms, *A Liberal Nation*, Sydney: Hale & Iremonger, 1982, p. 1.
7. D. Aitkin, B. Jinks and J. Warhurst, *Australian Political Institutions*, 4th edn, Melbourne: Longman, 1989, p. 185.
8. P. Weller, *First Among Equals*, Sydney: Allen & Unwin, 1985, p. 19.
9. Blau, *op. cit.*, p. 93.

The Basis of the Bargain

Surveying their patch, new prime ministers confront an interesting streetscape. To one side are the buildings of government, now firmly under their command. Less certain is a second set of institutions — the parliament and, beyond, the political party which has carried the leader to great office. The parliament is unreliable because government members owe a split allegiance — to the prime minister if they hope for advancement, but to the faction and party branches which provide their nomination. Forced to choose between loyalty to the incumbent and continued pre-selection, many will not hesitate to review present leadership arrangements. Hence, to maintain credibility the prime minister must perform adequately in the House, before regular party meetings when parliament is in session, at weekly cabinet meetings most of the year, at committee meetings almost every day and at any private meetings demanded or cajoled by factions and colleagues. Contact with parliamentary accomplices will thus be continuous and exhaustive, and with every disagreement the prime minister will be reminded that substantive political authority rests with the party room.

Yet the parliamentary group is at least small and reasonably disciplined. The broader party is much more dangerous territory. The imperatives of government and the interests of party members will often not coincide. In the late 1970s Malcolm Fraser felt good administration required retrospective tax laws which hurt his own constituency. His successor, Bob Hawke, found it necessary during the 1980s to suppress the wages of most of his party supporters in the name of the national economy. The electorate is bigger than the party. In opposition, parties can be united because they have nothing to lose; in government, leaders almost always upset their own. A new prime minister must find a reliable formula which respects the form — if not necessarily the content — of promises to the faithful.

If the expectations of the party offer a challenge to policy-making, then so too does the structure of the organisation. Australian political parties are not nationally based, but rather are aggregations of powerful state and territory branches. Consequently there is not one gang but several, allied on paper but pursuing aggressively their own state or internecine interests. There may be state premiers from the same party, able to speak authoritatively in public and to plead in private;[10] decisions will be affected by considerations such as state elections, the factional balance in particular areas, and mumbles from local branches. Surveying the mark, a leader would see looming a number of key party events, including national and state conferences, policy launches and closed national council meetings. Here are expected the formal stuff of

10. Weller (1985), *op. cit.*

leadership — commanding speeches, vision and a program — as well as the private deals which maintain accord within any organisation.

Given this formidable vista, how does a new prime minister keep control? A leader could easily be overwhelmed by the collection of interests and jealousies which comprise a functioning party. After all, the gang has no shortage of potential challengers, some with strong claims. It contains a parliamentary core which will see many decisions through the narrow prism of staying in power, and a wider constituency ready to be disappointed. Those claiming loyalty in the states and territories will, when expeditious, attack their own in distant Canberra for local advantage. All are ready to demand from — rather than give to — the new boss.

Fortunately the leadership bargain, like all good deals, brings returns to both sides. Members rely on the leader's skills; backbenchers cannot make or save a government, and their own careers depend on the party attaining and retaining office. If they destabilise a government they risk their own ministerial future and, perhaps, their re-election. Similarly, state governments depend on a favourable relationship with the national leader. Much state largesse is actually Commonwealth money, so a vindictive prime minister is a considerable threat to a vulnerable state premier. All in the party fear the barrenness of opposition. A party out of power has no opportunity to achieve objectives, dispense patronage or enjoy authority. A leader who can deliver office thus exerts a powerful attraction. The party must gamble on one person who can project the message and ensure the discipline required; if the wheel can turn it will carry everyone higher. This trade-off, subordinating individual hopes to a wider cause, is the basis of the bargain: the leader does not have to be good, or even popular, just successful.

Just as Thrasher and colleagues examined street gangs systematically from the different perspective of members, leaders and those in officialdom charged with policing the 'gang problem', one can now explore the leadership bargain from three angles. How does the office of prime minister look to backbenchers, to the party organisation and to the incumbent?

The View from Below

We possess some important biographies of prime ministers, including those by Crisp, Reid, Freudenberg and Walter.[11] Weller[12] has contributed

11. L.F. Crisp, *Ben Chifley: A Political Biography*, Sydney: Angus & Robertson, 1961; A. Reid, *The Gorton Experiment*, Sydney: Shakespeare Head Press, 1971; G. Freudenberg, *A Certain Grandeur: Gough Whitlam in politics*, Melbourne: Sun Books, 1978; J. Walter, *The Leader: a political biography of Gough Whitlam*, St Lucia: University of Queensland Press, 1980.
12. P. Weller, *Malcolm Fraser PM*, Ringwood: Penguin, 1989.

a unique study of prime ministerial power with his work on Malcolm Fraser. All provide insight into relations with the party from the perspective of the Lodge. Less numerous are observations from below — why backbenchers in particular accept the authority of a leader, and with what result.

Memories of Chifley's leadership, for example, are few. Former MP Fred Daly has provided one account of the first post-war prime minister, portraying a down-to-earth 'expert in human relations' who handled difficult ministers with ease, encouraged backbenchers by sitting with them in parliament and stressed the value of loyalty given and received.[13] Crisp notes that following the victory of war Chifley inherited a Labor Party organisation 'more happily united then for a generation past'.[14] As prime minister, Chifley held his parliamentary group together despite growing splits within the party and despite the bitter confrontation between a Labor government and the mining unions.

A more mixed view of a prime minister is offered in the recently published political memoirs of John Cramer (later Sir John).[15] Cramer entered political life during the Depression through the All-For-Australia League, worked within the Nationalist and then the United Australia Party, attained public office as the mayor of North Sydney, helped found the Liberal Party of Australia, became a backbencher and was minister for the army some years later. Cramer's reflections suggest a man still working through his relationship with the dominant figure of his time, Robert Menzies. Cramer is clearly both exasperated and awed by Menzies, whom he observed in defeat and then in extended triumph. He appears unhappy that Menzies is remembered as the 'father of the Liberal Party' when behind the scenes, as Cramer tells it, Menzies preferred the moribund Victorian-based UAP to efforts in Sydney to forge a new conservative party. Cramer portrays a reluctant Menzies forced into unity only when he could no longer resist the trend, and then skilful enough to claim credit for the work of others.

Given this less than flattering picture, what puzzles Cramer is the hold exercised on himself and his party by this leader :

> Lack of generosity of spirit was Menzies' biggest failing and the main reason why he never engendered a personal affection in his colleagues. I never knew him give genuine praise to anyone for their work or ideas. Worse still, he could very easily kill a new idea and then later bring it up as his own. He was clever — outstandingly so — but he lacked that human touch which drew men to him in a personal sense.[16]

13. F. Daly, *From Curtin to Kerr*, Melbourne: Sun Books, 1977, p. 37.
14. Crisp, *op. cit.*, p. 226.
15. J. Cramer, *Pioneers, Politics and People: a political memoir*, Sydney: Allen & Unwin, 1989.
16. *Ibid.*, p. 74.

As a backbencher Cramer was aggrieved to be passed over for the ministry; as a minister he discovered the prime minister inclined to go over his head. Cramer describes Menzies making decisions affecting the army portfolio, including the transfer of senior personnel, without discussion with the minister.[17] Yet Cramer cannot but admire the finesse with which Menzies retained his position. He is perhaps unsure how Menzies prevailed, though he mentions flattering private conversations designed to keep ministers on side, allowing members to sound off in the party room, and careful treatment of would-be rivals. It is a disappointment that Cramer still cannot draw on a substantive biography of Menzies as prime minister to explain the firm grip held over the party for so many years.

In the end Cramer attributes Menzies' good fortune with the party to the prime minister's character. He might believe Menzies aloof and distant but, he concedes, he was 'a man of tremendous ability', a leader 'far above his colleagues in personality and ability'.[18] During World War II Menzies was considered a loser, a man whose haughty style had lost office for himself and his gang. Yet Menzies survived this period of conservative collapse to become the embodiment of the party, the person who could 'fill the bill' and keep the Liberals in office. His character and his timeliness enabled him to prevail where his hapless successors did not. For as Cramer observes, reflecting on William McMahon :

> When members see the possibility of losing their seats they invariably blame their leader. Politics is a remorseless business and when the tide of public opinion turns against you, unless you can bring a miracle out of the hat, you must go down. Then no one cares tuppence about you.[19]

Cramer observed a triumphant leader. His parliamentary colleague, Peter Howson, watched in detail the fall of John Gorton. On Sunday 17 December 1967 Howson had just finished lunch when the phone rang: prime minister Holt was missing off Portsea.[20] Within a paragraph of describing the news his diary is busy recording speculation about the succession; politics is indeed a remorseless business. Several intense weeks of lobbying followed, chronicled in detail by Howson, particularly when his own ministerial position was threatened by pro-Gorton forces if he did not come out soon for their candidate.[21] Gorton prevailed and Howson duly lost his portfolio. He got mad first and even later. As an aggrieved backbencher, Howson spent three long years helping the new prime minister slowly to lose the confidence of his party. In May 1968

17. *Ibid.*, p. 185.
18. *Ibid.*, p. 54, p. 171–2.
19. *Ibid.*, p. 208.
20. P. Howson, *The Life of Politics*, D. Aitkin (ed.), Melbourne: Viking Press, 1984, p. 363.
21. *Ibid.*, p. 370.

Howson observed that Gorton was drifting away from his senior ministers, and must either learn to value their advice or face an eventual move to change the leadership.[22] In July he felt his concerns about Gorton's leadership echoed in comments by other Liberals such as Andrew Peacock and in August he was sharing with colleagues his 'unhappiness with the lack of leadership'.[23] By October 1968 Liberal backbenchers were speculating about possible successors.[24]

Gorton survived the year, a number of scandals within the party and a close election on 25 October 1969 when the conservatives were just returned after a loss of 15 seats. With the poll barely declared, forces within the Liberal Party mobilised to toss their leader. They were helped in the year ahead by Gorton's protracted brawls with various state premiers, all from the conservative side of politics. Though an initial challenge failed, in March 1971 the minister for defence, Malcolm Fraser, questioned the prime minister's loyalty and resigned. In a scene now part of political folklore, the Liberal Party met to consider the leadership issue. When a motion of no confidence in the prime minister tied at 33-all, with one informal vote, John Gorton used his casting ballot to remove himself from office. Shortly after Howson recorded the classic cry of the vindicated backbencher:

> When Gorton was elected three years ago I put in the diary what I thought would happen — and it happened. It has taken longer than I expected, and I think that in the battle that has gone on for so long the bitterness has entered a bit into my soul . . . I've had, throughout this whole time, to try to keep together a team whose aim was to get rid of Gorton and to get us back to the leadership that this nation deserves . . . Gorton was unfit to lead the nation. He has now been removed. We must ensure that he never returns to leadership.[25]

Gorton indeed is the exemplar of the leader who failed to carry his party. It seems all sections of the organisation could find fault with their prime minister — those experienced ministers dropped from his cabinets, the powerful state premiers disturbed by Gorton's 'centralist' policies, the party faithful who watched the conservative hegemony threatened by an apparently erratic and unpredictable leader. Peter Howson was only one of a number of backbenchers who believed he had a responsibility to campaign for Gorton's downfall. Nothing could be more undermining for a leader than a well-organised lobby, slowly obtaining the votes necessary for an execution. Yet as Reid noted, the great are not brought down easily; Reid concluded that 'Gorton's downfall was not planned by his opponents. It happened because of things he either did or did not do.

22. *Ibid.*, p. 432.
23. *Ibid.*, p. 450.
24. *Ibid.*, p. 470.
25. *Ibid.*, p. 705.

He was the architect of his own misfortune.'[26]

Gorton demonstrated the ultimate vulnerability of a prime minister, but also the advantages of incumbency. It is hard work to organise against the leader. Members do not wish to destabilise the party on which they depend, for the motto that 'division is death' holds grimly true in Australian politics. Further, backbenchers do not want to risk the eternal wrath of a prime minister through involvement in an unsuccessful coup. Howson knew he had no future under Gorton, but those with a glimmer of hope about their own prospects remained cautious about revolt. Gorton may have antagonised from the start of his reign, yet it still required more than three years and an unexpected crisis before a (bare) majority against him could be mustered.

The view from below stresses how much those in parliament rely on their leader. Daly clearly revered Chifley's quiet authority and tough persona. Cramer may not have liked Menzies, but he recognised his ability and enjoyed the benefits of prolonged government. Howson may talk of Gorton's leadership in terms of 'the nation', but his diary remains a running exposition of how much party confidence and direction are shaped by the prime minister. Both men were prepared to offer their loyalty, but they wanted in return stability, opportunity and success. Leaders who deliver these keep their side of the bargain.

The View from the Organisation

Gough Whitlam's victory in 1972 is often described as a triumph of both leader and a newly professional ALP. Guided by national secretary Mick Young, the 'It's Time' campaign relied upon a 'long exercise in regular collaboration' between the parliamentary leaders, their staff, the federal secretariat, the federal executive and the party's advertising agency.[27] Good relations with the organisation, though, did not follow Whitlam into office. New national secretary David Combe sought to maintain the links, but exchanges between Whitlam and ALP president Bob Hawke were not always warm. Indeed, within a year of the election Hawke and the Australian Council of Trade Unions (ACTU) were campaigning against the government over a referendum on prices and incomes.

Party organisations and, in particular, the national executives of Labor, the Liberals and the Nationals, seek to be factors in the political equation. They see their task as representing the long-term interests of the party and its members. This includes reminding governments of the basis of their support. A strong-minded federal president may seek to captain the team from the sidelines, rivaling the parliamentary leader for

26. Reid, *op. cit.*, p. 393.
27. Freudenberg, *op. cit.*, p. 224.

media attention and so setting up internal conflict. During the late 1980s, for example, it seemed Melbourne businessman John Elliot struggled to subordinate his impatience and ambition to the wider cause. As federal president of the Liberal Party Elliot expressed his own, much publicised, views on policy, and appeared at times equivocal about parliamentary leader John Howard. Elliot did little to dampen speculation about his own imminent entry to parliament, the leadership and the Lodge. No doubt Elliot saw his distinctive style as necessary to revitalise a party defeated in three successive federal elections, but those sections of the party accustomed to a more subdued public role for the organisation found the changed emphasis disturbing. Elliot's term as federal president expired in October 1990, and he did not seek re-election. His successor opted for a more low-key role and left policy announcements to a new parliamentary leader, Dr John Hewson.

Not all officials aspire to Elliot's profile, but in government and opposition alike senior party workers expect a voice in policy and tactics. As a newly elected prime minister, Gough Whitlam assumed a relatively free hand to implement his platform. Bob Hawke, soon president of both the party and the ACTU, saw it differently. As Freudenberg records, 'Hawke's mistake was to put the entitlement to consultation too high. Whitlam's mistake was to put the political advantages of consultation too low.'[28] As the Whitlam government ran into increasing economic and political problems, Hawke's exasperation — and sometimes public disputes — with the leader grew. Walter records a gradual shift, as Whitlam moved from dominating his party to difficulties not just with Hawke but with senior ministers and the caucus.[29]

In his account of the years 1972 to 1975, Gough Whitlam makes no reference to disagreements between prime minister and party president. He records only internal party disputes in Victoria during the late 1960s involving Hawke, and notes Hawke's opposition to a 'no new taxes' pledge in the 1972 campaign speech, before Hawke became national president.[30] The authorised biography of Hawke is less flattering about the relationship. After the debate about taxes, Hawke offended Whitlam by suggesting that he study economics. As D'Alpuget observes, 'the rivalry between them was to become intense.'[31] When the party president criticised a government decision, the prime minister emphasised that Hawke could not expect to be consulted about economic policy. Responding to a question at a National Press Club lunch, Whitlam remarked: 'Mr. Hawke's advice was not sought. It will not be sought . . . The president of the federal executive of the Labor Party does not

28. *Ibid.*, p. 284.
29. Walter, *op. cit.*, pp. 254–5.
30. G. Whitlam, *The Whitlam Government 1972–1975*, Melbourne: Viking, 1985, p. 197.
31. B. D'Alpuget, *Robert J. Hawke*, Ringwood: Penguin, 1984, p. 212.

determine such matters — is not consulted on such matters.' It is said that as he sat down, the prime minister suggested, *sotto voce*, something like 'that will show the little runt.'[32] The uncertain jurisdictions of leader and party president contributed to the perception of a divided administration.

When Hawke later became prime minister, he did not repeat the mistake of public brawls with the organisation. Hawke was careful to work well with national secretaries McMullan and Hogg, and to consult widely with the ACTU. The campaigning ability of the national secretariat, and its role in helping Labor against the odds in the 1987 and 1990 elections, cemented further the relationship between party organisation and leader. Hawke remained careful about working closely with factional leaders, stressing the importance of continued stability.[33] In this Hawke encouraged, and benefited from, the emergence of national factions within the party. By including every faction in deals, and by rewarding discipline, the prime minister carried his party through potentially destructive policy changes including conference resolutions which now allow uranium mining and privatisation of some public assets. Hawke consistently persuaded the party to fall in line with government policy. His achievement contrasts with the problems Whitlam experienced in convincing the ALP to adopt his platform proposals during the 1975 Terrigal conference.

Keeping the peace between the prime minister and party requires not only an astute leader, but the continuous work of sophisticated party bureaucrats. The professional and discreet party servant, offering timely advice but otherwise focusing on the logistics of organisation and campaigning, was the model employed by long-time Liberal functionary Tony Eggleton. An English migrant who began his political career as press secretary to Robert Menzies, Eggleton became federal director of the Liberal Party in 1975 and retained the post until April 1990. He chose a low public profile but remained a crucial link to the party for leaders from Fraser to Hewson. In government Eggleton could expect to be consulted whenever questions of government action turned to political considerations. Eggleton characterised his relationship with Malcolm Fraser as difficult but rewarding; Fraser 'worked at being prime minister day in and day out, hour in and hour out. Your phone could ring any time of the day or night. He was a tough taskmaster and a lot of people found it very hard working for him.'[34] Yet Eggleton persisted, and played an important role in rallying the numbers within the parliamentary party for Fraser when he faced a leadership challenge from Andrew Peacock during 1982. So close was the working relationship that Eggleton

32. *Ibid.*, p. 244.
33. P. Kelly, 'Leadership, Factionalism and the Prospects of the Hawke Government', *Canberra Bulletin of Public Administration*, 12 (2), 1985, p. 98.
34. *The Australian*, 7 April 1990.

helped prepare the prime minister's briefs for parliamentary question time, as well as supplying daily briefs from the party to the leader on sensitive issues.[35]

Observing the links between key party organisation officials and other players within the ALP, Parkin notes a range of possible relationships — conflict, circulation, co-optation, consensus, compliance and concessions.[36] All of these are possible, perhaps simultaneously, between party leader and organisation. No prime minister can satisfy all demands made in the name of the party, but a prime minister with a sense of history can not afford to alienate the organisation which selects parliamentarians, arranges their election campaigns and keeps open dialogue with party members. The party organisation represents the wider constituency, giving it voice and transmitting its opinions — along with its own assessments — to the leader. Used skilfully, the occasions provided by the party help a prime minister keep, or at least appear, in contact with the broader movement. The party provides an important channel of communication when government contacts fail. Bob Hawke used the party to convey messages to state Labor governments, and to remind them of their responsibilities to the federal party. State parties, in turn, use conferences and private meetings to signal their concerns to the leader in Canberra.

The party organisation, in short, cannot easily be separated from the office of prime minister. Both are part of the same web of relationships, a web which links the aspirations of local branches, the interests of state divisions and the hopes of those in parliament. The organisation provides institutional support for a prime minister, but it is also sensitive to party and public opinion. An organisation which worked to maintain Fraser's position in 1982 seemed to abandon Gorton in 1971. Like its parliamentarians, the organisation values success; anything less and the leaders are not keeping their side of the bargain.

The View from the Top

The perspective from backbenchers and the organisations indicates the obligations and ambitions of those who surround the prime minister. What of the view from the Lodge — how do prime ministers perceive their relationship with the party? Fortunately Weller, in a recent and detailed study of a prime ministership, has provided some evidence about how one incumbent worked with his party.[37]

35. Weller (1989), *op. cit.*, p. 165.
36. A. Parkin, 'Party Organisation and Machine Politics : the ALP in perspective' in A. Parkin and J. Warhurst (eds), *Machine Politics in the Australian Labor Party*, Sydney: Allen & Unwin, 1983, p. 23.
37. Weller (1989), *op. cit.*

In Weller's opinion, Malcolm Fraser 'fully appreciated the importance of the Liberal Party to his future; he accepted the principle that a good leader needed to maintain cohesion and solidarity within the party'.[38] Weller identifies at least nine sets of relationships between Fraser and the Liberal Party — those with backbenchers, party whips, the parliamentary leadership, ministers, the national secretariat, the federal president, the executive of the party, the state divisions and, of course, the Liberal branches within his own electorate. All demanded time and attention. Yet the parliamentary leader does not command institutional authority outside the House. Fraser could dominate his milieu when necessary, but his influence diminished with distance from Canberra. Hence Fraser, like all leaders before and since, could not exercise the same level of control over the state divisions of the party as he did over those near him in the cabinet and the party room.[39] Within the wider party, his was a position of respect, but not necessarily of power.

Party room meetings, suggests Cramer, can be 'a good outlet for members who [are] disgruntled or wanted to let off steam'.[40] Prime minister Fraser may not have always enjoyed proceedings, but he recognised their importance, attended as often as possible, and rarely used his authority to keep items off the agenda. If significant numbers of backbenchers dissented from a cabinet decision Fraser might agree to revisit the issue, or convene a meeting of the disaffected to talk through the topic. Backbenchers reported his style in the party room as firm but not dogmatic. Fraser usually prevailed — not least, as one backbencher put it, because 'after all he is the prime minister; you largely sink or swim by him'.[41] Less charitably, some suggest that Fraser only fought for those issues he cared about, and almost always obtained the result he sought. When asked to pass judgment in April 1982, the backbench split evenly between Fraser and challenger Andrew Peacock. It required the votes of ministers and parliamentary leaders to maintain the prime minister's position.

Fraser's links with the backbench were assisted by the party whips. These office-holders serve two purposes. They ensure the government's majority in the parliament and, equally important, they work to maintain the prime minister's ascendancy within the party. The whips kept Fraser informed about backbencher opinion. They tested the numbers when trouble loomed, and cajoled Fraser into regular contract with backbenchers who might otherwise have been ignored. In return the whips enjoyed regular access to the prime minister, a chance to demonstrate their ability and, if fortunate, eventual elevation to the ministry.

38. *Ibid.*, p. 149.
39. *Ibid.*, p. 174.
40. Cramer, *op. cit.*, p. 120.
41. Weller (1989), *op. cit.*, p. 156.

The whips do not just keep an eye on the backbench; they provide a prime minister with corridor opinion about cabinet performance and, one presumes, gossip about particular ministers. As the senior parliamentary representatives of the party, ministers are an important asset, and a constant danger, to a prime minister. They must be treated as colleagues and watched with wariness. As Weller relates, Fraser was careful to observe the proprieties of the cabinet system and to consult his ministers.[42] He turned up well briefed, and used the chair to express forcefully his own views. Perhaps as much by exhaustion as by art, Fraser was able to dominate cabinet. Ministers staggered under a load which left them ample opportunity to express opinions but little time for plots or treason.

Somehow amid the meetings, parliament and the official duties of a prime minister, Fraser found opportunities to work closely with Tony Eggleton and to encourage the federal secretariat to develop policy advice independent of that supplied by the public service. Eggleton in turn maintained close contact with the federal and state division presidents, feeding them survey data and conveying their concerns and suggestions to the prime minister. Senior federal and state party officials could look forward to occasional dinners at the Lodge, and to Fraser attending important divisional councils. Both were a mixed blessing, since Malcolm Fraser in a combative mood would like to debate policy proposals and to win the argument. This habit, particularly at state divisional meetings, did not always endear him to officials. For despite the hard work the prime minister devoted to the party, 'Fraser could never control the state divisions; they remained as semi-autonomous fiefdoms.'[43] When Fraser sought to influence local pre-selections he was rebuffed. When he became involved in coalition disputes at state level he simply earned animosity, or proved ineffective. As a collection of autonomous branches, state divisions have little to gain by allegiance to a remote prime minister when more immediate local concerns are at risk.

In a persuasive analysis Little portrays Fraser as an intensely competitive figure, a man shuffling between principle and opportunity, narrow in his belief that politics finally is about 'contest-and-control', firm in his convictions about right and wrong.[44] Little accurately observes that these characteristics can produce instability and discord. Yet the details suggest that Fraser sought to anchor his government in a strong relationship with the party. Potential disharmony was addressed by endless consultation, in which a prime minister involved himself in every available party forum. As leader of the gang, Fraser knew he could command respect but had to work hard for allegiance.

Within the party room Fraser employed a key device open to a

42. *Ibid.*, p. 106.
43. *Ibid.*, p. 168.
44. G. Little, 'Fraser and Fraserism', *Meanjin*, 41 (3), 1982.

Liberal leader in securing backbench support — the prospect that one day the prime minister will elevate a member to the ministry. This power of patronage ensured backbenchers were keen to impress the prime minister with their ability and their loyalty. Outside parliament Fraser insisted on regular meetings with the organisation, accepted a steady flow of policy advice from the federal secretariat and sought a close relationship with senior party officials. Though the will to contest sometimes overcame the need to listen, prime minister Fraser successfully carried the organisation though seven years of government. Unfortunately for his party, the prime minister then employed a prerogative of office — the right to call an election — and suffered the consequences.

Viewed from the top, the leader faces a formidable array of obligations and expectations. A prime minister, though, has some crucial resources. These include institutional support from the party organisation and parliamentary whips, a prestige which can be bestowed on party functions and officials, and an impressive parcel of patronage rights to be deployed in maintaining position. Indeed Blau suggests it is the 'distribution of rewards that most directly effects the legitimacy of leadership'.[45] For a Liberal prime minister the rewards to be dispensed include the power to appoint ministers. Within the ALP ministers are selected by caucus, but the right to assign portfolios, and to rearrange the structures of government, remains a prized privilege. The prime minister influences not just government decisions but the agenda of cabinet, so that the concerns of one faction can be favoured and others withheld. The leader's position may depend on the whim of the party room, but while in the job it offers advantages which can be used ruthlessly to stay on top.

Weller's study is unique. We do not possess the same detail on other recent prime ministers. Despite the millions of words written on Whitlam's last days in office we lack equivalent information about the months and years before. One potential source, the diaries of Clyde Cameron, were stolen from his garage in July 1982, so denying us an insider's view of Whitlam operating as prime minister.[46] No studies have yet been published on the tenure of Bob Hawke, though the fact that his cabinet included several former political scientists encourages hopes for diaries which illuminate the relationship between leader and party.

Given this absence of data, the Fraser experience tends to be taken as paradigmatic. It is more difficult to judge therefore whether some innovations under Hawke were particular to his style or will mark future Labor governments. The role of caucus, for example, was diminished by a national factional structure; decisions were instead negotiated between factional leaders, rather than within the parliamentary party or at the time

45. Blau, *op. cit.*, p. 202.
46. Reported in C. Cameron, *The Cameron Diaries*, Sydney: Allen & Unwin, 1990, p. ix.

of biennial conferences. Since prime ministers find it difficult to control the broader party, this change suggests some reduction in both prime ministerial and party room authority.

Such a reading, though, may be overstated. The move to stitch deals through party factions rather than parliamentarians simply shifted the forum in which some policy disputes were resolved; even then the national factional leaders were all themselves members of parliament. This practice can be seen as significant — or it can be interpreted as primarily concerned with imagery, since the importance of appearing united made the Hawke government reluctant to be seen at odds internally; private deals enabled the caucus to ratify, rather than make, decisions. It will require more prime ministers before we know whether a change has become a trend.

Prime Ministers and Parties

The street gangs of the 1920s and 1930s are long gone, along with studies of the genre. If any of those young boys, who once stared defiantly at Thrasher's camera, still survive they are old men now. If unlucky, they may even be victims of their successors, the packs which flourish in some American cities. Contemporary gangs tout more frightening weapons, and may deal in illicit drugs, but they are likely to follow the example of earlier generations in structure and organisation. Leaders still prevail through opportunity and exchange, gangs still value success and shun the vanquished. While the externals change, the characteristic patterns of organisation, and leadership based on transaction, remain.

So it is with prime ministers. The pressures of office may have increased, along with the quality of accommodation, the size of staff and the importance of the media, but the basic relationship between leader and party was unaltered from Chifley to Hawke. The mechanics of governing evolved but the bargain did not. Parties still offer allegiance in return for the prospect of office. Prime ministers employ the resources they have, notably patronage and prestige, in return for support and even loyalty. This is still a compact between leaders and led, a social exchange in the interests of collective success, a transaction between a party room which wants leadership and a prime minister who needs a majority.

That deal allows a range of possibilities. No one leadership style will always prevail; as on the streets, there is a sense of the leader being right for the times, of a prime minister who 'grows out of the gang'. Thus the prime ministers of the last 50 years are a reasonably diverse group and it is common for a long-serving leader to be characterised as outdated, wrong for changed circumstances. Even within one reign, there may be a cycle of leadership, from high points after election victories to times when power and popularity ebb.

Such variation remains possible because the basic dynamics of the post are largely unchanged. The cabinet process may have become bureaucratic, but prime ministers work within the same constraints as their predecessors did. Though the party may be more sophisticated in polling and election techniques, it still relies on a single individual who can embody, and sell, the message. The exchange between leader and led remains the basis of the bargain. The story of prime ministers and parties is not a trajectory toward some new and higher form, but an endless iteration of old and familiar themes. A leader who fits the times, can inspire the gang and will take it to success still has a chance to walk down these mean streets.

4

PRIME MINISTERS AND PARLIAMENT: PATTERNS OF CONTROL

John Uhr

'Parliamentary government is government by speaking. In such a government, the power of speaking is the most highly prized of all the qualities which a politician can possess: and that power may exist, in the highest degree, without judgment, without fortitude, without skill in reading the characters of men or the signs of the times, without any knowledge of the principles of legislation or of political economy, and without any skill in diplomacy or in the administration of war.'

—— Macaulay on William Pitt, 1859

Prime ministers each have a distinctive mode of executive control over parliament, derived in different measures from the state of their party in parliament and of their domination over their parliamentary party colleagues, together with such vital features as the quality of opposition leadership, the relevance of minor or third parties and Senate independence. There is no single model of prime ministerial political management: Chifley's artfully mute reliance on 'the numbers', Menzies's zestful display of divide and rule, Whitlam's mandatory indignation and open challenges over constitutional legitimacy, Fraser's demanding moralism and Hawke's clever consensualism — each of the classic leaders illustrates a typical mode of control appropriate to a specific set of political circumstances likely to recur at irregular intervals in the cycle of control.

Constitutional Perspectives

This chapter analyses the patterns of political management exercised by prime ministers over parliament, using an analytical history in which each of the five major forms of prime ministerial leadership are compared on a common set of categories. Overall, these categories of political management are the basic elements which taken together illustrate the range of devices to which recent executives have resorted in the quest for parliamentary control. These control devices constitute a kind of illustrated manual of parliamentary management and stand as something of an invitation to rulers on modes of rule appropriate to different parliamentary circumstances.

Not all readers will think such an enterprise at all sound or 'appropriate'. Decent-minded citizens and anxious legislators might think that a listing of proven control measures will only serve to embolden ambitious executives and assist their quest for domination of parliament. My general response is that all parliamentarians, opposition, minor party and independent as well as government members, here have an open opportunity to learn about the repertoire of executive ruses and to enlist that information in the cause of more effective parliaments, should that really be part of their concern. Besides, many of my illustrations of executive ploys show political incompetence and draw at best only negative lessons on how not to manage parliamentary affairs. My perspective is not that of an enthusiast for executive power at the expense of legislative power and responsibilities. My interest is in illustrating the zone of acceptable tolerance in the ever-changing balance between executive and legislative powers. Given the prime ministerial focus of this book, my immediate intention is to illustrate the variety of devices invented for parliamentary control or relied on by recent prime ministers. The chapter is informed, however, by an overriding interest in the developing character of Australian constitutionalism, especially in the liberal opportunities provided by the Australian Constitution for parliament to set whatever terms and conditions it sees fit in the relationship between it and the executive.

As Reid and Forrest amply explain, the Australian parliament has actively promoted the very ethos of party government which it appeals against when called upon to account for its own ineffectiveness.[1] Parliament has wilfully surrendered much of its power to the executive and has only itself to blame for much of the imbalance between the two branches of government. Perhaps further illustrations of its capitulation might serve to render it less liable to executive capture in the future.

Against the Grain of Governance

History is on the side of executive control of parliament, even if constitutional theory rates parliament as the institution of control over the powers and agents of government. The grain of parliamentary government as it has historically developed runs against active and powerful parliaments: resisting the political devices of prime ministerial management runs counter to the spirit if not the letter of parliamentary

1. G.S. Reid and M. Forrest, *Australia's Commonwealth Parliament, 1901–08*, Melbourne University Press, 1989, pp. 9–46.

constitutions. Perhaps the first great authority to recognise this was the eminent German social theorist Max Weber who, in search of lessons of governance relevant to post-war reconstruction in Germany, examined the inner logic of the British parliamentary model.[2] Weber's perspective is almost tragically sympathetic to the 'charisma' of chief executive leadership, yet it serves to frame our analysis by unveiling (i) the organisational capacities inherently available to parliamentary chief executives at the expense of non-ministerial members and (ii) the expected sources of opposition to schemes of prime ministerial control of parliament.

In trying to energise parliament in a manner consistent with both executive responsibilities and public interests, Weber unearthed the institutional tendencies with which executives have to learn to live. By calling on parliaments to lift their game and bring the best out of their executives, Weber helped form that coalition of interests which executives have to manage, whatever their ambitions. While Weber thought that parliaments had unused potential to help develop better qualities of executive leadership, serving prime ministers rarely see things this way. Weber at least has the virtue of clarifying their sources of likely opposition.[3]

Populist Ploys

The ideal model of parliamentary government indicates an odd tension between the minor principle of resistance to arbitary government and the major new principle of executive legitimacy through extra-parliamentary populism — or 'plebiscitarianism' to use Weber's category of modern caesarism. The model parliamentary executive is exemplified by Gladstone, who for Weber captured the ethos of leadership in mass democracy: the plebiscitarian or what we might call the 'soft caesar' principle. Gladstone's executive regime represented 'best practice' in the liberal use of parliamentary power.[4]

Although Gladstonian executives were true exemplars of the inner logic of parliamentary government, Weber reckoned that the UK model proved that the success of their governing powers actually required a high degree of 'positive politics' by non-ministerial parliamentarians in order to cultivate executive leadership compatible with liberal

2. M. Weber, 'Politics as a Vocation' in H. Gerth & C.W. Mills (eds) *From Max Weber*, London: Routledge & Kegan Paul, 1947, pp. 103–7.
3. See Reid and Forrest, *op. cit.*, p.7; also J. Uhr, 'Parliamentary Measures Evaluating Parliament's Policy Role' in Ian Marsh (ed.) *Governing in the 90s*, Sydney: CEDA, forthcoming; R. Eden, *Political Leadership and Nihilism*, Tampa: University Press of Florida, 1983.
4. M. Weber (1947), *op. cit.*, pp. 103–7.

constitutionalism. In Weber's eyes, Westminster regimes required strong parliaments as the breeding ground of mature political leadership, as a mean between the 'negative politics' of immaturely anti-executive institutions on the one hand, and the dangerously 'charismatic' populism typical of immature political leadership on the other.

For Weber, the model of executive leadership in parliamentary regimes was provided by Britain, where parliamentary activity was the essential schooling in political education for executive responsibilities. The political development of executive government required active parliamentary participation, which can be expected to be resisted from two quarters — one in the governing party, the other in the ruling bureaucracy — each of which requires artful executive management. Drawing on his own political experience as an adviser on techniques for 'taming princes', Weber described the patterns of parliamentary organisation most suited to effective, as distinguished from efficient, executive rule: effective rule being that which gave effect to the potential of the constitutional order, whereas efficient rule was that which minimised opposition and non-executive influence in producing the desired policy output for the least inconvenience to the executive.

To Weber, the British Commons was proof that an effective parliament can help in disciplining and training leadership along preferred policy paths. Weber's constitutional orientation remains a model for those taking their bearings from the requirements of effective governance, as distinct from efficient administration alone. Most approaches typical of executive and parliamentary studies tend to ignore Weber's realistic framework, although his approach to the realities of power and policy is consistent with an interest in responsible governance which is characteristic of the best of these two schools of institutional analysis.[5]

Obstacles to Parliamentary Leadership

The development of parliamentary government faces immense opposition from among the existing power-holders. Weber singled out two of the most vested interests: that of 'the typical party functionary' interested in partisan docility, and that of 'the like-minded interests of the civil service' fearful of pretenders to power. Weber recognised that bureaucratic state organisations necessarily have policy tasks, which can only really be accomplished under the leadership of politically responsible heads acting as ministers over 'the top ranks of the bureaucracy', so that 'parliament's first task is the supervision of these

5. See J. Blondel, *Comparative Legislatives*, New Jersey: Prentice-Hall, 1973; H.J. Marsfield, *Taming the Prince: The Ambivalence of Modern Executive Power*, New York: Free Press, 1989; P. Weller, *First Among Equals: Prime Ministers in Westminster Systems*, Sydney: Allen & Unwin, 1985.

policy-makers'. Parliament is the necessary 'countervailing force' against the 'power interests of the administrative policy-makers'.[6]

Weber's lesson for executives is that leadership will inevitably collide with an active parliament on the two fronts of party discipline and public service neutrality. Vigorous executives will prepare for the worst by reinforcing partisan commitments and team loyalty, and by preventing parliament from too direct or frequent access to public service chiefs. The common existence of party committees might well indicate a strategy of executive co-optation, rather than party democracy; just as the existence of government guidelines regulating the conduct of officials as witnesses might indicate a strategy of containment rather than co-operation.

In the Weber vision which haunts scheming executives, 'strong' parliaments engage in 'positive' politics through the twin strategies of leadership accountability (ministerial responsibility broadly understood) and administrative control (administrative responsibility broadly understood). Neither accountability program requires strict parliamentary domination of government; both do require, however, the public accounting by agents of government of their policy stewardship. Weber emphasises that both programs require a varied set of institutional activities, differing in each parliamentary setting. Examples of the first strategy are regular question periods, committee examination of legislative proposals, detailed budget examination and plenary debates on policy and ministerial capacity. An example of the second is committee cross-examination of senior bureaucrats to determine parliamentary confidence in their administration of public policy.

To the extent that Weber is either correct or influential, his itemisation of the vital signs of an effective parliament can serve to alert executives to matters requiring careful management. Without a prime ministerial agenda of business, parliaments will tend to make their own tasks and challenges, some of which might well check and balance executive interests. The fact that these mechanisms of accountability are aimed at the executive arm of government and bolstered by the rhetoric of public representation is unlikely to convince executives that compliance is the only form of co-operation. Weber's articulation of active parliamentarism helps to explain some of the clever forms of executive co-optation to which the Australian parliament has succumbed.

Modes of Political Management

There is no simple formula for parliamentary leadership: individual chief executives arrive in office with distinctive policy agenda and varied

6. M. Weber (1968), 'Parliament and Government in a Reconstructed Germany, Appendix 2' in G. Roth and C. Wittich (eds), *Economy and Society*, New York: Bedminster, 1968, pp. 1417–27.

constitutional convictions. All want policy change, and all require institutional compliance from parliament; yet few obtain all the changes they desire and none receives the compliance expected by executives possessed of and frequently by popular mandates. Although there is no model of parliamentary control, there are characteristic modes of executive domination, some more successful than others, some more wholesome than others. Each leadership mode is a response to a specific set of political circumstances, and it is important before examining the repertoire of control to compare the remarkably different landscapes of leadership, within which each mode of control should be appreciated.

Chifley: Unassuming Bicameral Boss

The prime ministership of Chifley inherited many of the favourable parliamentary circumstances won by the Curtin government. Most notably, Chifley himself had been, in Curtin's own terms, 'GOC House Strategy': all the more successful for being fair and considerate to the opposition, provided that it accepted the usual parliamentary forms.[7] The period between the two elections contested by Chifley as prime minister (1946-9) was, given the earlier episodes of party fragmentation, remarkably stable in parliamentary representation of parties. The Labor government was in control of both houses of parliament for only its second and, as it happens, its last, time since federation. As Sawer notes, the 1946 election, the last Senate election held on the pre-proportional representation scheme of simple preferential voting, 'produced its last absurdity': government 33, opposition three.[8]

Chifley's government during this period passed more legislation than any earlier parliament, and much of it is arguably of the first rank of importance to Australia's political development. The opposition had very few opportunities to defeat government proposals, although Chifley was reluctant to alter his tolerance and support for the appropriate forms and due processes of parliamentary business. Opposition leader Menzies later wrote that Chifley always 'hoped to be underestimated, with advantage'.[9]

The prominent theme of this government was post-war reconstruction, in which the government passed many items of legislation widening the powers and regulatory responsibilities of the

7. L.F. Crisp, *Ben Chifley: A Political Biography*, Sydney: Angus & Robertson, 1961, pp. 226, 254–63.
8. G. Sawer, *Australian Federal Politics and Law, 1929–1949*, Melbourne University Press, 1963, pp. 157–85.
9. R.G. Menzies, *Afternoon Light*, Melbourne: Cassell, 1967, p. 130; Crisp, *op. cit.*, p. 225; G. Souter, *Acts of Parliament*, Melbourne University Press, 1988, p. 380.

federal welfare state. This Labor government also inherited an able team of senior public servants committed to the Curtin-bred agenda of social and economic reconstruction. Weber would have been pleased: the national welfare agenda helped cement party solidarity, and the partnership with the public service worked to overawe parliament, so much so that Menzies retained almost all of Chifley's agency heads.[10]

Menzies: Divide and Rule, especially Divide

The very length of Menzies's tenure as prime minister makes it difficult to characterise succinctly. Certain features, however, stand out as illustrations of his basic tactic of artful confrontation designed to divide and rule. Menzies's assumption of office in 1950 began with new forms of parliamentary control characteristic of his regime: establishment of the office of leader of the House as the prime minister's chief tactician, and the introduction of the House's first set of permanent standing orders. The culmination of the Menzies era is also marked by complementary tactical developments: the 1963 revision of House standing orders and the recurrent use of electoral weapons against an obstructive Senate.

Menzies was at home in parliament: after all, he had received a rare apprenticeship through his elected experience first in the Victorian parliament, then in the Commonwealth as a minister before first becoming prime minister from 1939 to 1941. He rose from the parliamentary ashes by founding the Liberal Party and refining his talents as opposition leader to both Curtin and Chifley. At home in parliament, he naturally believed 'that the prime art of politics is that of persuasion which cuts deep into the popular mind and heart'. Menzies understood that leadership is distinguished from helmsmanhip by the use of strategy over and above tactics, even flexible strategies over rigid tactics.[11]

Holt, Gorton and McMahon: Muddles, not Models

Menzies resigned in early 1966, to be followed in office by Holt. Indicative of the pent-up restlessness of the last Menzies years were the 1967 referendum measures: one, which was successful, to confer additional legislative power on the federal parliament in Aboriginal affairs; the other, unsuccessful, to sever the constitutional nexus between the size of the two houses. While liberal measures unfolded, Liberal control over the Senate folded up — in response to the growth of the Democratic Labor Party (DLP) as minor party and 'honest broker', and

10. Crisp, *op. cit.*, pp. 226, 254–63.
11. R.G. Menzies, *The Measure of the Years*, Melbourne: Cassell, 1970, pp. 8–9; Menzies (1967), *op. cit.*, p. 130.

the increase in Senate rebels like Wright, Wood and Cormack who moved all the more independently in the post-Menzies twilight.[12]

It is noteworthy that it was during this changing of the executive guard that the Senate first experimented with and then formally established a committee system. Typical of the clash between executive and Senate at this time was the VIP flights affair, which helped pave the way for opposition parties to obtain control of the Senate at the 1967 half-Senate election, just a few months before Holt's death. Gorton's free-wheeling style paid its price at the 1969 elections which Labor almost won, and another minor party, the Australia Party, arrived in the Senate.[13]

The disrepair within government ranks encouraged Whitlam to push to the outer limits the capacity of the Senate to check the executive government. McMahon's predictable destiny as prime minister from 1971 was 'to preside over the disintegration of a Government that had been far too long in office'.[14] Characteristic of institutional developments was the involvement of the Liberal president of the Senate in establishing a committee system designed for Weberian purposes to the extent that it aimed at reintroducing responsibility into executive policy leadership. One effect of Liberal mismanagement generally and Labor's revitalisation of the Senate was that poisoned chalice delivered to Whitlam at the 1972 election: a Senate even further fragmented and beyond executive control, with five DLP and a record three independent senators. The game of executive control was only just beginning in earnest.

Whitlam: The Mights of Mandate

The Whitlam case is special in so many ways: a leader who used parliament in preference to cabinet as the forum for his prime ministerial agenda of legislative-led reform; a leader who had so clearly mastered the arts of parliamentary politics as opposition leader that as prime minister he felt he knew the worst that could be thrown at him, which proved to be wrong; a former opposition leader who had experimented with Senate obstruction and thereby opened new paths for subsequent oppositions; a leader who appointed and sacked a Speaker who failed to protect him, and a governor-general who failed to protect him and sacked him first; and perhaps just as importantly, a leader who returned to the office of opposition leader, an indication of his preference for and career devotion to parliament as the centre of political life. Like Chifley, he stayed on as

12. Souter, *op. cit.*, pp. 456–8, 472.
13. *Ibid.*, pp. 471–89, 495.
14. G. Freudenberg, *A Certain Grandeur*, Ringwood: Penguin, 1987, pp. 241–3.

opposition leader, but more as a caretaker of his party than as an undertaker of the government.

Upon election, Whitlam established the famous duumvirate with Barnard, his deputy prime minister; Lionel Murphy, the Senate leader, was most definitely excluded, not on personal grounds but as part of Whitlam's determination not to concede anything to the power of the upper house. Whitlam's very escalation of the 'mandate' rhetoric was at base a targeted and deliberate 'reply to Senate obstruction'.[15] As is well known, Whitlam lost; but despite this strategic defeat, former Liberal leader and treasurer John Howard still regarded Whitlam as 'certainly the most impressive parliamentary performer of all the prime ministers I have had anything to do with'.[16]

Fraser: Political Moralism and Public Management

Malcolm Fraser came to the office of prime minister not simply from the lesser office of opposition leader, but as a former minister under earlier Liberal governments. Knowing something of executive responsibilities, Fraser in opposition appreciated the defective nature of the Australian system as it affected preparation for ministerial office. Hence, when in opposition he appeared before the Labor-inspired joint select committee on the reform of the committee system to argue for the introduction of an expenditure committee in the House of Representatives. Although the eventual committee report of 1976 was lukewarm on this particular idea, prime minister Fraser proceeded to introduce just such a committee within the first year of his office.

Fraser's repeated insistence on integrity in public office and his alleged 'moralism' gave renewed prominence to 'responsibility' as his prime ministerial theme.[17] In this context, Fraser's establishment of his pet project of the House Expenditure Committee reflects his genuine interest in providing members with a forum for learning more about the value for money of public expenditures by scrutinising the bureaucracy responsible for managing the system of public expenditure.

Fraser's prime ministerial treatment of parliament is a bit of an enigma: coming to power through an extraordinarily bold justification of a 'checks and balances' thesis, Fraser tended to adopt the 'rump' Liberal policy of 'manage cabinet and let parliament take care of itself'. His instruments of rule did not really include parliament, attaching greater

15. J. Howard, 'Reflections on the Cabinet Process', in B. Galligan, J.R. Nethercote and C. Walsh (eds.) *The Cabinet and Budget Processes*, Canberra: Federalism Research Centre, 1990, p. 25.
16. G. Little, 'Leadership Styles: Fraser and Hawke', in B. Head and A. Patience (eds), *From Fraser to Hawke*, Melbourne: Longman Cheshire, 1989, pp. 9–15.
17. Howard, op. cit., pp. 24–5.

importance to cabinet, the party and the public service. Fraser was acknowledged as by nature a committee rather than plenary person, and his 1979 establishment of a cabinet co-ordination committee is seen by many of his ministerial colleagues as proof of his comparative advantage in non-parliamentary forums. Fraser was more at home in cabinet committees than in parliament, and 'was at his most persuasive round a table'.[18] Only in the former could Fraser exercise his energy for consensus and his mania for locking-in his colleagues through exhaustive co-optation.[19]

While Fraser focused on cabinet and strictly enforced ministerial responsibilities for public management — in declared contrast to the lack of integrity of the Whitlam ministry — his record-large backbench experimented with fragments of parliamentary power, such as estimates and legislative committees, spurred on by the reform agenda of former Liberal leader and Speaker Billy Snedden, whose program gave some concrete shape to Fraser's implicit recognition of the need for new forms of legislative responsibility.

Hawke: Waging Pre-emptive Peace

The 1983 Labor Party coup which unseated Hayden as the then leader of the opposition and substituted Bob Hawke did not do so for reasons of any defects in Hayden's parliamentary performance; and even Senator Button as coup commander expressed doubts about Hawke's 'capacities to lead the party successfully'. The Labor parliamentary caucus had spurned Whitlam's offer of leadership to Hawke after the 1975 defeat. Even with Hawke's entry into parliament in 1980, caucus maintained its distance, right up until early 1983. Fraser served in parliament for 20 years before becoming party leader, Whitlam for 14 and Hayden for 16. Hawke served for only two years, and over that brief parliamentary time he failed to impress many of his colleagues with skills appropriate to that theatre of politics.[20]

Yet within a day of becoming opposition leader, Hawke released *Labor and Quality of Government*, the Labor blueprint on machinery of government and public service reforms, prepared under Senator Evans's supervision.[21] Hawke inherited a machinery of government policy which expressed genuine interest in parliamentary reform. Expressing a view from the opposition benches, that document looked more kindly than

18. See P. Kelly, *The Hawke Ascendancy*, Sydney: Angus & Robertson, 1984, pp. 46–7, 60–6; and P. Weller, *Malcolm Fraser PM*, Ringwood: Penguin, 1989, pp. 129–32, 144–7.
19. Kelly, *op. cit.*, pp. 3, 108–9, 146, 214–16, 336.
20. *Ibid.*, p. 401.
21. G. Little, *loc. cit.*, pp. 23, 27.

Labor traditionalists might have desired on the public accountability agenda of parliamentary, especially Senate, committees. Upon election, Hawke justified his puzzling statements about 'the need for parliamentary reform' by reference to the policy work which had preceded him. While Hawke's executive practice soon focused on a modified corporatist style, his parliamentary practice was delegated to his two leaders in the two Houses, where politics continued as usual.

Hawke's successful 1983 campaign had the slogan of conflict resolution and national reconciliation, yet it is in the very nature of parliaments to foster division and irreconciliation. It used to be said that the Whitlam government won parliament but not power; oddly perhaps, Hawke won power but not parliament which, because of its institutional support for oppositional modes of dispute and division, his government tended to bypass wherever possible. By nature and experience, Hawke was a populist fixer in search of consensus; the parliamentary ethos was unsuited to the display of his mediating skills and might indeed have prematurely rusted them.[22]

Characteristic of the Hawke years are public events rather than parliamentary episodes; not so much the passing as the bypassing of parliament, as evidenced by such events and developments as the national economic summit of April 1983, even before the new 'Hawke' parliament had assembled, followed by the establishment of the Economic Policy Advisory Committee along corporatist lines, the tax summit of July 1985, and the government's dramatic response to the Gulf war without parliamentary involvement, so much in contrast to the vigorous parliamentary debates in other allied nations.[23]

The Hawke stamp was felt in his support for the parliamentary restructuring associated with the introduction of increases in the size of parliament, public funding of parties, modified list-voting in Senate elections, legislation for members' staff, and the establishment of the Electoral Commission as public watchdog.[24] Supplementing this interest in 'streamlining' the public management of parties in parliament, Hawke resorted to the traditional referendum route to bring further 'rationality' into the parliamentary process: establishing the Constitutional Commission to garner support for the failed 1988 attempts to extend the parliamentary term, guarantee one-vote-one-value, and insert a mini bill of rights in the constitution.[25]

The flavour of the Hawke experiment's lasting success in managing parliament is best found in the 1987 changes which formed part of the

22. G. Maddox, *Australian Democracy in Theory and Practice*, Melbourne: Longman Cheshire, 1985, pp. 95–6.
23. Reid and Forrest, *op. cit.*, pp. 121–31.
24. B. Galligan and J.R. Nethercote (eds), *The Constitutional Commission and the 1989 Referendum*, Canberra: Federalism Research Centre, 1989.
25. Sawer, *op. cit.*, pp. 185–6, 207.

post-election public administration changes. The parliamentary package was aimed at executive efficiency through a settled division of labor between executive offices and the rest. It included the establishment of the two-tiered ministry, reintroduction of the offices of parliamentary secretaries and the final establishment of a committee system for the House (originally designed to act as a component of a comprehensive system of joint committees). It is very rare for a government to survive four successive elections, and some credit must be given to the contribution made by these new devices to the reinforcement of executive professionalism, understood in the sense used by the then Hawke treasurer, Paul Keating, when he stated to parliament that traditional practices like question time were privileges extended to parliament by a busy executive, not enduring requirements of public accountability.

Repertoire of Control Strategies

There is a set of basic strategies which prime ministers have used to try to control parliament. Few strategies have worked as cleanly as expected, and over time parliament has become vastly more fragmented with intensified bicameral disputes, a web of committees overlap and competition, and the entry of vocal new minor parties, making it so much harder for executives to manage, let alone dominate. Consider the contrast between Chifley and Hawke: the former able to push legislation through parliament and broadcast, literally, a message of balanced competence, but unable to control the external political environment; the latter conceding the obstructive powers of parliament and focusing energy instead on the media to the masses, tending to leave parliamentary management in the hands of each minister.

While the legislative process remains broadly the same, the requirements for parliamentary leadership alter, providing no enduring model of executive success. This section illustrates typical control strategies; considerations of space alone work against an exhaustive catalogue. The examples are given as typical of executive strategies in response to specific circumstances, and not as a record or history of executive ploys.

Appointing Sympathetic Umpires

Power has to be exercised through other people, and prime ministers need many lieutenants in order to manage their forces. Three basic public offices require special consideration, because of their formal importance in the parliamentary process: the 'presiding' offices of governor-general, Senate president and House Speaker. The historical record suggests that this traditional rendering of their formal order of rank coincides with their political potential to interfere with prime ministerial control. Each prime minister has learnt to respect the power if not the occupant of these offices, and most have attempted to frame their parliamentary setting with reliably 'sound' allies.

Persons appointed to high public office frequently slip the noose, and act as public trustees rather than delegates of government. Consider Chifley's use of the power in 1947 to appoint as governor-general a serving New South Wales Labor premier, McKell. The opposition was predictable but McKell proved not to be a Labor stooge, even to the extent of later ignoring Labor's cries when in opposition not to grant prime minister Menzies his 1950 double dissolution.[26]

Inherited occupants are very much a mixed blessing for ambitious executives. The Curtin government had appointed Rosevear as Speaker as a consolation for not having been made a minister, only to witness his tenure as that of 'an unsatisfactory Speaker, often partisan, often addressing members of the opposition in an over-bearing way' and involved as a polemical ex-Lang factionalist in committee stage debates on legislation. Chifley put up with no-confidence motions in Rosevear and his deputy, Clark, and may have been thankful that the Speaker was so often absent, frequently as assistant to the minister for supply.[27]

Menzies's experience was no more satisfactory. His election was followed by the election of Cameron as Speaker, one who loudly proclaimed his commitment to the Westminster convention of a non-political Speaker and his determination not to participate in party-room meetings. But as one historian says: 'That, of course, had probably been his colleagues' main purpose in electing him'.[28] Cameron did not really intend to avoid politics altogether, as was established by his personal attack on governor-general McKell in 1950. Somewhat independent but mainly unpredictable, Cameron offended many in turn, including the prime minister on occasion, although he remained wily enough to survive Menzies's 1953 successful and rare motion of dissent against the Speaker's ruling. As for the office of president of the Senate, when available in 1951, Menzies appreciated its new importance to the success of governments and scouted out the possibilities of a number of his ministers before the Senate Liberals finally secured their own preferred candidate, Mattner.[29]

Upon the termination of McKell's term of office in 1953, Menzies appointed the British soldier, Sir William Slim, returning to the non-Labor practice of appointing distinguished British public officials to the office. McKell's tenure had not given any evidence of the partisanship

26. *Ibid.*, pp. 117, 207; Souter, *op. cit.*, pp. 365–6, 381–2.
27. Souter, *op. cit.*, p. 408.
28. Reid and Forrest, *op. cit.*, p. 43; Souter, *op. cit.*, pp. 416–17, 427.
29. Freudenberg, *op. cit.*, p. 311.

originally feared by Liberals. Still, Menzies's sentimental preference for British vice-regents safely matched political convenience.

Three prominent but independently-minded Labor public officials helped make the political environment unmanageable for prime minister Whitlam: first, Speaker Cope, who was eventually sacked by Whitlam after his refusal to back down from a ruling adversely affecting the government; secondly, Senate leader Murphy (admittedly elected by caucus and not appointed by the prime minister), who repeatedly attracted opposition attacks and was actually censured by the Senate, an indication of his inability to control or moderate opposition forces in that chamber; and thirdly, governor-general Kerr, who exercised his official responsibilities by trumping Whitlam's own populism when in 1975 he sent parliament back to the people through the extraordinary double dissolution, after first sending Whitlam to the opposition benches.

The Cope incident is a good example of the parliamentary pathology, one in which the 'parliamentary in-fighting, intrinsically a side show, took centre stage'.[30] Having 'named' minister Cameron, Cope lost the support of his own party for the suspension motion and resigned; but a related casualty was opposition leader Snedden, whose inability to profit from this parliamentary mess encouraged his rival, Fraser, to launch his second and successful campaign for the leadership of the opposition — thereby forcing Whitlam to deal with a much more pugnacious and formidable opponent.

Fraser's two appointments as governor-general made eminent sense as acts of restoration after Kerr's destructive effect. Sir Zelman Cowen healed the wounds in public reputation by getting out of Canberra into the mainstream of the community, so that Sir Ninian Stephen was able to restore the legitimacy of the more delicate side to do with the office's powers of parliamentary dissolution. It was Barwick from the High Court who in 1975 legitimised the Kerr-Fraser alliance; and it was former High Court Justice Stephen who in Fraser's last desperate electoral gamble in 1983 used his official discretion to request further information from the prime minister to prove the point that parliament had in fact become unworkable. Fraser had come to power through the 1974 and 1975 double dissolutions; his 1983 fall from power coincided with his unconventional disregard of the capacity of the governor-general to make up his own mind on the alleged 'unworkability' of parliament.[31]

The circle had come as complete as it ever would, Fraser's appointee now putting the prime minister and his followers on public notice that the constitution provided an avenue for requests, not demands, for double

30. Kelly, *op. cit.*, pp. 390–2.
31. D. Hamer, 'Some Proposals for Senate Reform' in G. Hawker *et al.*, *Working Papers on Parliament*, Canberra: Canberra CAE, 1979, pp. 17–31; D. Hamer, 'Australia's Commonwealth Parliament', *Legislative Studies*, 4 (2), 1989.

dissolutions. Presumably this vice-regal action, so soon made public through the *Hansard* publication of the official correspondence, also put the Senate on notice that not every act of legislative independence could be regarded as a necessary instalment in an electoral war, and that opposition parties might as well begin to focus on their legislative responsibilities between elections.

The other decisive Fraser appointment was of former Liberal opposition leader and arch-rival, Sir Billy Snedden, as Speaker. Regardless of whatever sense this appointment made politically in isolating rivals, it became a classic case of the office making the man: Snedden's self-interest propelled him to advertise and promote a shopping list of parliamentary reforms which acted as a protective foil for the latest generation of Liberal 'rumps' — 'wets' like Allan Missen as well as 'drys' like John Hyde. Snedden's much professed parliamentarism sounded innocent enough, but it lent credibility within the governing Liberal Party to a reform push, which forced the House for example to try out estimates and legislative committees, and the Senate to stay the course in filling out its scrutiny armoury with such innovative weapons as the Chaney-Missen-led Scrutiny of Bills Committee, against the expressed wishes of the party leadership.[32] Speaker Snedden's defence of the rights of the backbench had its anti-Fraser tendencies, as when he provoked Fraser's one parliamentary outburst of fury, when he refused to insist on Bob Hawke withdrawing a reported claim that Fraser was a liar.[33]

The distinctive Hawke contribution to umpiring was the appointment of his party predecessor and defeated rival for office as governor-general upon the retirement of Fraser's appointee. The Fraser solution of promoting a former party opponent to parliamentary office had proven awkward, and Hawke was only too keen to see Joan Child elected as the first female Speaker. Hayden's appointment was unprecedented in treating the vice-regal office in the manner of the High Court as a gift for retiring (or retirable) colleagues. The appointment not only rewarded a highly regarded parliamentarian, it helped erase memories of the 1983 disloyalty while destabilising one of the prime minister's rival party factions. Hawke displayed the same interest in picking winners while confusing his parliamentary opponents through his securing the appointment of Malcolm Fraser as Australia's 'eminent person' on the British Commonwealth team to Southern Africa.

32. P. Weller (1989), *op. cit.*, p. 180.
33. P. Dunleavy, G.W. Jones, B. O'Leary, 'Prime Ministers and the Commons: Patterns of Behaviour, 1868–1987', *Public Administration*, 68, Spring 1990, p. 128.

Leaders and the Led

The office of leader of the House was also established in 1951, loosely modeled on prime minister Churchill's hiving off of the two spheres of executive duties during the war.[34] The Australian office was to be held by a minister appointed by the prime minister with additional specific duties to manage government business through the House. The position was the child of Menzies rather than the House, and required no parliamentary resolution or order. Later it became a conventional part of the parliamentary office scene, recognised and remunerated through the government's statutory office for official salaries. The *House of Representatives' Practice* now describes the responsibilities of the prime minister working through this office, as distinct from that of the Speaker, as having 'ultimate authority and responsibility for the management of the House'.[35]

Fraser appointed the national party leader, Ian Sinclair, as House leader. Sinclair illustrates the executive allegiance of the office and its potential to protect the prime minister from adverse parliamentary comment and activity. Sinclair officially defended the steady growth of parliamentary committees but conceded that Australian executive governments have 'been relatively free from direct parliamentary participation in their affairs'. He further argued that committees readily 'abuse their function of criticism', interfering with the government's 'proper responsibility to govern and to govern efficiently'. He exemplified the Fraser ministry's management of parliament through his refusal to appear before the Rae Senate Committee inquiring into the Asia Dairy affair, and his failure to police the 1978 Fraser commitment to respond to parliamentary reports within six months.[36]

Hawke's choice of Mick Young as House leader made good sense in terms of the combination of Young's genuine interest in more effective forms and procedures and his Chifley-like enthusiasm for using the numbers. While in that office, Young prepared the ground for reforms later introduced by his successor, Kim Beazley, while advancing the government's interests in more predictable patterns of business, even to the point of arranging the House timetable to match better the interests of his cabinet colleagues.[37]

34. See J.A. Pettifer, *House of Representatives Practice,* Canberra: AGPS, 1981 p. 97. It was misquoted in Reid and Forrest, *op. cit.*, p. 157.
35. I. Sinclair, 'Government, Parliament and Administration' in J.R. Nethercote (ed.) *Parliament and Bureaucracy*, Sydney: Hale & Iremonger, 1989, pp. 70, 75; G. Evans, 'Scrutiny of the Executive by Parliamentary Committees', in J.R. Nerthercote, *loc. cit.*, pp. 90–1.
36. J. Uhr, 'Parliament and Administration,' in *Australian Commonwealth Administration,* Canberra CAE, 1984.
37. Menzies (1967), *op. cit.*, p. 304; Sawer, *op. cit.*, p. 171; Souter *op. cit.*, p. 378.

Sitting on the Standing Orders

An important measure of Chifley's management of parliament was the introduction of the radio broadcasting in July 1946, just 12 sitting days before parliament was dissolved approaching the election of that year. Although a joint parliamentary committee had reported in favour the year before, the Chifley government accepted the argument from New Zealand's earlier Labor government initiative of broadcasting: only in this way could Labor governments overcome the power and bias of conservative-controlled newspapers. Menzies's opposition party supported the initiative, sensing that Labor's reputation would not be enhanced by greater public attention to Chifley's stolid, uninspiring performances.[38]

In 1950 the Menzies-led House adopted quite faithfully the proposed standing orders as recommended by the Standing Orders Committee in 1949. The enlarged House required streamlined procedures, and the first permanent standing orders reduced the speaking time at the disposal of ordinary members and ministers — probably not without an aim of improving the ability of the listening audience to follow debates. The numbers required for support for a 'matter of public importance' motion were slightly increased, although the rules actually made such discussions more accessible and popular because, as matters of indeterminate discussion rather than formal debate, they bypassed normal requirements for debates to be determined by an act or resolution of settled parliamentary will on matters of public policy. Also relaxed was the traditional requirement that government urgency motions be supported by a set minimum of votes, thereby making it easier for governments to jettison the normal conventions of non-urgent consideration.[39]

More fundamental were the standing orders changes of 1963, which made governing very much easier for all subsequent prime ministers. The then House leader, Harold Holt — himself a later prime minister — brushed off the mild opposition objections to the obvious ceding of further parliamentary powers to the executive. The main example affected the House's financial procedures, which were reformed to prohibit any member other than a minister from even introducing proposals relating to taxes or duties. A second example was the reversal of priority for committee-stage examination of bills before the House, henceforth no longer required unless so ordered by the House. Since this change, over three-quarters of all legislation have been exempted from committee-stage consideration in the House.[40] A third and final example was the

38. Reid and Forrest, *op. cit.*, pp. 156–7.
39. *Ibid.*, p. 161.
40. J. Uhr, *Questions Without Answers*, Canberra: Australasian Political Studies Association, 1982.

consolidation of the rules for question time in their current form so as to guarantee that this whole accountability exercise remains a non-onerous ministerial game of enduring 'questions without answers'.[41]

Maintaining Legislative Initiatives

Menzies illustrates the mastery of the legislative initiative through his appeal to public safety against opposition subversion. His typically adventurous strategy was exemplified by the 1950 passage of the Communist Party dissolution bill, clearly aimed less at the Communist Party and more at wrecking the fragile unity of Chifley's opposition Labor Party.[42] A number of state branches of the Labor opposition party declared their general support for an anti-communist bill, and Menzies looked on in pride as the opposition fought out publicly its parliamentary position on the government bill. Fearful of triggering a double dissolution, the opposition-controlled Senate passed the bill, only to see the act later declared unconstitutional by the High Court. This extended example drawn from the Menzies early years properly describes his government's typical legislative strategies of controlled confrontation against the opposition, the Senate and the courts, all the while justifying executive expansion in terms of public safety.

Whitlam was proud of the daring energy of his government in acting to implement the Labor agenda of social and economic reform. The first year is indicative: the House sat for more hours than it had in 50 years, a record 203 of the 253 bills introduced were passed, and it took an uncharacteristically patient Whitlam over two hours to read into the *Hansard* record a list of legislative and administrative achievements. Opposition in the House was pruned by Whitlam's use of the guillotine, but the price was high in that it helped force the opposition to seek more drastic remedies in the Senate. The other side of the heavy legislative coin minted in year one was the Senate's amendment of 19, rejection of 13 and deferral of seven bills.[43] And the other side proved the winning side, despite Whitlam's novel use of a joint sitting to have passed bills which occasioned the 1974 double dissolution. The example of the 'king hit' sitting in 1975 on the loans affair well illustrates the dangers faced by Whitlam's attempts to maintain every initiative. The special sitting ploy backfired when the Senate stayed on for another week airing all the anti-Labor elements which Whitlam had hoped to exhaust through his 'put up or shut up' invitation to the House.

41. Crisp, *op. cit.*, pp. 381–97.
42. Souter, *op. cit.*, pp. 513, 518.
43. Reid and Forrest, *op. cit.*, p. 209.

Taming the Senate

Created by Chifley, the modern Senate demanded priority of containment by all successive prime ministers. Menzies began the saga of Senate reform of the powers of the Senate, typified by his establishment in 1954 of the joint committee on constitutional review, which duly reported in 1958 on a variety of measures which had the likely effect of weakening the powers of the Senate relative to those of the executive government. One of the final acts of the Menzies prime ministerial era was the peace treaty between the House and the Senate in relation to the powers of the Senate over the budget. Under treasurer and House leader Harold Holt's famous 'compact' of 1965, the government conceded the right of the Senate to amend a broad category of budgetary matters thereafter included in a second appropriation bill.[44]

In between these institutional reforms, Menzies tried to accommodate a potentially obstructionist Senate. Unlike Chifley, Menzies began his tenure without a government majority in the Senate; with the introduction of proportional representation, he knew that there was every possibility that his government could never depend on obtaining or retaining a Senate majority and would have to work with a 'hung' Senate. New circumstances required new forms of parliamentary management to diffuse the clear potential of the 'new Senate' systematically to obstruct government legislation.

Menzies devised and perfected the strategy of 'the threatened election' by apparently but carefully playing into the hands of the Senate's anti-government majority; he orchestrated intercameral dispute with the aim of moderating further Senate opposition by arranging the constitutional preconditions for a double dissolution. The last double dissolution had occurred in 1914, and Menzies is to be credited for recognising the renewed relevance of the threat of such complete parliamentary elections as a powerful weapon in the hands of the executive, capable of threatening electoral retaliation against recalcitrant senators.[45]

Menzies relied upon the Senate's disagreements over a 1951 Commonwealth bank bill to engineer his first and characteristic double dissolution. It was an important test case because the Labor-controlled Senate attempted to frustrate the government's election plans by delaying rather than rejecting the bill through referral to a select committee. The irony is that Menzies won out because he was able to persuade the Labor-appointed governor-general that such a ploy satisfied the 'failure to pass' test required under s57 of the constitution.[46]

44. Menzies (1970), *op. cit.*, ch. 5.
45. Souter, *op. cit.*, p. 418.
46. *Ibid.*, pp. 438–9, 457–8.

The important short-term effect of the 1951 double-dissolution election was that it gave Menzies a majority in both houses, but the long-term effect was that it introduced into the armoury of prime ministers the threat of a double dissolution in parliamentary circumstances judged as 'unworkable' by an ambitious executive. The real threat of the double dissolution lay in its likely swamping of the expected anti-government by-election effect of a normal half Senate election when held out of step with an election for the House.

Menzies was soon to recognise that under the testy circumstances of the Labor split, threatened double dissolutions ran the risk of enhancing the power of the breakaway minor party. The prime minister therefore did not always make real his electoral threats, although his bargaining position was all the stronger when, as was frequently the case, the electoral preconditions had been arranged and the opposition in the Senate was kept guessing, preoccupied and nervous about meeting the electorate prematurely.[47]

A potential flaw in Menzies's strategy was the very real possibility that double dissolutions might result in evenly divided Senates, thereby negating any prospect of a government regaining control over parliament as a whole. Menzies never gave up the search for a structural reform to the problem of Senate obstruction. An early attempt was the 1950 referendum bill on avoidance of double dissolution deadlocks, not passed by the Senate and not put to the people.[48]

Apart from the constitutional issues of structured adversity between the two houses — which Whitlam, like Menzies before him and Fraser after him, sought to have reformed through referendum — Whitlam faced an almost unmanageable task in adapting to the opposition's refusal to accept his notion that his government possessed a popular mandate. Opposition Senate leader Withers, right from the outset of the Labor government, ridiculed the prime minister's mandate thesis as nothing but 'temporary electoral insanity', threatening 'the national interest' which the Senate must protect 'by exercising its undoubted constitutional rights and powers'.[49]

As early as the time of Whitlam's first budget, Withers was advising the leader of the opposition in the House that the Senate could defer consideration on supply, thereby incapacitating the government and engineering a change of government.[50] Whitlam's counter-management strategy was epitomised by the 'Gair affair', a move cleverly designed to wreck the third party while regaining the Senate balance of power but, as executed, no match for the opposition's ability to exploit to the limit the

47. *Ibid.*, pp. 413–14.
48. *Ibid.*, p. 511.
49. *Ibid.*, p. 515.
50. Freudenberg, *op. cit.*, p. 291.

black letters of constitutional politics. The idea was not to destroy the already stale DLP but to increase the number of winnable Senate positions available at the expected 1974 half Senate election. Whitlam and Murphy acted alone and in secrecy, to their detriment. As is now apparent, 'Whitlam was playing in the wrong league'.[51] The opposition was far more cunning; it forced a double dissolution by refusing supply, losing the election but gaining valuable experience for the more fateful 1975 supply crisis.

Whitlam also suffered under Murphy's Senate leadership, whose reformist energies as attorney-general were outbalanced by his imprudent raid on the Australian Security Intelligence Organisation (ASIO) and the opposition's ability to keep alive public doubts about his judgment and character, such that Whitlam's apparently clever appointment of Murphy to the High Court only served to trigger the awful mechanics leading up to the 1975 dismissal.[52]

Fraser's prime ministership was established through Senate obstruction, and he was rewarded with those six rare years of bicameral control from 1976 to 1981. Unfortunately, the route to power had its institutional price: Fraser's Senate Liberals were among his most public critics. His insistence on ministerial proprieties had a tendency to rub both friends and opponents the wrong way, particularly given Fraser's own track record of white-anting and discord. Two party allies who should have been assets in managing the unprecedented majorities in both Houses became Senate thorns in Fraser's parliamentary side: Peter Rae as a kind of 'angel's advocate' for liberalism, and Chipp as leader of the breakaway Liberal party, the Australian Democrats, whose representation in the Senate steadily increased, eventually holding the balance of power and denying Fraser his Senate majority in 1981. In 1982 the Democrats moved to oppose the government's bills to extend sales tax — characteristic not so much of the Senate's supposed obstruction as of its unpredictability.[53] It is also ironic that Labor senator Gareth Evans's justification of the early success of Senate committees in modifying government policy or administration claimed that this was achieved by creating 'the preconditions for others to act rationally'.[54]

The Hawke government bedded in an executive trend in avoiding half Senate elections by stockpiling intercameral disputed legislation in the event of a need for an early election. Hawke thus turned the fact of Senate obstruction into something of an electoral asset, minimising the likely effects of a by-election and retaining the maximum likely Labor representation in the Senate. The early elections of 1984, 1987 and 1990

51 *Ibid.*, p. 264.
52. Kelly, *op. cit.*, pp. 155–6.
53. Evans, *op. cit.*, p. 83.
54. *Ibid.*

were all double dissolutions, the preconditions for which were carefully established soon after the formation of each new Hawke government.

Using the Numbers

When all else fails, read the instructions or, better still, the riot act: executives are there to execute, and Australian leaders just love to 'use the numbers', even when prudence would counsel otherwise.[55] As an ill-considered instance of Chifley's determination to hound parliamentary opposition when it strayed from the innocent due processes of the House, some mention can be made of the Fadden affair of 1948. The opposition Treasury spokesman had quoted from apparently top-secret government papers supporting his case that the USA was unwilling, for fear of leaks and general insecurity, to provide full intelligence briefings to Australia. Government security officials interviewed Fadden at Parliament House, provoking an unsuccessful motion of privilege by Fadden who not surprisingly complained about government interference with his parliamentary duties. The case for secrecy was little more than one of ministerial convenience effectively protecting government ministers against public discovery of 'their administrative errors'.[56]

Chifley liked to trump an opposition's use of the Marquess of Queensbury rules with what he openly called Rafferty's rules, which nicely captures the spirit of the executive perspective on parliamentary process. As Chifley put this underlying logic: 'The fact is that in parliament — if you have the numbers you can do what you think ought to be done.'[57] When reduced to a House majority of one after the 1961 election, Menzies made great use of the gag and guillotine rules in order to weaken opposition tactics. Menzies's clever sense of the theatre of parliament had at a very early stage encouraged him to use urgency and guillotine motions as effective staging props designed to help send a sense of grave national importance to the electors.[58]

Capturing Parliamentary Reform

The Representation Act of 1948 enlarged parliament in a way that advantaged Labor at least in the important short-term battle over control of the Senate. The House was increased from 74 to 121, the Senate from 36 to 60. Part of the House ploy was to bolster constituency security for existing members through guarantees that 'safe' zones would be retained.

55. Souter, *op. cit.*, p. 208.
56. Crisp, *op. cit.*, p. 218.
57. Crisp, *op. cit.*, p. 393.
58. Reid and Forrest, *op. cit.*, pp. 120–1; Souter, *op. cit.*, pp. 396, 403.

Senators from each state were increased from six to ten, but with seven to be elected at the next regular Senate election. The allied Commonwealth Electoral Act of 1948 introduced proportional representation for Senate elections, a noble enough principle possibly intended 'to enhance the status of the Senate' as claimed by attorney-general Evatt at its introduction; but one devised, according to Menzies, 'for a particular purpose at a particular time' with the aim of giving Labor power in the next Senate 'to resist and obstruct its opponents'. Sure enough, Labor lost government at the general election but retained control of the Senate, 34 to 26. Chifley's Speaker, Rosevear, argued that a PR-based Senate was a 'gold brick' destined to bring disaster.[59]

Menzies often sought to expand the powers of the federal parliament, but he implicitly accepted the Weberian strategy of calling the bureaucracy to public account. A prominent example is his 1952 resurrection of the Public Accounts Committee, suspended during the Depression as an economy measure. The very electoral success of Menzies's governments created problems in managing the government backbench. Under Menzies and his successor Liberal governments, small groups of independently minded House and Senate members tried to carve out a place for themselves in a system of parliamentary checks and balances against the conventions of executive domination.

Later governments fought back with executive preferment by creating places as assistant or junior ministers, or parliamentary secretaries, or simply keeping people busy with committee assignments. Menzies seemed not concerned to respond to these elements of restlessness within and his last years saw the steady growth of the 'backbench rebel' prone to vote against the government, particularly on matters of government regulation adversely affecting civil liberties. House backbenchers like Turner and Wentworth regularly struck poses of independence; more strategically placed senators like Wright and Wood often helped make up opposition majorities to amend or defeat government proposals.[60]

The political utility of parliamentary reform is well illustrated by Fraser's quite personal establishment in 1976 of the House Expenditure Committee, loosely modelled on that in the UK which was then about to be abolished and replaced with a set of portfolio-specific committees.[61] The fact that some authorities regard this committee as having made 'only a token contribution to parliamentary control'[62] does not necessarily mean that the prime minister had intended its contribution to be no more than that of a token. Furthermore, the committee's work in paving the way for the parliamentary acceptance of program budgeting and

59. Souter, *op. cit.*, pp. 457–8, 464, 466, 475.
60. Reid and Forrest, *op. cit.*, p. 376–8.
61. Weller (1989), *op. cit.*, 156–7.
62. Reid and Forrest, *op. cit.*, pp. 380–1.

evaluation is quite consistent with Fraser's original expectations of its performance. Early in the life of his first government, Fraser agreed to the establishment of a comprehensive system of party committees for backbenchers.[63]

One popular academic interpretation is that Fraser was simply attempting to deflect backbench energies away from paths of potential rebellion into anything of minor if useful consequence which would act as a buffer, protecting the ministry from the rest of the parliamentary party. Perhaps a more credible interpretation is that Fraser wanted to repair some of the House's defects as an institutional training ground for ministers, consistent with his earlier recommendations — and indeed with those of the 1976 Report of the Coombs Royal Commission — on the need for greater public attention to matters of public expenditure.

The risk of playing with the fire of reform is illustrated by the Fraser executive group's intransigence in meeting the demands of Senate committees: such as the 1982 requests for appearances by House leader Ian Sinclair before the Asia Dairy inquiry by senator Rae's Finance and Government Operations Committee, and the 1982 attempts by chairman Missen to have permanently established his new experimental Civil Liberties Committee on the scrutiny of bills. The link between the Fraser government's acceptance of House committees and their reluctance to feed or encourage Senate committees is not hard to find: House bodies are ultimately under the control of whoever controls the House, whereas Senate bodies — even when that chamber is controlled by government senators, as was the case from 1976 until 1980 — have an unpredictably independent life of their own, as prime ministers Gorton and McMahon had discovered.

Between these two extremes Fraser learned to live with backbench demands for legislative and estimates committees in the House, at least experimentally from 1979 to 1981 until they were wound up by House leader Killen, the former champion of legislative pre-eminence. Prominent reform voices came almost always from members who were never to make it to the Fraser ministry; the question is whether Fraser rewarded only the silent loyalists and whether some like senators Rae and Missen were blocked because of their committee independence.

The Hawke years saw one major episode of parliamentary reform when after the 1987 election the government introduced sweeping reforms to the House committee system, with an expectation that the Senate system would combine to form a unified parliamentary system of committees. Such a model of House-dominated joint committees had been evident in those new specialist committees, such as those on ASIO, the National Crimes Authority (NCA) and the Electoral Commission. Despite the predictable Senate preference for running its own duplicate

63. Souter, *op. cit.*, pp. 445–7, 489, 522; Reid and Forrest, *op. cit.*, p. 498.

system, the 1987 changes gave the House a range of important new committees, and committee positions, designed to shadow the newly-amalgamated government departments. To an extent, this made it easier for governments to keep the whole House busy on an agenda of the executive's chosing, as committees could only be activated by ministerial or House reference.[64]

Containing the Opposition

Prime ministers are frequently the creatures of their opposition leaders, especially if the opposition forces can steal the initiative and unsettle the legitimacy of, or public confidence in, the government: Chifley eventually succumbed to Menzies and Whitlam lost out to Fraser, who was defeated by a rampantly populist Hawke. But perhaps the best guide to a containment policy for an active opposition comes from the story of the inability of the three immediate post-Menzies prime ministers to cope with Whitlam, whose time as opposition leader illustrates the limits to executive control of the parliamentary agenda.

Three facets of Whitlam's career as opposition leader deserve comment, each indicating a growing mastery of parliamentary politics. The first is the culmination of the learning of the 1950s: his early mastery of the rhetoric of confrontational debate, a style of parliamentary politics suited to the testing of ministerial responsibility as the exemplary activity of parliamentary life. A telling example is Whitlam's artful hounding of attorney-general Barwick, who was later as chief justice to assist Kerr in sacking Whitlam. Second is the fatal experimentation with extending the conventional reach of Senate powers with that chamber rarely controlled by governments: for example under Murphy's Senate leadership in the case of VIP aircraft in 1967; and Whitlam's insistence in 1970 that a Labor-controlled Senate could constitutionally, and consistently with responsible government, defeat money bills. Third is the Whitlam domination of question time when in opposition to the rump Liberal leaders, especially under McMahon, leading up to the historic electoral victory of 1972.[65]

Constitutional Reframing

Almost every prime minister at one time or another experiments with a program of constitutional reform to clear out anti-executive obstructions within the parliamentary system. This is the ultimate weapon, designed to reframe the parliamentary process along new lines more compatible

64. Sawer, *op. cit.*, p. 191.
65. *Ibid.*, pp. 176, 212–13, 216; Crisp, *op. cit*, p. 323–42.

with executive responsibilities. It is the least successful control strategy, frequently indicative that the government of the day has lost power or legitimacy within the institution.

With the establishment of the Chifley government, both government and opposition recognised that with the end of the war and the passing of the war powers remit it was now an open question as to the exact scope of federal legislative jurisdiction. To a considerable extent, government and opposition fought over the merits of extending the legislative powers available in the constitution, rather than fighting about those procedural powers clearly then available to parliament. The opposition was only a few degrees more wily in its brand of populism in calling on the people to resist constitutional change; although later when in government Menzies resorted to the same convenient executive ploy of power through plebiscite.

Even before the 1946 election which gave popular legitimacy to Chifley's inherited mandate, the Chifley government targeted constitutional amendment as a preferred political activity, while the Menzies opposition eagerly took its battle outside parliament to defend its more classically liberal interpretation of limited government. Three proposed amendments were put at the 1946 election, when only one, that relating to power over social services which attracted opposition support, was successful. This social services power was primarily useful in allowing the government to put beyond constitutional doubt the package of existing social welfare legislation: no new legislation of substance was passed as a result of the constitutional amendment.[66]

The constitution can just as easily be used against as for the benefit of prime ministers, and judges are less controllable than other politicians, a risk well illustrated by the major revisions of the Chifley statute book. Significant items of Chifley legislation were challenged in the High Court as unconstitutional, such as laws on airline and bank nationalisation. The most prominent example is the Banking Act of 1947, which attempted to nationalise the private trading banks and gave rise to Chifley's famous 'light on the hill' image of Labor's socialist program. Three state governments and the private banks successfully brought action in the Bank Nationalisation Case, arguing that the government's prohibition breached Section 92 of the constitution. One authority states that the Chifley government 'was frustrated by judge-made doctrine rather than by clear constitutional restrictions to an extent not equalled since the Deakin period'.[67]

Menzies operated on principles remarkably like Chifley's 'power through plebiscite' practices. Examples include the unsuccessful 1951 referendum seeking legislative power over communist parties in response

66. Sawer, *op. cit.*, p. 191.
67. *Ibid.*, pp. 197, 213–14, 216: Crisp, *op. cit.*, pp. 323–42.

to the High Court's rejection of Menzies's Communist Party Dissolution Act as unconstitutional. The referendum proposal would have provided the federal parliament with the legislative power which the High Court had stated as necessary to render the 1950 act constitutional. Although the government-controlled Senate eventually passed the resolution, it was not carried at the referendum.

Almost as part of the prime ministerial model, Whitlam pursued the referendum road in extending the legislative powers of the federal parliament, or in attempting to reduce the independent power of the Senate. Referendums on prices and incomes failed in 1973; a further four proposals relating to the powers of the two houses failed in the 1974 referendums.

Fraser attempted only one package of referendum proposals, and was successful in three out of the four proposals. Yet again, an executive government sought to contain the unmanageable Senate, this time by adjusting the electoral cycle to bring about simultaneous elections for House and both half and full Senate elections. This was the only unsuccessful proposal; successful constitutional changes included the important regulation of the process by which state governments fill casual Senate vacancies (filling a hole Fraser himself exploited when in opposition but now threatening to be of more value to new oppositions), lowering the retirement age of judges (thus allowing governments greater opportunities to appoint their own candidates to the highest court) and, finally, including territory voters in future referendums.

The Hawke years showed just how difficult constitutional alteration had become, despite extensive executive commitment to the preparation of better plans of management for parliament. The newly elected Hawke government introduced but could not secure passage of a feasible proposal for a fixed term parliament. At the 1984 elections voters defeated a proposal for simultaneous elections. By 1985 the government had established a constitutional commission, which had considerable effect on the choice of the unsuccessful 1988 referendum proposals, including that for extending parliamentary terms. The root idea was to give governments more time between elections to weather parliamentary and public opposition, but the track record of popular rejection might indicate that governments are even less trusted than are parliaments.

Conclusions

Max Weber argued that the qualities of parliamentary leadership reflected the on-the-job learning obtained by rising executives during their earlier committee assignments when tracing the paths of public accountability. In Weber's anxious world view, liberal democracies require of their parliamentary leaders a period of training in parliamentarism, for which the best preparation is a backbench career as an active committee auditor of government. Of the eight Australian prime ministers examined here, no more than three had lengthy backbench careers but perhaps only two had any extended experience as active committee members: Whitlam and Fraser. The others fell upon ministerial or party office too quickly to serve as committee members.

Perhaps even more pertinent is this chapter's epigram from Macaulay, suggestive of the limitations of the rhetoric of leadership and expressive of the frailty of all parliamentary institutions. Leaders of parliamentary governments have every opportunity to speak, even though parliamentary oppositions have few incentives to listen. The scheme of leadership training desired by Weber was designed to respond to the genuine fears about executive incapacity raised by that great parliamentarian, Macaulay. The experience of the Australian prime ministership strongly suggests that the community will be better governed to the extent that leaders are listeners as well as speakers. Devising an appropriate institutional framework for responsible leadership can usefully begin with something like this chapter's unpacking of the executive devices for parliamentary convenience.

5

PRIME MINISTERS AND THE MEDIA

Clem Lloyd

More than any other factor, the conduct of the contemporary Australian prime ministership has been shaped by the impact of television. This television imperative has not emerged in any dramatic rewriting of the prime minister's job description. The process has been more a gradual evolution still falling short of political maturation. Television is no longer one of the technical instruments at the prime minister's disposal but a fundamental part of the prime ministership's political environment. The British analyst Colin Seymour-Ure has observed that by the early 1990s television had become, in a general sense, a forum of political accountability.[1] This is not yet as evident in Australia as it is in the United Kingdom or, more significantly, the United States. Technically, the principal sources of political accountability for the prime minister remain the cabinet, the parliament, the political party, the election campaign and the general media (including radio and print as well as television). What is important is the impact that television is having on prime ministerial accountability to these political elements. Thus prime ministerial performance in cabinet, parliament and political party is assessed in a context of authoritative and competent television performance. The other news media, radio and the political press, are also influenced by television in their judgments of prime ministers. The establishment and maintenance of prime ministerial power increasingly rests on television.

Seymour-Ure suggests that the development of television has had three important effects on prime ministers. First, it has shifted the job description to more emphasis on media appearances and relationships. Linked to this switch of emphasis has been an enhancement of the prime ministers' role as opinion leader and mobiliser. Finally, television has drawn prime ministers away from their parliamentary bases.[2]

Undoubtedly, the growth of the political media, particularly television, has realigned the prime ministerial workload, but just how remains unclear. Is the prime minister spending less time in the cabinet, the parliamentary chamber, the party room, or the electorate? Or is the

1. Colin Seymour-Ure, *The British Press and Broadcasting since 1945*, Oxford: Basil Blackwell, 1991, p. 176.
2. *Ibid.*, p. 182.

greater media load met by increasing the length of the working day? The scope for short-cuts is limited. There is less call for a prime minister to spend time in the chamber than there was even 20 years ago, but cabinet sitings have increased substantially. With election campaigning on a virtual permanent footing, incessant electorate demands are made on the prime minister, particularly by television.

Has the impact of television taken prime ministers away from their natural parliamentary base? The Australian answer would certainly be 'No'. The convention by which Australia's federal executive government functions solely within Parliament House has ensured that the prime ministers' essential media work is conducted conveniently from this parliamentary base. Furthermore, the televising of question time from parliament since 1990 has reinforced this reliance on a parliamentary base. Unlike Westminster, there is no specific provision for prime ministers' questions. Potentially, each question time is the prime ministers' question time unless they are absent or parliamentarians ignore them. Televised question time gives that venerable political institution some of the character of American presidential press conferences, with parliamentarians filling the role of the White House press corps. The strains of televised question time have offset to some degree the economies of media scale emerging from the prime minister's parliamentary base, close to the federal parliamentary press gallery (also known simply as the press gallery). Before looking at the technical aspects of the media/prime ministerial relationship, some account of its historical development is necessary.

The Television Prime Ministership

The rise of the television prime ministership in Australia can be chronicled with reasonable precision. The first Australian television programs were broadcast late in 1956. The first authoritative use of the medium to attain the prime ministership and assert, even enhance, its prerogatives was made by John Grey Gorton in his successful thrust for the prime ministership early in 1968. Gorton's innovative use of television to promote his claim to the prime ministership was breathtaking by customary standards of Australian political communication. Through television Gorton, prominent in parliamentary and party circles but largely unknown to the Australian electorate, presented himself as a personable and potentially effective political leader:

> Gorton's chief weapon was television. Alone of all the candidates he realized that, in the extraordinary circumstances existing in the nation, the numbers

in the Party room could be influenced by pressure from the people. And that meant using television.[3]

By using television, Gorton overcame at one stroke the disadvantages of a limited electoral perception. The favourable response to his appearances helped convince a majority of the Liberal Party to vote for him as prime minister. Gorton's use of the medium marked a new era in which the increasing impact of television altered the dynamics of prime ministerial power.

Some notion of the relative impact of television on Australian prime ministers can be gathered from the table in the introduction to this book (page 3). The only Australian prime minister since 1945 not affected by television presentation, as distinct from television policy, was Ben Chifley, who was prime minister when the war ended. His successor, Sir Robert Menzies, the inaugurator of Australian television, was already in his sixties when his government presided over the introduction of the first services in late 1956. Thus, Menzies's long prime ministership (1949–66) included a decade in which television emerged as the principal news medium.

Menzies's immediate successor, his close colleague Harold Holt, was 48 when television started. Although Holt was younger than Menzies, his federal political career was of comparable duration and he had been a federal parliamentarian since the 1930s. John McEwen, who was interim prime minister following Holt's death and deputy prime minister for several years, was 56 when television began. The remaining coalition prime ministers, Gorton and William McMahon, were respectively 45 and 48. Gough Whitlam, Australia's first ALP prime minister since Chifley, was 40. His successors, Malcolm Fraser of the Liberal–National Party coalition and Robert Hawke of the ALP, were young men in their twenties. Paul Keating was just 12.

A clear trend emerges of Australian prime ministers increasingly steeped in the ethos and practices of the television era. Chifley, Menzies Holt and McEwen were redolent of an era of print media dominance. Chifley, of course, did not have to adjust to television but Menzies, Holt and McEwen had to learn from the beginning. Menzies mastered television although he did not have to exert himself when responding to its demands in these establishment years. The austere, craggy-visaged McEwen, a rough-hewn figure from the Australian country, recognised television's potential political importance but responded awkwardly to its demands. Holt and McMahon also lacked composure and confidence before the cameras.

The younger Gorton was more flexible, being able to approach television without hindrance from media predilections. Whitlam had an

3. Graham Freudenberg, *A Certain Grandeur: Gough Whitlam in Politics*, Melbourne: Macmillan, 1977, p. 119.

instinctive preference for print media and parliament, but, like Gorton, he had the flexibility to adjust. The political careers of Fraser and Hawke advanced virtually in step with the development of television, bestowing on them priceless opportunities to exploit it. (A not dissimilar pattern emerges in the United Kingdom, where the established political titans, Attlee and Churchill, were 63 and 71 respectively when TV services resumed in June 1946. The British prime ministers most attuned by age and generation to television were Harold Wilson [30], Edward Heath [29] and Margaret Thatcher [20]).[4]

Prime Ministers, Media and Milieu

Although Australia is a polity of the Westminster persuasion, it has made some important divergences in practice, particularly the concentration of the executive government within the physical milieu of Parliament House. Since the federal parliament moved from Melbourne to Canberra in 1927, the executive government has functioned wholly from parliamentary offices. In Canberra, a cabinet room and administrative offices for ministers were provided in an administrative building near the temporary Parliament House. It was more convenient, however, for the cabinet to meet in the parliamentary building and for ministers to administer rudimentary departments from offices within it. (The core of the public service remained for many years in Melbourne, which was the provisional capital between 1901 and 1927.)

With both the parliament and the executive accommodated in a single building, it was common sense for the press to cover both institutions from the press gallery. When the first federal parliament met in 1901, the press was allocated gallery space to report parliamentary proceedings and adjoining offices for 'writing up' parliament and items obtained in the parliamentary halls and lobbies. In the Australian parliament, however, there has been no equivalent of the Westminster lobby of political journalists. The British lobby developed in the 1880s from the mingling of political journalists with parliamentarians in the House of Commons lobby. Here, a small group of privileged journalists was permitted to gather political news on a non-attributable basis. This 'lobby' of political journalists emerged as a powerful elite distinct from colleagues reporting parliamentary proceedings. Over more than a century the lobby has acquired prestige and a distinct mystique. It has had an incalculable influence on the conduct of British politics and on the conduct of the prime ministership in particular. It retains significance in British political journalism, although criticised as increasingly vulnerable

4. Colin Seymour-Ure, *op. cit.*, p. 184.

to political manipulation. Some political journalists have tried to work outside its conventions.[5]

Why did a lobby system not emerge in Australia's federal parliament? The most plausible explanation is that when the lobby began to evolve at Westminster, the press galleries in the colonial parliaments were too small to permit any similar division of function. Furthermore, there were no areas of exclusive parliamentary space comparable to the House of Commons lobby. Australia's first federal parliament was housed in the building of the Victorian state parliament and much of the former colonial legislature's convention and practice was adopted. Thus, the press gallery structure, rules and conventions of the Victorian parliament were largely adopted by the new federal parliament. The Westminster division of function between gallery and lobby was not emulated.

When the parliament moved to Canberra a unitary press gallery was retained, covering both parliamentary proceedings and the executive government within Parliament House. Over the 60-year occupation of the 'temporary' Parliament House the news value of parliament was eclipsed by a prime ministership increasingly prepared to manage the media where it could. When the Australian parliament moved to its permanent building in 1988, prime minister and cabinet were sumptuously accommodated in its precincts. The usurpation by the executive government of parliamentary space was accepted by parliament with only perfunctory challenge. The media was installed in an equally commodious adaption of traditional press gallery formats.

There was some speculation that the new arrangements might at last create a division of function upon Westminister lobby lines. The new Parliament House provided a hall for the exclusive use of parliamentarians, a possible mechanism for a lobby system. This did not materialise for two reasons: a belief that the traditional press gallery system in Australia sufficed for the collection of political and parliamentary news; and a suspicion among Canberra political journalists that a lobby system would inhibit independent news collection and expose them to increasing manipulation by the executive government.

Another important factor in the functioning of the Australian prime ministership has been the absence of a working residential milieu for the prime minister. There is no equivalent of 10 Downing Street or the White House in Australian politics. The relatively modest prime minister's dwelling in Canberra, known appropriately as the Lodge, was intended as a temporary residence. It has retained a transitory quality although occupied by Australian prime ministers for more than 60 years. The Lodge has remained an essentially private residence, with the prime minister's formal office and personal staff accommodated in the

5. See the analysis of the lobby in Michael Cockerill, Peter Hennessy and David Walker, *Sources Close to the Prime Minister,* London: Macmillan, 1984, particularly pp. 31 ff.

parliament building. The prime minister's press office is part of the prime ministerial office in Parliament House. Journalists' formal contacts with the prime minister's residence are confined to occasional social events, although informally a few privileged journalists may visit it to play billiards or provide musical entertainment. There is no Australian equivalent of the Downing Street press office or White House press office, each headed by a powerful press secretary.

Despite these differences, the Australian prime ministers and political journalists work within the framework of what is demonstrably a Westminster model. The differences between the Australian and American systems are, of course, much more fundamental. In Canberra the press gallery covers both parliament and executive government, with the principal focus on the executive government. In Washington the reporting of the legislature is undertaken by a separate press gallery system. There is no equivalent in either Westminster system for the White House press corps which concentrates exclusively on the president as the incarnation of executive government. The US president has no legislative role and his party status is largely symbolic. His media relationships are reflected solely through the prism of the White House. By comparison, Australian and British prime ministers merge the roles of political party leader outside parliament, prime minister in parliament, and head of the executive government. Each requires a different media configuration, with the head of the executive government much the most important.

Australian prime ministers are not assured of automatic supremacy in the media. They may be only one of several news-makers in the ministry and have to compete for media time and space with powerful colleagues who aspire to their jobs, or seek to promote different emphases in public policy. The British prime ministership, of course, is vulnerable to similar competing centres of power within the executive government. The countervailing influence, however, of an expert prime ministerial press secretary operating under lobby conventions provides the British prime minister with sounder mechanisms for co-ordination and management of media strategy than Australian prime ministers have had at their disposal.

The Media Endowment

By 1945, the conventions governing the relationships between Australian prime ministers and the media had acquired a certain stability from more than four decades of practice. They may be summarised thus:

1. Prime ministers accepted principal responsibility for the presentation of the federal government in the media, and for

conduct of formal relationships with the media. The prime ministers did not, however, invariably accept an overriding responsibility for co-ordination of media strategy and presentation.
2. The prime ministers also accepted the principal responsibility for the presentation of party policy through the media, particularly during election campaigns.
3. The principal media institution involved in the prime ministers' relationship with the media was the federal parliamentary press gallery.
4. Prime ministers appointed press secretaries and established a press office within their personal offices to facilitate their media relationships.
5. Prime ministerial press conferences provided a formal, albeit irregular, conduit between prime ministers and media.
6. The media increasingly recognised the likelihood that prime ministers, or their delegates, would increasingly try to manage and manipulate them.

The remainder of this chapter is directed in a loosely organised way to eludicating these propositions.

Media and the Prime Ministership

In the early years of representative government in the Australian colonies, the press was a primary recruiting ground for parliamentarians. Australia's first generation of provincial newspapers was largely established by itinerant printers who also wrote much of the content. When responsible government emerged in the 1840s and 1850s, many of these journeyman printers had become affluent publishers, men of influence in their communities and natural political candidates. Colonial politics also attracted talented metropolitan newspapermen such as Henry Parkes (premier of New South Wales), George Higinbotham (attorney-general and chief justice of Victoria) and Graham Berry (premier of Victoria). This fusion of journalism with politics flourished only briefly and was extinct long before the Australian federation was established in 1901. Three Australian prime ministers — Alfred Deakin, James Scullin and John Curtin — worked as journalists, although their journalism was supplementary to their principal avocations. Thus Australia has not developed a tradition of direct political participation by prominent journalists. There have been no Beaverbrooks, Northcliffs or Robert Maxwells, no R.H.S. Crossmans or Michael Foots in Australian federal politics. In the early 1990s, there were no journalists in the Labor cabinet or even in the governing party. The opposition parties included only one journalist who was also a member of the shadow cabinet.

Undoubtedly, this lack of a journalistic tradition in federal politics has hampered media strategy, notably by giving too much influence in media presentation to public servants unskilled in these matters.

Australia's first post-war prime minister, Ben Chifley, had never worked as a journalist although he was a member of a provincial newspaper board. Chifley conducted open and generally attributable press conferences for press gallery journalists. During World War II the press had shown restraint, muting its political criticism in furtherence of the war effort. When the war ended, however, a torrent of vituperate press criticism broke over the hapless Chifley. Invariably courteous and temperate in his political style, Chifley was affronted by the searing criticism directed at his prime ministership. He was particularly galled because he felt that he had treated newspaper management promptly and fairly over crucial issues such as access to newsprint supplies and scarce overseas funds for capital re-equipment. Chifley was usually able to mask his exasperation, although he sometimes vented it publicly, as his biographer, L.F. Crisp, records:

> Chifley spoke with unusual asperity in the House [of Representatives] of 'paid stooges who with pen and tongue and radio voice are prepared to sell the cause of truth and their own souls at a lesser price than that for which Judas sold his Master — that is, when one takes into consideration the increased cost of living since biblical times'.[6]

Chifley, however, preserved a fundamental respect for press freedoms, declining to countenance the calls of fiery subordinates for reprisals. He did complain to senior press management about what he considered complete untruths, saying that the half-truths did not worry him.

Chifley's government was defeated in 1949 by a resurgent coalition of Liberal and Country parties led by Menzies, who had been prime minister previously from 1939 to 1941. During his first prime ministership Menzies had been dismissive of the press, declining to hold regular press conferences or to co-operate with photographers. As opposition leader during the ALP governments of Curtin and Chifley (1941–9), Menzies's attitude to the press swung a full 360 degrees. From a remote prime minister he became an accessible opposition leader, admitting senior political journalists to his circle of convivial intimates. As the political fortunes of the Liberal Party revived after the war, Menzies assiduously cultivated newspaper management, exploiting the increasing unpopularity of Chifley's Labor government and ensuring a regular flow of political news to the press.

As opposition leader, Menzies was a keen student of political journalism, observing the decline of verbatim reporting and noting that a handout had to be given in advance for a speech to be reported. He

6. Quoted in C.J. Lloyd, *Press and Parliament*, Melbourne University Press, 1988, p. 43.

dabbled in journalism, writing articles from America for Sir Keith Murdoch's *Melbourne Herald*, but finding irksome the disciplines of regular journalism. He assessed his own performance at press conferences, praising the perceptiveness of questioners and proving susceptible to flattery by journalists. Menzies was the first senior Australian politician to appreciate the coming significance of television as a political tool. During an extensive visit to Britain, Europe and the United States in 1948, Menzies accurately prophesied its impact: 'This system will sweep the boards before long.'[7]

When Menzies regained the prime ministership in 1949, he gradually drifted from the co-operative bonhomie that he had extended to the media as opposition leader. His approach was reinforced by unexceptionable principles of political conduct whose impact on political news-gathering was threefold. High-level political discussions, particularly those with international leaders, were not disclosed by Menzies for reasons of confidentiality. Matters of significant policy content were not disclosed because they had first to be referred to cabinet. And matters of more general significance were not disclosed because they had first to be referred to parliament. A later Liberal Party prime minister, Malcolm Fraser, has given a vivid account of a press conference in Washington where Menzies skilfully deployed all three strategies:

> He came in with an overcoat on, kept it on because he had a cold, took out a cigar, lit it and blew out a great tail of smoke. 'Now what do you fellows think you want to know?' 'Sir, you've just had confidential discussions with the president. Can you tell us about them?' 'Young man, you've just answered your own question.' 'I don't understand you, Sir?' 'Didn't you call those discussions confidential? Do you expect me to advise you of their substance before I have spoken to my colleagues in Australia?' 'Sir, is there any particular purpose in your being in the United States at this time?' 'Do you expect me to tell you that before I have informed the Australian Parliament?' 'Sir, is it correct that a decision has been made to send half a dozen Caribous to Vietnam?' 'The same applies, young man, if it were, I wouldn't be advising you at this point. Right, is there anything that you fellows want to learn?'[8]

Menzies's insistence on making important statements in the parliament exemplified the convention that the electorate should be informed largely through the parliamentary institution. It also reflected his great relish for the parliamentary forum and his command of its theatrics. Menzies was more successful in asserting the primacy of the parliament than was Winston Churchill in post-war Westminster:

> [Churchill's] Edwardian style decreed that prime ministers should communicate with the nation only through the medium of parliament. The

7. *Ibid.*, p. 173.

Number Ten Press Office was abandoned. But this harking back to an older conception of parliamentary propriety lasted all of six months.[9]

For Menzies it lasted all of 17 years. Menzies's mastery of parliamentary discourse and his retention of major statements for parliament was also the essence of his media strategy. By carefully controlling the release of information Menzies evolved a system of news management whose effectiveness has never been equalled in the Australian prime ministership. He kept a tight clamp on his cabinet, conceding an independent right to disclose policy decisions and comment broadly only to the leaders of his coalition partner, the Country Party. The press was virtually reliant for government political news on Menzies's parliamentary pronouncements, his press statements and his increasingly rare press conferences. Menzies, through his press staff, exercised total control over release and presentation of government news.

Menzies's control of a predominantly print media was not diminished by television, although his splendid political skills had been honed in parliament. He was an intuitive television performer who adapted readily to the new medium. Menzies had a fine platform and parliamentary presence because of his leonine bulk and finely modulated voice. He was just as commanding when seated before the cameras. None of Menzies's successors approached his skills in reading a text to camera, essentially all that was required of him in the early years of television. TV interviewing was in its infancy; besides, Menzies would have considered it below the dignity of the prime minister to submit to demeaning questions from television interviewers. Menzies's expression could be succinct, even epigrammatic, and he would have adjusted comfortably to the tyranny of the '20-second grab', but evolving television news-gathering techniques made few demands on him.

Chifley had lacked the ruthlessness to extract political concessions from newspaper proprietors in return for public policy benefits, but not so Menzies. Advantageous political timing gave his government the final decisions over the allocation of Australia's commercial television licences, and great newspaper companies such as Herald and Weekly Times, John Fairfax and Sons, and Consolidated Press were principal beneficiaries. Retention of these licences was controlled by the federal government, providing psychological reinforcement for the natural inclination of the newspaper management to support conservative governments. Menzies had another implicit inducement before the press proprietors: access to imperial honours which tantalised senior newspaper management. These glittering prizes were awarded sparingly, but invariably with a sound tactical sense. Menzies kept the influential and

8. Patrick Weller, *Malcolm Fraser PM: a Study in Prime Ministerial Power*, Ringwood: Penguin, 1989, p. 194.
9. Cockerill *et al.*, *op. cit.*, p. 63.

strongly supportive media baron, Frank Packer, dangling for some years before bestowing a knighthood on him.

Once Menzies departed, the system of tight media control which he established began to evaporate. It depended heavily on Menzies's mantle of omniscient authority which his successors could not hope to match. Besides, the rapidly developing electronic media was becoming more demanding and the outlines of its future political status were already discernible. Menzies's immediate successor, Harold Holt (1965–7), was shrewd enough to realise that the prime ministership had to be brought into closer touch with the electorate. In his early days as prime minister Holt adopted a populist approach, generating interviews and picture opportunities in the tabloid press which Menzies had largely spurned. Holt also acknowledged the importance of the political media and strove to build better links with it. He retained general public and media support in the first year of his prime ministership, culminating in overwhelming victory after the 1966 general election campaign. A congenitally affable man, Holt's authority as a parliamentary and media performer diminished when he faced a new opposition leader, Gough Whitlam, a superior performer in both parliament and the media.

Holt drowned off the coast of south-east Australia in December 1967. The contribution of television to the election of his successor, John Gorton (1968–71), has already been noted. An erratic but seminal prime minister who tried to innovate in public policy without ever quite knowing how, Gorton was never able to capitalise on his initial media success. He was perpetually hampered by incoherence in developing new policy proposals and in presenting them through the media. Gorton's public performance was sometimes populist and uninhibited to a degree unacceptable even to the relatively relaxed Australian electorate. His public performance could be lackadaisical; even during crucial election campaigns Gorton's foibles exposed the prime ministership to unaccustomed media ridicule, with journalists gleefully picking up his convoluted expositions of public policy.

Gorton resigned as prime minister in mid-1971 after his party denied him its continued confidence. This followed a tumultuous sequence of political squabbles in which the media played a prominent role. The issues are too complex to summarise adequately here, but the crisis hinged on the resignation of Malcolm Fraser, then defence minister and subsequently prime minister. Fraser left the government and attacked Gorton in parliament, alleging that the prime minister had been given the opportunity to quash damaging press reports about Fraser but had failed to do so. Freudenberg has speculated that this issue was 'trumped up' by a conspiracy of political and media interests in order to 'bring Gorton down':

There was, in fact, nothing intrinsic to this issue to require . . . the resignation of a minister, much less the destruction of a prime minister. If a minister were to resign every time a prime minister refused to repudiate damaging press articles, no government would survive a month.[10]

Gorton's failure to cultivate and secure the support of influential press interests, particularly Sir Frank Packer's Consolidated Press group, contributed significantly to his downfall.

William McMahon, who succeeded Gorton, was prime minister for only 18 months before the general election of December 1972 ended the 23-year ascendancy of the coalition government established by Menzies. In his mid-sixties by the time he became prime minister, McMahon lacked physical distinction, his physiognomy making him a cartoonist's delight. His public performance was hindered by deafness and a consequent monotony of intonation. In some respects, his problems with television were similar to those of the British prime minister, Sir Alec Douglas-Home, who, like McMahon, was unable to master the auto-cue. If Gorton's political freshness seduced the media for a time, McMahon suffered because media proprietors and journalists knew him too well. For more than 20 years he had been an assiduous cultivator of senior management and a vigorous importuner of journalists by telephone. For his pains he was treated much more harshly by the media than was Gorton, as Freudenberg observes:

For all his life-long cultivation of proprietors, McMahon's press support was minimal and grudging. His last prop was removed in 1972 when Sir Frank Packer sold the Daily Telegraph to Rupert Murdoch. Murdoch had committed his papers to a change of government. He telephoned McMahon in London to tell him of his deal with Packer: 'I can promise, prime minister, that I will be as fair to you as you deserve'. In the background Packer warned: 'If you do that you'll murder him.'[11]

An important factor in McMahon's defeat had been the high level of press gallery support stimulated by Gough Whitlam during six years as opposition leader. Whitlam had acquired experience of television as a panellist on an early current affairs program and he was a confident television performer. In 1969, the ALP under Whitlam as opposition leader permitted direct TV coverage of the 1969 ALP federal conference and the leader's policy speech launching Labor's 1969 election campaign. The intrusion of the TV cameras into Australian politics largely dates from these two pioneering ventures. Despite his modernity and innovatory acceptance of television in politics, Whitlam also had something of Menzies in his media approach. Like Menzies, Whitlam believed in the primacy of parliament as the crucible of national debate and source of political information. Unlike Menzies, however, Whitlam did not use parliament as a stage and mechanism for media control. His

10. Freudenberg, *op. cit.*, p. 186.
11. *Ibid.*, p. 221.

approach to parliament, and through it the media, was essentially didactic, as his close associate Graham Freudenberg has pointed out:

> More than any other Australian parliamentarian, Whitlam has committed himself to and exploited parliament's teaching and informing functions. For Menzies, parliament was a stage. For Whitlam, it [was] the best platform in Australia. Television, radio, the press, party meetings, conferences, seminars, public meetings were all important, but parliament remained the supreme forum . . . in his sustained use of parliament for the exposition of a cause, Whitlam can well lay claim to the title of the supreme [Australian] parliamentarian of his time.[12]

For much of his prime ministership Whitlam provided the media with greater access to the prime ministership than has any other Australian prime minister except John Curtin. The strong links built up with working journalists during opposition were generally maintained despite the strains of prime ministerial office. Whitlam could be terse and impatient with the media but he mostly accommodated its demands, particularly when expositions of his cherished programs were involved. His relationships with media proprietors proved much less durable. Rupert Murdoch, who supported him enthusiastically in his drive for the prime ministership, had become his most inveterate critic by mid-1975, and this antipathy contributed to Whitlam's downfall.

In many respects, the Whitlam years marked a watershed in the relationship between prime ministers and the media. The prime ministers from Chifley to Whitlam had been essentially reactive rather than proactive in their media attitudes. Prime ministers largely approached the media on the basis of well-established conventions without trying to change the ground rules. Following Whitlam, the growing dominance of television created opportunities for discriminatory media policies which were essentially manipulative. The American television journalist Dan Rather said that John F. Kennedy knew how to manipulate but lacked the will; Lyndon Johnson had the will but not the knowledge; and Richard Nixon and his staff had plenty of both.[13] In the contemporary Australian context, Malcolm Fraser had both the will and the knowledge to manipulate the media. Bob Hawke had the knowledge but, as prime minister, largely refrained from employing it to manipulate except during election campaigns.

Hawke had come to parliament relatively late in life, winning the prime ministership after only two years as a parliamentarian. His previous career had been concentrated on the trade union movement, which he had served for many years as industrial advocate and president of the Australian Council of Trade Unions (ACTU). Hawke had also been

12. *Ibid.*, p. 79.
13. Mark Hertsgaard, *On Bended Knee: the Press and the Reagan Presidency*, New York: Schocken Books, 1989, p. 45.

federal president of the ALP. His biographer, Blanche d'Alpuget, credited him with sweeping away the 'debris of a century of trade union neglect of public relations':

> . . . he was . . . 'articulate, logical and tough' . . . and an exotic. His Rhodes scholarship and his swashbuckling personality dazzled the Press. From the moment of his election [as ACTU leader] the news media was mesmerised by Hawke. Within a couple of years his face and brazen voice were among the best known in the nation; within five, they were recorded in the brain cells of the whole society.[14]

Thus Hawke entered federal politics as perhaps the most publicised figure in Australian federal politics, accumulating a huge media capital through consistent accessibility and co-operation. He was acutely sensitive to the nuances of media presentation and what journalists wanted, confident and sometimes arrogant in his media appearances.

In contrast, Fraser owed little to the media before he became prime minister, feeling that he had been a victim of Gorton's media manipulation. As opposition leader in 1975 Fraser, with his senior political colleagues and staff, had used the media skilfully to discredit the Whitlam government and prepare the way for the constitutional crisis which ultimately made him prime minister. In no sense, however, did this give him any sense of obligation to the Canberra press gallery, which he considered too closely aligned with Whitlam. Fraser's contempt for the press gallery was largely shared by Hawke, who felt that he had achieved the prime ministership despite its indifference to his aspirations. Despite their differing political ideologies, the prime ministerships of Fraser (1975–83) and Hawke (1983–91) represented a virtual continuum of media manipulation. Fraser developed the fundamental tactics; Hawke refined and maintained them.

Prime Ministers and the Press Gallery

As an institution established in parliamentary space, the press gallery is subject to parliament's authority. In theory, the executive government has no power to regulate the press gallery except through parliament. In practice, however, the press gallery largely runs its own affairs under its constitution and in consultation with the parliamentary officers. This practice has worked well and since 1945 there has been little abuse by the media of conventional rights and the limited regulation imposed by parliament.

The absence of a lobby-type organisation, either as a subsidiary of the press gallery or working in close conjunction with it, has seen the press gallery's relationship with the prime minister develop on different lines

14. Blanche d'Alpuget, *Robert J. Hawke*, Melbourne: Schwartz, 1982, p. 175.

to Westminster. The essence of the Westminster relationship is the non-attributable briefing of lobby members by the prime minister's chief press secretary acting as the prime minister's delegate or surrogate. Twice a day lobby journalists leave Westminster for 10 Downing Street for these briefings. The relationship between the prime minister and the media is largely conducted outside the parliamentary milieu. This traditional arrangement gives the prime minister's press office valuable feedback from lobby journalists on whichever issues are running. Thus, this system of non-attributable briefing is both a convenience for political journalists and a prime source of political intelligence for the prime minister's office.

In Washington, the briefing of the White House press corps by presidential press aides operates with different objectives. The crucial aim is to establish the 'line of the day' for the media, particularly television, as early in the day as possible. Journalists are briefed in accordance with this strategy as early as 9.15 a.m., with the prime target being the evening news bulletins of the television networks. This strategy has had a remarkable strike rate since the accession of Ronald Reagan in 1981:

> During the Reagan years, it was the rare network evening news telecasts that did not include at least one White House story. It had not always been so; Washington coverage during previous Presidencies had featured a more varied diet of stories, with some originating on Capitol Hill, some in the State Department, some elsewhere in the federal bureaucracy. The trend towards delivering the main Washington story through the prism of the White House can be traced back to the Nixon years, but it was greatly stimulated by the arrival of the Reagan administration, with its prowess as a supplier of attractive visual images.[15]

Lacking both daily briefings according to lobby rules and briefings designed to set the daily television agenda, the media strategies of Australian prime ministers seem essentially *ad hoc* by comparison. Without formal media procedures, Australian prime ministers have been free to develop their own ways of dealing with the press gallery. Chifley provided access to the press gallery by regular press briefings, mostly attributable, alternating the times to suit morning and evening newspapers. Menzies was much more sparing in permitting formal access and his dealings with individual journalists grew increasingly rare. Over the 17 years of the Menzies prime ministership, a generation of younger journalists emerged in the press gallery who had no direct contact with the Australian prime minister. There were, however, isolated occasions such as press gallery dinners when Menzies unbent and mingled convivially with journalists.

15. Hertsgaard, *op. cit.*, p. 45.

Holt encouraged more regular access by the media, but there was also a discriminatory element in his approach. He was wary about full-scale press conferences with a general right to question, preferring to brief a small group of press gallery journalists known personally to him and representing the principal media organisations. Effectively, this meant that two representatives of each office attended Holt's briefings on an invitation basis. Holt also recognised that by the mid-1960s electronic media was well established in the press gallery and their special needs had to be met. If he made an important statement for attribution at a briefing, he summoned TV and radio reporters to his office and repeated the remarks for the cameras and tape recorders.

Gorton's dealings with political journalists were less formal and generally less amiable. He continued the briefing sessions initiated by Holt, but they were less regular, and he also used the 'by invitation' convention to exclude journalists who incurred his disfavour. He preferred direct television interviews and background briefings for individual journalists. Gorton's relations with the press gallery deteriorated markedly through his three-year prime ministership. During the 1969 election campaign he described some gallery journalists as 'slimy white things that crawl out of sewers', arguably the most offensive epithet ever levelled publicly at press gallery journalists. McMahon avoided formal contact with the press gallery as much as possible, restricting on-the-record press conferences and even background briefings to fewer opportunities than those offered by Gorton, Holt and even Menzies. McMahon relied heavily on his press office to 'square' journalists and he persisted with a long-established practice of phoning senior journalists and media management to badger them with a litany of suggestions and complaints. The press gallery's annual general meeting in September 1972 criticised the lack of attributable information coming from McMahon and reminded him of an undertaking given when he became prime minister to hold regular on-the-record press briefings.[16] (Whitlam's formal approach to the press gallery is considered in the following section on prime ministerial press conferences.)

Fraser's relationships with the press gallery were awkward at the personal level and his media management techniques were greatly resented by journalists. He was not inaccessible, however, and was prepared to grant lengthy interviews to print journalists for publication and to brief them on public policy issues. Fraser and his press staff were also responsible for notable innovations in the prime minister's relationship with the press gallery. After his sweeping success in the 1975 election campaign, Fraser translated several effective campaign techniques into the daily conduct of his press relations. These were largely drawn from US campaign practice, particularly that of Richard Nixon, but there were

16. *Lloyd, op. cit., p. 249*

other influences, including the strict control of news release applied by Menzies. Essentially, the Fraser strategy revolved around two changes in basic procedure. In effect, Fraser inverted the Holt practice of briefing senior journalists and then calling in the cameras to repeat attributable comments. Fraser made his comments directly to camera and then circulated transcripts of his comments to the general media. This began a process of monitoring and transcription which has become crucial in the conduct of prime ministerial politics in Australia. Fraser also encouraged the tactic of 'door-stopping', an *ad hoc* mechanism by which clusters of journalists sought comment in public places. Properly handled, 'door-stopping' is an invaluable technique for prime ministers because they can grant or decline comment, according to circumstances. Fraser elevated this *ad hoc* process to virtual formal status, with the adoption of regular times and places for 'door-stop' opportunities and the monitoring and distribution of his comments in print format.

Early in his prime ministership, Hawke made a commitment to holding attributable press conferences in preference to non-attributable briefings and 'door-stopping'. While Hawke held more frequent press conferences, he also sought to limit the subject matter discussed, an approach eventually abandoned as unworkable. Essentially, Hawke's media practice combined relatively frequent on-the-record press conferences with a development of 'door-stopping' into virtual mini-press conferences, also monitored and quickly distributed in print form. He used saturation television and radio exposure to exploit major policy announcements.

Prime Ministers and Press Secretaries

The prime minister's press office in recent years has usually employed two senior journalists with support staff. Prime ministers have shown some disposition to appoint at least one journalist experienced in electronic media, although not invariably. For many years, the prime minister's press office was located opposite the cabinet room near the entrance to the prime minister's private office. With Whitlam as prime minister in the early 1970s, the press office was shifted into the press gallery area, making it more accessible to political journalists. In the new Parliament House, however, the press office is incorporated into the prime minister's private office. In some respects, this inhibits direct contact between press secretaries and journalists. Inevitably, journalists who frequent the press office regularly are suspected of cronyism, currying favour, or blatantly swapping intelligence. The vast dimensions of the new Parliament House, with the prime minister's press office two floors below the press gallery quarters, also constrain direct contact.

Inevitably, much of the communication around the new Parliament House is done by phone or fax.

The role of the press secretary in Australian federal politics originated after World War I when a government press officer was appointed by prime minister W.M. Hughes. Previous prime ministers had been assisted informally on publicity and promotion by working journalists who were not staff appointments. By the early 1930s, it was established practice that prime ministers should recruit a senior journalist to serve as press secretary in their private office. By comparison, the prime ministerial press secretary did not emerge in Westminster until after World War II, when Clement Attlee and Winston Churchill made the first appointments. The prime minister's chief press secretary at Westminster, however, has developed into a more powerful and influential figure than the Australian counterpart. So also, of course, have the highly publicised White House press secretaries.

Despite his remoteness, Menzies was never without a press secretary. His press secretaries included some able journalists, but their role was confined mainly to monitoring, intelligence-gathering and distancing the prime minister from the media. Their anonymity created a trend which has persisted down to the present. Prime ministerial press secretaries in Australia are usually glimpsed on television as unobtrusive figures close to their political masters; the label of 'minder' has immense relevance and resonance in the Canberra model. Prime ministerial press secretaries do not appear on the electronic media or conduct attributable briefings or write their memoirs. While not non-entities, most have been shadowy figures whose considerable influence has been little recognised. Only two have gained a degree of public recognition: Graham Freudenberg, who was Whitlam's press secretary for several years, and Tony Eggleton, who served Menzies, Holt and Gorton. Freudenberg's public profile was probably due more to his distinction as a political speech writer than his contribution as press secretary. Eggleton attracted nationwide publicity as the government's principal spokesperson in the aftermath of Holt's drowning. With the exception of Eggleton, who was a career public servant, prime ministerial press secretaries have mostly been recruited from either the press gallery or the ranks of party apparatchiks.

According to Margaret Thatcher's chief press secretary, Bernard Ingham, the role has three principal functions: to serve as spokesperson for prime ministers and, where necessary, the government as a whole; to advise prime ministers on their presentation program and the government as a whole on overall presentation of its policies and measures; and to co-ordinate the government's presentation program at official, as distinct from ministerial, level.[17] By comparison, the role of the Australian prime ministerial press secretary is more limited in concept and

17. Bernard Ingham, *Kill the Messenger*, Sydney: Harper Collins, 1991, p. 190.

fragmentary in execution. Although the press secretary may brief political journalists on behalf of the prime minister and, on occasions, the ministry, the scope is more attenuated than the lobby system provides. Clearly an informal briefing system without the inbuilt safety mechanisms conveyed by lobby rules is less authoritative and effective than regular briefings of a quasi-official nature. Furthermore, the obtaining of feedback becomes more randomly selective when it is conducted outside the exchanges permitted between press secretary and journalists under a system of regular, formal briefings.

Apart from briefings, which are essential for the performance of any spokesperson's functions, the prime ministerial press secretary has little formal responsibility for the co-ordination of overall government presentation and media strategy. Where co-ordination has been undertaken in recent years, it has usually been the responsibility of the appropriate government information agency. (These have been the Government Information Unit [GIU] created under Fraser, and the National Media Liaison Service [known as ANiMaLS] established by Hawke).[18]

Two other factors have constrained the authority and effectiveness of prime ministerial press secretaries under Hawke. With a private office largely driven by career public servants, it has sometimes been difficult for the prime minister's press office to assert itself, even where crucial issues of media strategy and presentation have been involved. Thus, Ingham's ability to tell a public servant or even a minister interfering in media strategy to get the hell out of his area is constrained in Australia, where too many senior public servants fancy themselves as experts in media presentation. Another inhibition was the appointment by Hawke of principal political advisers who, without exception, were senior journalists. Inevitably, this created an alternative source of media counsel for the prime minister.

Prime ministerial press offices have been troubled in recent years by the emergence of alternative power sources in other ministerial offices. These have relied heavily on influencing the media, particularly press gallery journalists. The most important examples have been foreign minister Andrew Peacock's challenge to Malcolm Fraser in 1982 and treasurer Paul Keating's sustained challenge to Bob Hawke from December 1990 to late 1991. Peacock's challenge was defeated convincingly in the party room, and so at first was Keating's, although he was ultimately successful. There were pervasive feelings that both prime ministers had been vulnerable because the challenger had captured excessive media support. This impression was particularly strong over the first challenge to Hawke, prompting a review of the media relations

18. Derek Parker, *The Courtesans: The Press Gallery in the Hawke Era*, Sydney: Allen & Unwin, 1990, pp. 39–40.

policies of the prime minister's private office. The obvious explanation was that Hawke had always been unpopular with much of the press gallery, that he was fundamentally contemptuous of the institution, its journalists and its practices. Keating, however, had acquired a meticulous working knowledge of the press gallery over more than 20 years. No other federal politician had ever matched the familiarity with its mores and consummate mastery of its mechanisms that Keating acquired; certainly not Hawke. The challenges and related media activity exposed the vulnerability of the prime ministerial press office, particularly Keating's challenge which, with media assistance, was established on what was virtually a continuous footing. Press gallery support was crucial to Keating's ultimately successful challenge which saw him replace Hawke as prime minister in December 1991. There is no longer any guarantee that the prime ministership automatically conveys pre-eminence in media relations on behalf of the executive government.

Prime Ministers and Press Conferences

President Theodore Roosevelt is credited with introducing the press conference in the early years of the twentieth century. In his characteristic idiom he described it as a 'bully pulpit'.[19] Presidential press conferences have generated a large academic literature in recent years. Elmer Cornwell analysed presidential press relations, wading through volumes of transcripts of presidential speeches, press conferences and correspondence. He concluded that press conferences were the most valuable source material in understanding different styles of presidential leadership:

> [Only the press conference] shows a president in action under conditions likely to illuminate his mind at work and his techniques. Speeches and statements, which are premeditated and calculated (and often ghost written), are a poor substitute . . . [P]ress conference transcripts stand alone as first hand records of presidential 'action' and reflection.[20]

Media analyst Ron Dorfman suggested that the 'quasi-spontaneity' of the news conference was more likely than any other medium to display a president's 'confusion or glibness or irrationality or genius or grace'.[21]

Australia's prime ministerial press conferences can be analysed according to regularity, content or style. The principal aspects of regularity in the Australian context have been indicated earlier in this chapter. Only Chifley and Whitlam adhered consistently to the practice

19. Hedrick Smith, *The Power Game*, London: Collins, 1988, p. 397.
20. Carolyn Smith, *Presidential Press Conferences: A Critical Appraisal*, New York: Praeger, 1990, p. xviii.
21. *Ibid.*

of holding multi-media press conferences regularly and on-the-record. (With Chifley, of course, press conferences were confined to print and radio journalists.) Other prime ministers have made commitments to such formal press conferences but have largely failed to observe them. This does not mean that prime ministers such as Fraser and Hawke have not participated in a wide range of media contacts. Hawke, in particular, held numerous press conferences. Fraser also held relatively frequent press conferences, although he preferred the ubiquitous 'door-stopping'. The crucial point is the willingness of prime ministers to submit themselves regularly to the uncertainties of attributable press conferences, with no limitations on subject matter and opportunities for follow-up. Chifley and Whitlam apart, all other Australian prime ministers have called press conferences at times of their own choosing and with a large measure of control over the topics for discussion.

Comparable analyses of press conference transcripts drawing conclusions about style, competence and prime ministerial stature have not yet been attempted in Australia. It is possible here to make only some general comments about prime ministerial press conferences, focusing particularly on patterns of questioning. The relationship between Chifley and political journalists at press conferences was too intimate to encourage adversarial questioning. The notion of an adversarial relationship between journalists and the Olympian Menzies was derisory; it simply would not have been tolerated under the conventions of his prime ministership.

Menzies's approach to press conferences in his years as prime minister, when television was well established, is best illustrated by his airport conferences when he returned from overseas missions. A large group of multi-media journalists and technicians would assemble in the airport conference room. After a few minutes, a press secretary would appear and announce that Sir Robert would make a statement to the cameras but not answer questions. When the great man entered, the media would rise in a body and stand until he was seated. A few respectful queries would be directed to the prime minister's health and how he had endured the flight. Menzies usually answered with a certain grace; 'Not bad for an old man' was a standard response. Menzies would read his statement with mellifluous expressiveness, collect his papers, acknowledge the presence of party colleagues such as William McMahon who invariably attended to greet the returning chief, and rise to his feet. The more foolhardy or less inexperienced journalists might try to fling a question Sam Donaldson-style at the prime minister. Menzies would stare them down, or make a contemptuous guffaw and perhaps a brief dismissive comment before striding from the room. This was accepted as routine prime ministerial performance by the media. As Malcolm Fraser observed many years later about Menzies's press contacts, '. . . if you did that today you'd get headlines of all sorts of terrible kinds.' [22]

Such press conferences did much to establish Menzies's mystique with the media and instil awe, even fear, among journalists who encountered him. Holt and McMahon gave few opportunities for adversarial press conferences, but Gorton exposed himself, to his detriment, to the public questioning of a new breed of confident and increasingly aggressive political journalists. His problems were accentuated by his ineptitude with detail and occasional lack of comprehension bordering on the absurd. At one legendary press conference on an overseas mission he confused the South-East Asian Treaty Organisation (SEATO) with an Indonesian general. Adversarial questioning culminating in media ridicule was largely responsible for Gorton's increasing aversion to press conferences.

Whitlam largely set the tone of his press conferences by a lengthy preliminary statement containing policy and administrative detail of varying value to journalists. This tended to take the edge off what American analyses of press conferences call 'the opening salvo'. He was also adroit in selecting questioners and restricting follow-ups. Consequently the tone of his press conferences was generally respectful, although there was an increasingly adversarial edge through 1975 as Australia plunged into constitutional crisis.

Fraser's media management strategies provoked resentment among political journalists and his press conferences became increasingly adversarial. The full measure of media dissatisfaction, however, was not vented until his final election campaign in March 1983 when he was clearly heading for defeat. His biographer, Phillip Ayres, has sought to account for the manifest glee of several journalists at Fraser's impending defeat:

> Fraser's relations with the majority of journalists had never been very good, partly because he preferred kerb side interviews to longer, more formal interviews, (although his answers to questions were frequently long and detailed), but chiefly because many of the younger journalists instinctively disliked Fraser as the man who had preciptiated the collapse of the Whitlam Government. Whatever the reasons, there was some culpably uneven coverage of the principals in this [1983] election.[23]

The virtual gloating of some journalists was contrary to accepted media conventions of impartiality and equity. It displayed a certain lack of grace among journalists who had not sought to confront Fraser when he was at the zenith of his powers. It also reflected an element of pay

22. Quoted in Weller, *op. cit.*, p. 194.
23. Philip J. Ayres, *Malcolm Fraser, a Biography*, Melbourne: William Heinemann Australia, 1987, p. 430.

back for media management which political journalists endured but never accepted.

Hawke called more frequent press conferences than Fraser, and generally permitted a wide range of questioning. Generally, his press conferences were less adversarial than Fraser's. Although essentially co-operative, Hawke responded pugnaciously to any hint of adversarial questioning. His essential gregariousness generally made his press conferences more congenial than those of Fraser.

Prime Ministers, Management and Manipulation

Media manipulation is easier to identify in retrospect than it is to conceptualise. In the United States an extensive literature has developed pointing to extensive media manipulation during the Nixon and Reagan presidencies in particular. (It should also be noted that these periods of extensive manipulation were linked by the often bumbling media ineptitude of the Ford and Carter presidencies.) The essence of media manipulation in the 1980s, particularly its emphasis on television, has been evoked by a former White House press officer, Leslie Janka:

> As opposed to Kissinger and Haldeman and that crowd, whose view was that you control the media by giving them bits and pieces [of information] the Reagan White House came to the totally opposite conclusion that the media will take what they feed them. They've got to write their story every day. You give them their story they'll go away. As long as you come in there every day, hand them a well-packaged, pre-masticated story in the format they want, they'll go away. The phrase is 'manipulation by inundation'. You give them the line of the day, you give them facts, access to people who will speak on the record And you do that long enough, they're going to stop bringing their own stories and stop being investigative reporters of any kind, even modestly so.[24]

It is questionable whether 'media by manipulation' so defined is feasible in the peculiar circumstances of the Australian prime ministership. Unlike the US presidency, it is virtually impossible to siphon off what is exclusively prime ministerial news from what is government news, legislative news, political party news, policy news, or general political news. Even in the highly manipulative Reagan White House, the 'manipulated' news from the executive government was 'moulded' into a legislative framework.[25] Under the Australian system, prime ministers have an undeniable advantage in generating news coverage, particularly on television, but it is by no means a monopoly. Prime ministers have to share news opportunities with their government colleagues and with the government party in the legislature.

24. Hertsgaard, *op. cit.*, p. 52.
25. *Ibid.*, p. 158.

Furthermore, they have to compete for news opportunities with the opposition parties. In such circumstances, even the most adroit 'manipulation by inundation' simply would not work.

There is, of course, one important exception: the election campaign. During an election campaign, the Australian prime ministers function very much as presidential figures. The election strategy and its media sub-strategy is focused exclusively on prime ministers to the virtual exclusion of all other ministers. Because the campaign is dominated by television and the vital network news services in the early evening, the fundamental manipulative tactics of 'line of the day' and early picture opportunities apply. When studying accounts of how media manipulation has been applied to promote the US executive government through the president, one could almost be reading about prime ministers' role in Australian election campaigns. Here, the paramount nature of the prime ministership and media strategies dependent on it have been demonstrated in levels of competence and effectiveness rivalling US presidential elections and eclipsing so far the efforts of British political parties.

While effective manipulation of the media by prime ministers and their support staff is largely confined to election campaigns, media management has been widely practised, not always successfully. There is a certain subtlety in deciding just where media management, which is an accepted part of political practice, tips over into media manipulation, which is considered undesirable. Media management is inherent in the operations of the British system, as Bernard Ingham conceded in his autobiography *Kill the Messenger*. Ronald Reagan's former press secretary, Larry Speakes, has also frankly acknowledged the importance of media management in the conduct of the presidency:

> My job was like that of anyone in the public relations business, to tell the press only what my client, in this case, the president of the United States and his top aides, wanted me to, while the job of the press was to try to find out everything, and I do mean everything, including the intimate details of President Reagan's health. We had our innings and they had theirs.[26]

Australian prime ministers and their staffs have engaged in a variety of media activities which, in certain combinations, could be construed as manipulation, management or both. This is a rough check list:

1. The timing of news and particularly picture opportunities to meet the requirements of television.
2. Avoidance of regular press conferences accessible to all media, but particularly suited to the demands of adversarial print journalists.

26. Larry Speakes, *Speaking Out: Inside the Reagan White House*, New York: Charles Scribner, 1988, p. 217.

3. An emphasis on 'door-stopping' and other impromptu interviews which mostly yield little or no hard news, and have only limited opportunity for follow-up questioning.
4. Agenda-setting through a 'line' or 'story of the day', sold to television network journalists in the knowledge that other media will probably follow the story.
5. Creation of quasi-government information units with extensive monitoring capability to pump out news material favourable to the executive government
6. Direct prime ministerial contacts with senior media management, sometimes in a context of important public policy decisions affecting the media.
7. Leaking to selected journalists by the prime minister or his delegates.

If all of these tactics were applied consistently by an Australian prime minister, it would undoubtedly constitute a high order of media manipulation. Applied singly, or in lesser combinations, the activity would mostly fall within the bounds of acceptable news management. The important exceptions would be prime ministerial leaking and the grey area of prime ministerial relationships with media proprietors.

It has long been accepted that leaking, defined as the unofficial disclosure of official information, has been practised at the highest levels of executive government in the United States and the United Kingdom. The distinguished US journalist, James Reston, once described government as the only known vessel that leaked from the top.[27] The former British cabinet minister, Sir Ian Gilmour, concluded that most leaks came from No. 10 because the general level of information was 'always highest at the centre' (Gilmour may have been jaundiced by his falling-out with Margaret Thatcher.)[28] British prime minister James Callaghan described the difference between leaking and briefing to a colleague: 'Leaking is what you do, briefing is what I do.'[29] The line between briefing and leaking is often extremely fine indeed, depending very much on the motives of the perpetrator.

It would be misguided, however, to assume that prime ministers who gave the greatest number of unattributable briefings to journalists were those most likely to leak. Leaking at the prime ministerial level raises the prospect of serious consequences if the leak is detected and identified. Similar strictures apply to political colleagues or staff officers delegated by the prime minister to leak. Furthermore, a staff officer who leaks without any authorisation from the prime minister is in an exceedingly vulnerable position. There have been instances of reckless leaking from

27. Hedrick Smith, *op. cit.*, p. 441.
28. Cockerell *et al.*, *op. cit.*, p. 137.
29. *Ibid.*, p. 115.

prime ministerial offices. It is extremely difficult to prove, however, that such leaks have been deliberately intended to manipulate the media with the prime minister's express authority.

Fraser and Hawke maintained close links with media proprietors. Hawke in particular has been criticised by political colleagues and elements of the media for his alleged closeness to 'media mates'. Advantageous public policy decisions from the governments of both prime ministers benefited media proprietors like Rupert Murdoch and Kerry Packer. It is arguable to what extent these relationships have been reflected in favourable media coverage. The media generally turned swiftly against Fraser when it became apparent that Hawke would lead the ALP in the 1983 election campaign. This realignment occurred before Hawke had an opportunity to influence media policy. There were substantial 'winners' and 'losers' from media policy during the Hawke years, but these can be attributed in part to a major shake-out of the media industry during the 1980s and also to demonstrable incompetence in several media managements. The maintenance of relationships with the highest levels of media management developed very much into a prime ministerial prerogative.

Prime Ministers, the Media and Power

Without question the growth of the media, particularly television, over the past 20 years has significantly increased the workload of the executive government. In the '2000 days' that press secretary Larry Speakes worked for Ronald Reagan, the president had 535 sessions with the press — more than one every five days. The press contacts comprised 257 interviews, 216 question and answer periods which were essentially 'door-stop' interviews; 39 fully fledged press conferences, and 23 other media briefings in the White House briefing room.[30] Similar statistics have yet to be compiled for the Australian prime ministership, but almost certainly they would indicate a greater media workload. In the judgment of some analysts, Reagan's media load was relatively light compared with those of some predecessors and his successor, George Bush. Margaret Thatcher's chief press secretary, Bernard Ingham, estimated that in just over ten years at No. Ten he gave about 5000 formal briefings to groups of journalists and probably about 3000 to individual journalists who telephoned or buttonholed him.[31]

Ingham's industriousness undoubtedly suited the policy-oriented Margaret Thatcher who had little intuitive feel for the media:

30. Speakes, *op. cit.*, p. 234.
31. Ingham, *op. cit.*, p. 190.

Mrs Thatcher's natural habitat was not the media. She regarded journalism as the haunt of the brittle, the cynical and the unreliable.[32]

Like Sir Robert Menzies, however, Mrs Thatcher, recognised that a 'free press' was fundamental to the British constitutional settlement, that the public had to be informed and that journalists had to be accommodated:

She would do her duty to the Government she led by giving broadcasts, granting interviews and meeting editors and journalists to explain her policies and even throw the occasional party for groups of journalists.[33]

On this evidence, Thatcher did her duty to the media more conscientiously than did Menzies. She was conducting the prime ministership, however, in an era of an omnipresent, if not omnipotent, media, an era when political communication was overwhelmingly reliant on television. Her continuing power as prime minister depended as much on reaching the electorate through the media as it did on her implacable public policy commitment, her authority in the Tory Party and her performance in parliament. Menzies owed a debt to the press for getting him the prime ministership, a debt he largely ignored as prime minister. He was assured anyway of virtually fawning press support. The power of his prime ministership resided in his immense prestige in cabinet, parliament and the party room and, through these institutions, the electorate.

At the other end of the scale from Menzies and Thatcher was George Bush, who relished media work and was prepared to give it priority, at least in the early part of his presidency:

Bush made himself available to reporters so often, both in impromptu and in formal sessions that he seemed to be emulating Lyndon Johnson's example in acting as his own press secretary.[34]

Until he became prime minister Bob Hawke largely acted as his own press secretary, a task that he discharged with consummate skill. His prime ministership, however, became marked by a certain withdrawal from the media. This did not mean that he ignored the media demands of the job. In fact, he met his commitments conscientiously, retaining much of the vitality and authority that marked his earlier years. In no sense, however, could his prime ministership be described as a media-aligned prime ministership. Hawke was not the 'television prime minister' that might have been expected from the media panoply of his political ascent. Certainly, Hawke used the electronic media to appeal to the electorate over the heads of an unenthusiastic Canberra press gallery, particularly during successful election campaigns. He did not, however,

32. *Ibid.*, p. 168.
33 *Ibid.*
34. Hertsgaard, *op. cit.*, p. x.

focus on media presentation to the extent of neglecting other onerous responsibilities of the prime ministership. A media-aligned prime minister strongly implies one who buys time for the media by trimming the time allocated to cabinet, parliament and party. When his prime ministership came under protracted challenge through 1990–1, Hawke did not increase his media activities significantly. If anything, he accepted stoically that he had largely lost the media battle, in the Canberra press gallery at least, to Paul Keating and relied on maintaining performance in the other areas of prime ministerial power — cabinet, party room, parliament and the broader electorate before finally losing power at the end of 1991.

Accepting that media growth has significantly increased the workload of the prime ministership since 1945, has it brought any commensurate benefits to the office in terms of power? In fact, the media returns and rewards have been relatively meagre. Media disfavour contributed significantly to the political downfall of Chifley, Gorton, McMahon, Whitlam and Fraser. Excluding McMahon, all would have been assessed by their peers as having some competence in media relations. The good media relationships of Chifley and Whitlam did not save them from crushing defeat. Fraser took the media strategy of the prime ministership into a new realm of news management, a venture that increased prime ministerial power for a time. (According to Parker, the effectiveness of Fraser's media strategy fell away sharply in the final years of his prime ministership.)[35] The media, however, did not spare him when a serious tactical blunder over election timing left him vulnerable. Of the others, Holt's death makes problematical any assessment of media impact on his prime ministership. He had a better understanding of media fundamentals than other prime ministers and he was liked by journalists. It is doubtful that he could have sustained the respect and support of the media over a longer prime ministership, however, McMahon's perceived media inadequacies sit somewhat oddly with the relatively slender margin of his defeat. Too much should not be made of this, however, as political communication in Australia has developed immensely in the twenty years since McMahon's government. Significant changes in communications technology, techniques of news-gathering, and popular taste should also be taken into account in any assessment of Menzies's now legendary ascendancy over the media.

There is also reason to doubt the overall effectiveness of the inherited framework for the conduct of the prime minister's media relationships. By any criteria, it is fragmented and unco-ordinated by comparison with the Westminister model and the US presidential system (taking account of the ability of the US system to focus primarily on the executive government). It might be argued that messy as the Australian system

35. Parker, *op. cit.*

often is, it offers less opportunity for extensive media manipulation as a reinforcement of prime ministerial power. This is true to some extent, but it ignores the expertise that the prime minister and the governing ALP have brought to dictating the crucial media agenda of federal election campaigns. It has been impossible to assert the same prime ministerial dominance in an environment mixing the politics of executive government with legislative and party politics. Possibly, these problems could be overcome by a prime minister prepared to act as his or her own press secretary and to subordinate all other considerations to media relationships as the basis of prime ministerial power. This could not be accomplished without significant realignment of prime ministerial priorities, a course likely to prove detrimental to the proper functioning of a prime ministership under essentially Westminster conventions. The system that has developed since 1945 has many imperfections. Certainly it could be made more efficient, but at the risk of removing checks and balances which, while constraining prime ministerial power, also limit the opportunities for blatant media manipulation.

6

PRIME MINISTERS AND THE ELECTORATE

Colin A. Hughes

Ben Chifley's first election as prime minister in 1946 differed in a number of respects from the 1990 federal election, Bob Hawke's third as prime minister. For one thing, the electorate was more than twice as large: there were only 4.7 million electors on the rolls in 1946 against 10.7 million in 1990. On the other hand, Australian electors were still spread about the country in much the same way: two states, New South Wales and Victoria, accounted for 48 of the 74 seats in the House of Representatives in 1946, and for 89 of 148 in 1990, electing 65 per cent of MHRs in 1946 and 60 per cent in 1990. All eight prime ministers, all nine if McEwen's brief interregnum is counted, over this period represented either New South Wales (Chifley, McMahon, Whitlam) or Victoria (Menzies, Holt, Gorton, Fraser, Hawke — and McEwen). Ten of the 11 leaders of the opposition also came from either New South Wales (Chifley, Evatt, Whitlam, Howard and now Hewson) or Victoria (Menzies, Calwell, Snedden, Fraser, Peacock), and only one from the remaining third of the country — Hayden from Queensland.

Moreover the two largest cities, Sydney and Melbourne, have dominated Australia's political map almost as much as the two largest states have done. While the classification of the occasional peri-metropolitan electoral division can be argued about, in 1946 there were 24 divisions in Sydney and Melbourne combined, which elected 32 per cent of the House of Representatives; in 1990 there were 53 such divisions, returning 36 per cent of the House. Thus the two largest cities' share of the House has risen even though their states' share has fallen. Of the 20 prime ministers and leaders of the opposition, counting those who held both offices twice, only Chifley and Fraser held country seats, as did McEwen; Evatt shifted from a marginal Sydney seat to a safe one in the country. Hayden's division can probably be classed as country and it certainly was neither Sydney or Melbourne. The other 15 sat for Sydney or Melbourne divisions. The highest political office in the land has been dominated, for the post-World War II period at least, by an especially influential third of the electoral divisions located in that third of the states which happens to have two-thirds of the population. Those who live in the largest states, and in the cities, are more likely to perceive the federal level of government as 'more important' than the state level[1], and it may be that territorial identification with the leading political figure reinforces that tendency.

Before 1946, there had been a few exceptions: Fisher and (briefly) Fadden and Forde from Queensland, Lyons from Tasmania, Curtin who although originally a Victorian had become identified with Western Australia (just as the South Australia-born Hawke was identified with Victoria). But the great majority of prime ministers and leaders of the opposition came from New South Wales (Barton, Watson, Reid, Cook, Hughes originally, Charlton as a leader of the opposition only, Page for an interregnum) and Victoria (Deakin, Hughes when he changed parties and fled south, Bruce, Scullin, Tudor and Latham as leaders of the opposition only). In the second half of the period since federation there has been only one exception coming from an outlying state, compared to three (or five if Fadden and Forde are counted) in the first half.

Why this has been so is not immediately clear. Neither Brisbane nor Perth has ever had many safe seats for either side, and a safe seat is a great help in accumulating seniority and avoiding too many parish-pump duties — but Adelaide has had a modest supply of both Liberal and Labor safe seats and failed to produce likely federal leaders. No doubt loyal support from one's own state helps secure party-room preferment and the more numerous delegations provide more help. Possibly the bigger states have tougher-minded politics which temper those who survive into more effective politicians; Lyons was often said to have been unhappy with the differences between the amiable relationships of Tasmanian affairs and the adversarial style of federal politics. No one has claimed that Australian parties choose their national leaders with native-son appeal in mind as American parties used to do when picking presidential candidates, but their choices certainly appear to have been skewed towards the big battalions and the pattern by which the electorate is spread around the country must matter.

The Structure of the Electorate

While the territorial mix has altered little, the composition of the Australian electorate has changed in ways more significant but less obvious, and these changes have had at the very least some potential to modify the behaviour of Australian prime ministers. Most conspicuous of the changes is that the predominantly Anglo-Celtic electorate of 1946 has been diversified by post-war immigration. Though this appears to have had relatively little impact on the party system or on voting

1. Clive Bean, 'Politics and the Public: Mass Attitudes towards the Australian Political System', in Jonathan Kelley and Clive Bean (eds), *Australian Attitudes: Social and Political Analyses from the National Social Science Survey*, Sydney: Allen & Unwin, 1988, p. 54.

patterns,[2] it has required some modifications in prime ministerial style. Menzies's unashamed concentration on and displays of affection for Britain and the United States, Australia's mother country and most powerful ally respectively, was replaced by Whitlam's two-pronged diversification of Australia's international relationships and cultivation of Australia's hyphenated electors. While neither of Whitlam's successors emphasised Australia's new diversity to quite the same extent in the international sphere, each pursued the emerging 'ethnic' lobby and its votes with enthusiasm, creating a special bureaucracy and set of programs to capture the new electors.

Earlier, such national-origin differences as there were in Australia had heavily religious connotations: the Irish and Italians were not only not British in the sense of being neither English, Scottish or Welsh, they were also Catholics and not Anglicans, Presbyterians, Methodists or Congregationalists. The tensions that had flared over Ireland during the Great War remained a noticeable undercurrent during the Depression, and broke out for the last time during the Labor Party's 'Split' of the middle 1950s and the subsequent debate about introduction of state aid to church schools, one of Menzies's more masterly political moves. Thereafter they died away and are largely meaningless to the younger generation. New religious affiliations are apparent in the community — Greek and Russian Orthodox, Muslims and North American fundamentalist Protestant sects to name only the more numerous and conspicuous. But more important electorally has been the general decline in religious commitment, an encouragement to the left, and the only politically significant phenomenon an alliance of ancient enemies when conservative Catholics and Protestant fundamentalists rallied around the pulpit in new minor parties for a last stand against the forces of secularism. The religious allegiance of prime ministers has ceased to be a matter of interest and the political reaction to one prime minister, Gough Whitlam, calling an especially devout state premier, Johannes Bjelke-Petersen, 'a Bible-bashing bastard' was mainly that it had been indelicate to say such things and to use such language publicly.

Industry and occupation changed too. In 1946 rural Australia was still a major political force. Approximately half the electoral divisions were still outside the six metropolitan areas (with which might be bracketed the largest provincial centres of Newcastle and Wollongong in New South Wales, and Geelong, Ballarat and Bendigo in Victoria). Moreover the Labor Party still did well in the rural seats: Chifley's comfortable majority in the House of Representatives where he held 43 seats out of 74 following the 1946 election was only marginally pulled

2. See James Jupp (ed.), *Ethnic Politics in Australia*, Sydney: Allen & Unwin, 1984; James Jupp, 'The Defused Issues: Ethnic and Aboriginal Affairs' in Ian McAllister and John Warhurst (eds), *Australia Votes: The 1987 Federal Election*, Melbourne: Longman Cheshire, 1988.

back by the country where he had carried 16 out of 36 divisions. By 1990, when the number of substantial provincial cities was larger and identification of rural seats becomes more difficult, rural Australia was much diminished and the Labor Party's chances in such seats had fallen on hard times. With perhaps 32 out of 148 seats classifiable as rural, Hawke carried only eight of them. It should be added that the current proportion of the population living on a farm or in a rural electorate does not settle the amount of political influence the rural interest may claim. A Saulwick poll in 1990 reported that only 6 per cent of respondents (4 per cent of Labor voters and 8 per cent of coalition voters) actually lived on a farm, 25 per cent had once lived on a farm and 30 per cent had visited a farm within the previous three years. A majority, 57 per cent, thought people who lived on farms had 'better lives' and only 12 per cent the opposite.[3] Nostalgia for the bush is a significant political factor.

The relative decline of rural Australia for political purposes is a complex story.[4] It concerns particularly the fortunes of the Country Party within the anti-Labor permanent coalition and the political consequences of John McEwen, who is probably the last leader of that party ever to be a serious contender for the leadership of the coalition as well. When the coalition had been forged in the early 1920s the Country Party component had been so valuable that the resulting government was truly the Bruce-Page government, an alliance of almost equal partners. Even when Menzies retired in the mid-1960s, forty years on, it was still appropriate for him to say that preserving the coalition was the first duty of a Liberal leader. The extent of the influence which the Country Party retained was soon demonstrated when McEwen successfully vetoed a leader the Liberal Party might otherwise have chosen, William McMahon, and later withdrew the veto and allowed McMahon into the position.

But by the second half of the 1970s the close rapport between Fraser, exceptionally a truly rural Liberal, and the three principal parliamentary figures in what was known by then as the National Country Party, Doug Anthony, Ian Sinclair and Peter Nixon, was a source of irritation to many in his party. By the later 1980s there was a continuous run on the political credit of what was now called the National Party — during which it sacked its parliamentary leader, something it had never done before, and the new leader succeeded in losing his seat at the following election, which was also unheard of — that reduced its votes and seats and left the partnership unbalanced to an extent never previously

3. *The Age*, 6 June 1990.
4. See Brian J. Costar and D.F. Woodward (eds), *Country to National: Australian Rural Politics and Beyond*, Sydney: Allen & Unwin, 1985; Brian Costar and Scott Prasser (eds), *Amalgamate or Perish: The Future of Non-Labor Parties in Australia*, School of Management, University College of Southern Queensland, Toowoomba, 1990.

experienced. The decline of the rural electorate certainly shifted the balance of power within the coalition and made a Liberal prime minister (or leader of the opposition for that matter) relatively more powerful.

A more recent transformation in the electorate, but again with some potential significance for the prime ministership, has been the equally steep decline of employment in manufacturing industry. In its earliest days the Labor Party sought support from manual workers in manufacturing, mining, agriculture and the pastoral industry alike and the numerical mix of these categories in each state shaped the character of the local state branches of the party. But, and this was especially true after World War II, employment in manufacturing grew whilst the other three categories stayed static or even declined. Consequently the party's image was increasingly tied to its urban blue-collar trade union affiliates and their members, and its economic policies to their need for tariff protection, even though the last party leader to come from anything like an industrial background was Chifley.

However Australian manufacturing was undermined by a combination of factors, including economic theory, government policy, changes in world trade patterns and its own inability to respond quickly to such changes. We can see this in the two largest of what are now often called Labor's 'heartlands', the electoral divisions of western Sydney and western Melbourne; between 1971 and 1986 (these being census years for which the data are readily accessed) in Sydney, while the total workforce was growing from 397,000 to 514,000, the number of those engaged in manufacturing fell from 138,000 to 104,000, or from 35 per cent to 20 per cent of the workforce. In the equivalent western sector of Melbourne, west of the Yarra, where workforce numbers were more or less static at 418,000 in 1971 and 423,000 in 1986, the numbers in manufacturing fell from 156,000 to 93,000, or from 37 per cent down to 22 per cent. In each so-called heartland a decline of 15 percentage points took place in as many years.

The implications for the Labor Party's survival in a recognisable form are considerable[5], as are the changes in the class-war warriors' roles previously played to the hilt by prime ministers and leaders of the opposition from both sides. Liberal leaders and Liberal doctrine both repudiated class lines and loyalties, while visiting the worst sins of class exclusiveness and bias on their opponents, and it was a Labor prime minister, Hawke, who had to adjust to the new situation. Hawke was much criticised in the process[6] for abandoning his party's roots and most devoted supporters.

5. Andrew Scott, *Fading Loyalties*, Sydney: Pluto Press, 1991.
6. See Dean Janensch, *The Hawke-Keating Hijack*, Sydney: Allen & Unwin, 1989; Graham Maddox, *The Hawke Government and Labor Tradition*, Ringwood: Penguin, 1989.

Although the proportion of the electorate who are women has changed hardly at all, the contribution which women make to Australian politics has altered and gender has taken on a new significance in politics and public policy.[7] In 1946 four women were elected to the Commonwealth parliament. Two widows, Enid Lyons and Doris Blackburn, occupied their late husbands' seats in the House of Representatives, Dorothy Tangney was re-elected to the Senate and Annabelle Rankin was sent there for the first time — two among 74 (3 per cent) and two among 36 (6 per cent) respectively. Following the 1990 election there were ten women (7 per cent) in the House of Representatives and 18 (24 per cent) in the Senate. Although such numbers were still well short of proportionality, and in respect of the House of Representatives the growth curve had showed a tendency to level off prematurely in the mid-1980s, the increase did make some difference to Australian political life.

The extent to which the prime minister was a central figure in the changes varied. Menzies had been the first prime minister to appoint a woman, Enid Lyons, as a minister but without portfolio; Holt the first to give a woman, Annabelle Rankin, a post with portfolio. Whitlam was the first to become involved in wider questions of the place of gender in politics and had made his personal office a centre for reform in policy and the bureaucracy. Fraser had tended to push the subject off to another minister. Hawke returned to personal involvement at the prime ministerial level, although not as consistently as Whitlam. Following the 1987 election he required the Labor Party's factions to review their ministry nominations to ensure that a second woman was included in the ministry, but spending restraints restricted his government's ability to continue inducing change in the bureaucracy and in sensitive policy areas. It is arguable that the Labor Party's deliberate cultivation in the 1970s of non-English-speaking immigrants and women, two sections of the electorate with which they had fared poorly previously, underpinned the party's run of election victories in the 1980s.

The proportion of young people in the electorate has been altered once, and that fairly substantially by the reduction of the minimum voting age from 21 to 18 in 1974. Apart from that one infusion of youth, the Australian electorate has been aging gradually as more individuals survive into their seventies and eighties and continue to be active citizens. Early development of the welfare state ensured that wooing elderly voters has long been seen as a necessary political activity, and probably little has changed in this regard in the last forty or fifty years. Accompanying television cameras now ensure that visits to

7. See Jocelyn Clarke and Kate White, *Women in Australian Politics*, Sydney: Fontana, 1983; Marian Sawer and Marian Simms, *A Woman's Place: Women and Politics in Australia*, Sydney: Allen & Unwin, 1984; Marian Simms (ed.), *Australian Women and the Political System*, Melbourne: Longman Cheshire, 1984.

institutions for the elderly get maximum publicity for prime ministers who do such things, but they can also savage a prime minister who snaps at an inquiring pensioner — as happened to Hawke during one shopping-centre political excursion.

An older electorate does not mean enthusiasm for older prime ministers. It is likely that the popularity of early retirement from the workforce and conversion to retirees' lifestyle makes it more difficult for a prime minister, however vigorous, to continue in office much past normal retirement age in the early sixties. Among the post-war prime ministers, only one stayed past 65: Menzies, who retired gracefully at 71. Chifley (who by then was leader of the opposition) and Holt died at 65 and 59 respectively. Gorton was forced out of the leadership at 59. McMahon, Whitlam (also leader of the opposition again) and Fraser each stood down following electoral defeat at 64, 61 and 52 respectively. None obviously overstayed his welcome, though it may have been that Menzies — who had had a very long innings indeed — was seen as increasingly out of touch with political fashion.

The electorate is aging slowly, but it has been educating itself quite rapidly. Menzies, whose own natural talents had been enhanced by the educational opportunities already available early in the twentieth century, repaid his debt by a substantial expansion of tertiary education in the 1950s and 1960s. The Labor Party overcame its early, and well-founded, suspicion of universities as the preserve of a well-to-do minority to become just as supportive. The consequence for electoral demography of so much expenditure has been that, whereas in 1971 two-thirds of the House of Representatives' electoral divisions had fewer than 5 per cent of their eligible population (defined as aged 15 and over) with some tertiary education, by 1986 the proportion had dropped to one-eighth. At the other end of the distribution pattern, in 1971 the relevant population of only one division in 12 included more than 10 per cent who had experienced some tertiary education, but by 1986 the proportion was one division in four.

A better-educated (at least as measured by quantity of exposure to formal instruction) electorate should be a more critical electorate, and because it is the younger electors who will have had more formal education, age variations in attitudes and opinions are likely to be greater than they once were. A better-educated electorate may also be more sophisticated and realistic about what governments can actually achieve. If that is so, it may be less likely to take immediate reprisals for any swings of domestic and international economic fortunes. Earlier generations nearly tipped Menzies out in 1954 and again in 1961 for allowing the economy to turn down briefly, and economic problems magnified the scale of Whitlam's defeat in 1975, but Fraser and Hawke both won re-election despite much more severe 'misery indexes' of unemployment and inflation combined. (That is not to say, of course, that recent prime ministers have been any more conscientious than their predecessors in educating the electorate to the realities of economic life, or any more frank in taking the electorate into their confidence as to what was likely to happen in the economy.) Further, a better-educated electorate is likely to be concerned about different issues, especially if more education has coincided with different jobs and more income; environmental issues for example have grown in importance.[8]

As a consequence of the growth in welfare spending and services, the number of persons employed by the private sector now barely equals the number of those who are employed by the public sector or receive their income as payments from the public sector. Public sector unions and welfare support groups have become powerful political actors by virtue of the electoral clout which they can bring to bear, but after the apparent failure of welfarism in the mid-1970s prime ministers are caught between the Scylla of voter expectation of increased benefits and the Charybdis of taxpayer resistance to more taxation. Menzies and his immediate successors could simultaneously keep Labor out of office by asking at large where the money would come from for Labor policies, and still retain the loyalty of the significant blocs of electors with a few well-directed election promises. Whitlam could expect that economic growth and income-tax-bracket-creep would painlessly deliver sufficient revenue to pay for an expanded public sector — an expectation which in the event proved mistaken. But after the oil shock of 1973 and the Hayden budget of 1975 public expectations changed. The shift in ideological predispositions away from spending and towards tax reductions, and from incremental public sector growth to cut-back and privatisation, put the next two prime ministers, Fraser and Hawke, in a very different position.[9]

Electoral Mechanisms

The mechanisms which shape electoral outcomes may matter just as much as the structure of the electorate itself. The alternative vote, known in Australia as preferential voting, had been introduced prior to the 1919 federal election and assisted the two anti-Labor parties to find an accommodation which allowed competition between them in some seats without too much risk of Labor slipping through a divided field.

8. Elim Papadakis, 'Minor Parties, the Environment and the New Politics' and Murray Goot, 'The Forests, the Trees and the Polls' in Clive Bean, Ian McAllister and John Warhurst (eds), *The Greening of Australian Politics: The 1990 Federal Election*, Melbourne: Longman Cheshire, 1990.
9. See Brian W. Head and Allan Patience (eds), *From Fraser to Hawke: Australian Public Policy in the 1980s*, Melbourne: Longman Cheshire, 1989; and Christine Jennett and Randal G. Stewart (eds), *Hawke and Australian Public Policy*, Melbourne: Macmillan, 1990.

Preferential voting's usefulness for the coalition was revived in the 1950s when it allowed the Democratic Labor Party (DLP) to retain a separate existence and yet deliver almost all its voting support to the coalition in the form of second preferences. Most recently preferential voting has performed a similar service to the Australian Labor Party, with Australian Democrat and Green preferences moving to that party. In each case the minister or ministers in the especially sensitive policy areas — defence and foreign policy in the DLP's day, conservation when the Democrats and Greens were calling the tune — appeared responsible for putting the deal together to guarantee delivery of the desired preferences. But ultimately the responsibility for the policy baits and perhaps for the deals would have to be the prime minister's.

Introduction of proportional representation to Senate elections from 1949 onwards initially smoothed out the excessive swings which had previously characterised winner-takes-all Senate elections. Previously one party could be left virtually excluded from one chamber of the parliament if it polled poorly at two successive elections. But after the 'Split' in the Labor Party in the mid-1950s, proportional representation took on a new significance. By means of PR the DLP could not merely take votes from the ALP and give them to the coalition as it could in House elections. It could actually keep votes cast for the Senate for its own use, secure the presence of its own members in that half of the parliament, hold the balance of power there, and thereby extract somewhat greater concessions from the coalition than it could normally get from manipulating preferences in House electoral contests. A handful of DLP senators, once elected, was more disciplined than hundreds of thousands of DLP voters were likely to be, if for example they had to be told to abandon the coalition and give their preferences to the ALP just to make the point that it could be done and so prove that the DLP still had some independence in how it would bestow its favours.

A few years after the DLP had disintegrated at the 1974 election and disappeared from the Senate, the Australian Democrats appeared on the scene. Their ideological enthusiasms were more varied than the DLP's, and their internal discipline made them less reliable as allies. For the first half-century of the Commonwealth parliament Australian prime ministers could expect that they could normally manage the Senate with little more difficulty than they managed the House, unless there was a rare bit of bad luck when staggered elections for the Senate produced a differently complexioned chamber, or there was some short-lived issue on which a few government backbenchers in the Senate were ready to be obstreperous. But from the mid-1950s the Senate usually required some management, and from the late 1970s a lot of management. While the government leader in the Senate carried the primary burden of such problems, it was the prime ministers who were ultimately responsible for getting the government's program through and also for avoiding being criticised in parliament to an embarrassing extent. Hostile senators could block legislation, but even when they did not go that far they could complain and condemn the government's performance.

The presence of a substantial minor party in the electorate, and the translation of that presence into power and influence through the electoral system, added one more to the prime ministers' bundle of roles — courting support outside their own party or coalition. Menzies had done it well, the Liberals who followed him were less successful. Whitlam preferred to sell a program direct to the electorate, though his one piece of horse-trading (displacing the DLP's leader with the offer of a diplomatic post) contributed to the destruction of that party. Personal relations were poor between Fraser and the Australian Democrats' principal founder, Don Chipp, and much better between Hawke and Chipp. At the grass-roots level Democrat preferences went increasingly to the ALP although this may have been in part because with a Labor government in office disgruntled coalition supporters were not prepared to risk giving their first preferences elsewhere.

One final point remains to be made about the electorate: Australia is governed as a federal system and consequently electors make each electoral choice subject to the additional complexity a federal system creates.[10] Perceptions of the federal element in the political environment vary. It is clear that there is disagreement about which level of government matters most to the public, and it is abundantly clear that there are many misapprehensions as to which level of government is in constitutional theory or administrative practice responsible for which functions. There is some evidence that many voters do not distinguish too carefully between the federal structures of each party and their state-level counterparts, but then it is arguable that this may be realistic. A threat to take revenge on the innocent part of the party may be almost as effective as a threat directed to the guilty part.

Attitudes to Leaders

Electors normally have opinions about the federal party leaders, the prime minister and the leader of the opposition, and these opinions matter at election time,[11] but they also have opinions about the local state equivalents, the premier and leader of the opposition, and they may even, if asked, have opinions about the premiers of states other than their own. They are unlikely to have opinions about many cabinet ministers,

10. Don Aitken, *Stability and Change in Australian Politics*, 2nd edn. Canberra: Australian National University Press, 1982, pp. 44-7.
11. Clive Bean and Anthony Mughan, 'Leadership Effects in Parliamentary Elections in Australia and Britain', *American Political Science Review,* 83 (4), December 1989.

whether federal or state, so that the most senior figures in the political arena stand out whatever the theory of cabinet government might suggest. But electors are likely to have opinions about the principal alternative to the leader in each party, the heir apparent or the most likely challenger; most of the time, being cautious and conservative by nature, they favour the incumbent in each party though there have been times, such as the unusual alternation of Andrew Peacock and John Howard at the head of the Liberal Party in the second half of the 1980s, when it seemed that as soon as one was made leader he would fall behind his rival in popularity.

Australian prime ministers have not been much talked about at a popular level,[12] and there is certainly nothing like the Americans' indoor sport of ranking presidents from George Washington to the incumbent. Thus there is little known about popular evaluations of the office and what is required of its occupants, and that little is now fairly dated.[13] However, some informed guesses can be made, and the following pages speculate about how the prime minister's roles, as these have been played by occupants of the position from Chifley to Hawke, might have been seen by Australian electors over that period.

The first bundle is of roles which are essentially constitutional and institutional. Australia is a monarchy, but it has an absentee monarch. There is potential for a secular trinity in the public mind: the absent monarch; her local representative, who for the quarter century since 1965 has been an Australian already known to some extent to the electorate, sharing duties as head of state; and the prime minister as head of government.

The monarchy has remained popular by comparison with an alternative republic, though the level of its popularity has moved a little. A poll in 1953, at the time of the coronation of Queen Elizabeth II when the monarchy was in especially high regard and the impact of non-British immigrants in Australia was still limited, showed 77 per cent of respondents pro-monarchy and only 15 per cent pro-republic. Five subsequent polls 1966-70, by which time non-British immigrants were a

12. Thus there have been few volumes which provide potted biographies of all occupants of the office: Colin A. Hughes, *Mr Prime Minister: Australian Prime Ministers 1901–1972*, Melbourne: Oxford University Press, 1976; Brian Carroll, *From Barton to Fraser: Every Australian Prime Minister*, Sydney: Cassell, 1978; Scott Brodie, *Statesmen, Leaders and Losers: The Twenty-three Prime Ministers of Australia*, Sydney: Dreamweaver Books, 1984; Lindsay Nance, *Prime Ministers of Australia*, London: Bison Books, 1989. Biographies of a single prime minister are much more common and are more discussed.
13. See Henry Mayer and Ross Curnow, 'Hunting the P.M.', *Australian Quarterly* 40 (1), March 1968; Ross Curnow and Henry Mayer, 'Hunting the P.M. — Country Style', *Australian Quarterly* 40 (4), March 1968; Colin A. Hughes and J.S. Western, 'Hunting the P.M.: The Sequel', *Australian Quarterly* 44 (1), March 1972; J.S. Western and Colin A. Hughes, *The Mass Media in Australia*, 2nd edn., St Lucia: University of Queensland Press, 1983.

significant factor, gave an average of 63 per cent pro-monarchy, 28 per cent pro-republic. Two polls in 1973, when the Whitlam government was still well regarded, showed pro-monarchy sentiment down to 51 per cent and pro-republic up to 37 per cent, the one period when the division of opinion has roughly matched coalition and ALP voting support — usually there are more monarchists than coalition voters. But since then there has been some recovery in support for the monarchy: 12 polls 1975–86 produced an average of 61 per cent pro-monarchy, 30 per cent pro-republic,[14] not very different from the ratio prior to the Whitlam years. Australian voters are likely to think of a presidential regime on the American model, with a combined head of state and head of government, and the preceding evidence suggests most would like to keep the two separate. On the other hand, a slight majority (55 per cent) in 1984–85 said the monarch and royal family were either not very important or not important at all 'to Australia' while 44 per cent thought them very important (16 per cent) or fairly important (28 per cent);[15] in Britain, nearly two-thirds had thought them very important.

When the Queen is present in Australia the governor-general recedes into the background. The prime minister publicly attends on the monarch and probably rises in public esteem because of the association. By contrast, governor-generals may be respected, even liked, but their stock of charisma is limited and certainly insufficient to enhance the prime minister's status with the electorate. On the one occasion they came openly into conflict, the electorate divided about equally between governor-general Kerr and prime minister Whitlam.[16] However at that point the governor-general had been deeply embroiled in partisan conflict by the intercameral and interparty dispute over supply. It is more than likely that normally the dichotomy of the dignified and apolitical — the monarch — and efficient and party political — the prime minister — works to the disadvantage of the latter. However, the extensive and diverse royal family, even at a distance, supplies domestic drama sufficient for media needs and allows prime ministers a fair degree of personal privacy.

Australia is a nation-state and as such is a member of a world system, and also of a worldwide Commonwealth of Nations and of a series of bilateral and multilateral alliances across the Pacific Basin. Relatively little is known about how the Australian electorate views these connections, apart from continuingly favourable attitudes towards the United States and Britain and shifting fears of possible threats with

14. George Winterton, *Monarchy to Republic: Australian Republican Government*, Melbourne: Oxford University Press, 1986, p. 13.
15. Bean, *op.cit.*, p. 52.
16. Terence W. Beed, 'Opinion Polling and the Elections' in Howard R. Penniman (ed.), *Australia at the Polls: The National Elections of 1975*, Washington: American Enterprise Institute, 1977, p. 247.

ideological (Russian) or racial (Japanese or Indonesian) or both (Chinese) overtones, and therefore of how foreign policy stances might have enhanced or detracted from the public estimation of particular prime ministers. Undoubtedly the Commonwealth link, and the British link which was its core, has diminished in the public mind and no contemporary prime minister would risk electoral popularity for British interests as Chifley did, or display acute Anglophilia publicly as Menzies did. Perhaps, though this is less certain, the American link has been undercut by a gradual drift from military dependence to economic hostility, though status as a serious actor on the world stage still comes from attendance on the US president, much less so from an appearance at the United Nations.

When the nation goes to war, or appears likely to, the role of national leader assumes a special prominence. Three levels of concern are possible. The major, life-and-death struggle as in World War II under Curtin has not been repeated since. The protracted, threatening but remote conflict — the Korean War, the Suez Crisis, Vietnam — can for a longish time engender support for the prime minister, with Holt's sweeping victory at the 1966 election a prize specimen. But even a minor diversion, as an ally of Britain still east of Suez in the Malayan Emergency or as a participant in United Nations peace-keeping, can translate into electoral approval depending to some extent on the auspices. Military commitments generally go down well with coalition voters, and when undertaken on behalf of the world can rope in a substantial proportion of Labor voters too.

Australia is a federation as well as a nation-state, and consequently the prime minister is head of one level of government frequently in conflict with other levels of government. There are the great traditional tournaments, like a premiers' conference and loan council meeting, which pit the prime minister against all the premiers, in theory at least though it is usually easy enough to split their ranks. And there are separate hand-to-hand encounters, often sought out by a premier who believes with some justification that this is what state electors expect and want. Prime ministers are the ultimate embodiment of 'Canberra', a relatively alien presence on the total governmental scene that extracts the largest share of taxes (even though much is subsequently returned), mismanages the economy so that unemployment and/or inflation are let loose upon the people, and fails to understand their needs because it is remote and cushioned against the adverse effects of its policies.

Wise prime ministers therefore need to spend a considerable proportion of their time moving among the people, visiting all parts of the country and being involved as participant or spectator in as wide a range of public activities as possible. Once this used to be done in a very low key:

Ben had come to me in the party room and told me he intended coming to my electorate in the Christmas vacation, to unostentatiously meet folk during my tour. There was to be no publicity at all; I was not to tell my colleagues at this stage. He just wanted to poke around knocking on doors . . .[17]

Subsequently, and especially after the advent of television, such tours and meeting of folk evolved into media circuses.

Australia is also a constitutional state with a written constitution which, even if the people have little knowledge of its contents and many are ignorant of its existence, matters considerably in day-to-day political life. Prime ministers sometimes contemplate changing the constitution but when they do they know they will require the electorate's approval. Chifley took four proposals to the people on two occasions and got one accepted. Menzies tried only once, lost and never tried again. Holt went to the people once and one of the two proposals was carried. Whitlam and Hawke each put a total of six proposals on two occasions without any success at all. Only Fraser managed a respectable record: three out of four proposals carried on the one occasion he tried.

So unproductive a record suggests some widespread distrust, but distrust of *what* is not immediately apparent. There is no evidence of affection or respect for the constitution, such as is identifiable in the United States, so it is unlikely to be a popular belief that the constitution could not possibly be improved that is at work. If it were solely that the people are federalists at heart and perceive any amendment of the constitution as likely to expand the federal jurisdiction (unless some immediate benefit for themselves is obvious, as was the case with the social services referendum in 1946), then it is hard to see why the Labor Party ever wins a federal election when it had until very recently been committed to expanding governmental activities.

More plausibly, there may be a distrust of politicians and governments *per se*.[18] Compulsory voting and political reality mean that someone has to be chosen to govern and therefore electors have reluctantly to choose the lesser evil, but the need to amend the constitution is never urgent and therefore can be avoided. Sometimes bipartisan support for an amendment can be secured and then if the issue is easily comprehended and reflects prevailing public opinion — in 1967 that something should be done for Aborigines, in 1977 that Senate vacancies should not be manipulated — then the electorate may be induced to vote 'Yes'. The prime minister's approach and personal popularity have nothing to do with the outcome.

Next, prime ministers are not only leaders of all Australians. Each prime minister is also leader of that particular section or part associated

17. Gil Duthie, *I Had 50,000 Bosses: Memoirs of a Labor Backbencher 1946–1975*, Sydney: Angus & Robertson, 1984, p. 60.
18. Bean, *op. cit.*, pp. 55–7.

with a political party (or coalition) and its associated interests. Class used to be the dominant cleavage in Australian politics, though its salience has diminished and — a point which has already been raised — this may have ended the prime minister's role as class-war warrior as it was once played by Chifley and Menzies. On this matter, Hawke's experience is critical. Did his long-standing popularity, at a level quite remarkable by Australian standards, mean that class cleavage no longer matters or that Bob Hawke in a unique way managed to transcend it? Commentators on the Australian party system have reported a transformation of its components from mass parties expressing the ideology and program of their syndicates to 'catch-all' parties for which these older commitments have been subordinated to 'responsiveness to the changes in the mood and opinions of the electorate at large'.[19] More likely, the two processes have fed upon each other: objectively class has declined in importance and parties have altered their stances in response and, by failing to reinforce class consciousness as they once did, contributed further to the decline.

Even though contemporary parties may have shed some of their ideological baggage, prime ministers remain the authoritative articulator of party doctrine. There have been times when a leader's doctrines have been the focus of widespread and prolonged attention. Chifley's socialism, Menzies's liberalism, Whitlam's reformism, Hawke's corporatism, were each something more than a bag of election promises and those prime ministers have a special significance because of their ideas. But there have been other times when ideas have flitted on and off the stage too quickly to matter to any but the most committed politics observer, and since 1977, when the changeover from Whitlam to Hayden took place, there has been no little convergence in ideological positions. In the absence of evidence, it is difficult to know whether this has been well received, or even noticed, by the electorate.

Though class has declined in importance, lifestyles have become more divergent in Australia. In the late 1960s it was still possible for a prime minister's off-duty conduct to cause political problems;[20] in the 1990s it is likely that similar behaviour would cause talk but have very little political fallout. Whatever they may choose to do themselves, prime ministers are expected to be interested in everybody and everything. They can go to the opera without fear of being accused of being a highbrow or a snob, but would be wise to go to the footie and the races more often. Thet are expected to be dutiful to the old and also interested in the next generation — though Malcolm Fraser's display of face-painting during a kindergarten visit had an inherent implausibility not seen since President

19. Dean Jaensch, *Power Politics: Australia's Party System*, Sydney, Allen & Unwin, 1989, p. 190.
20. Edward St. John, *A Time to Speak*, Melbourne: Sun Books, 1969, pp. 164-8; Alan Reid, *The Gorton Experiment*, Sydney: Shakespeare Head Press, 1971, ch. 10.

Coolidge was photographed in a Sioux war-bonnet. The media are likely to take an interest in any human interest story, such as a family problem or a new pet, involving prime ministers — but be less interested than if the principal were a pop star, a television soap-opera actor, or a member of the distant royal family. The prime minister's spouse is likely to receive some attention, but a leader of the opposition without one is not thought to be particularly handicapped in the political stakes. In short the public are mildly interested in the prime minister's personal affairs but not especially intrusive.

A connected matter is the prime minister's role as *parens patriae*. A popular model is the Lincolnesque 'man of the people', moving naturally among them and drawing strength from that contact — Chifley. Another is the leader of exceptional ability, able to stand comparisons on the world stage and towering above contemporaries at home — Menzies or Whitlam. But the obverse does not disqualify, though it may be a slight handicap. An aloof patrician, such as Fraser appeared to be, may be accepted; so may ordinary decent 'blokes' doing their best — Lyons was a great success in that part but Holt had more problems with it, so perhaps the audience has become more demanding. Finally, a transformation from Hal to Henry may be well received by the electorate. The larrikin tradition[21] still has its followers; Gorton failed to make the transition and this proved one of several problems for him, Hawke succeeded and turned his somewhat gaudy past into a political asset.

Most of the time prime ministers are the principal actors on an unequivocally political stage. For example, there has been a proliferation of pressure groups, and a growing intensity in their conflict. Again, probably the decline of class warfare and employer-employee hostilities encouraged the development. Prime ministers are likely to have special responsibilities as conciliator or adjudicator, not intervening in every issue but only those which have dragged on too long or have the capacity to hurt too many people. Some premiers have built reputations as stirrers and trouble-makers, but it is most unlikely that a national leader could get away with that role. One of Hawke's initial strengths was a reputation for successful conflict resolution brought over from his industrial career, and reprises from the older repertory always seemed to bring applause.

Curtin once observed that, like a football team, a cabinet needed a couple of members whose rough play attracted the crowd's attention and let the rest get on with winning the game. If the proposition was then anything more than a rationalisation of the difficulties he had with Ward and Calwell, it is of doubtful validity today. A happy and unified team is thought to be everything with the electorate, but a word or gesture out of

21. S. Encel, *Cabinet Government in Australia*, 2nd edn., Melbourne University Press, 1974, p. 170.

line sends the opposition into paroxysms of constitutional concern with the media not far behind, and the electorate then becomes sufficiently concerned or even alarmed for the tremors to register in the polls. Here may be a danger, for there may be sound political reasons for not enforcing cabinet or parliamentary discipline on a certain individual or at a particular time — but the public expectation of solid ranks at all times will impose heavy costs for tolerance that looks like weakness.

Because the electorate's attention is concentrated on a very small number of individuals, most members of a government are quite unknown except to a tiny fraction of the electorate. The exception is when they manage to produce a scandal or political calamity of some sort, in which event they may have a momentary notoriety. One consequence is that the number of serious or plausible rivals or challengers to the prime minister, or indeed to the leader of the opposition, is never more than two or three, who are likely to include the major political figure from the other of the larger states — so a New South Wales leader will be threatened by a Victorian potential challenger and vice versa. Menzies, late in his time as prime minister, and Hawke, relatively early in his, were undisputed for some years, but as each of the major parties permits overnight revolutions[22] the potential for challenge is always there and the media are attentive to the possibility. Two high points of the political drama are dumping an incumbent or getting a new leader, often both in combination. The process is more difficult when the party leader is prime minister, rather than leader of the opposition, but is not impossible.

Another high point is the election campaign when the involvement of the electorate with the prime minister and the alternative prime minister becomes more intense. As spectators there is little citizens can do, apart from talk to friends and neighbours, write a letter to an editor or telephone a talk-back compere. If they are sufficiently bored, it is easy enough to switch the set off and ignore the drama entirely. But in the case of an election, eventually they will have to hold up a card and award marks for performance. Reinforced by compulsory voting, this demands closer attention — though the nature of an election campaign ensures that the messages come looking for their audience.

During the period reviewed here, campaign techniques have gone through three main phases. First was the traditional (except for the Liberals' innovative campaign in 1949[23]) which depended on party workers, print and radio messages, and personal appearances and longish speeches by the prime minister. Then there was a transition period, starting with the Labor Party's 1972 campaign, when television took over as the principal medium and the prime minister's effectiveness was

22. See Patrick Weller, *First Among Equals: Prime Ministers in Westminster Systems*, Sydney: Allen & Unwin, 1985, ch. 3.
23. Stephen Mills, *The New Machine Men*, Ringwood: Penguin, 1986, pp. 87-94.

determined on television. Most recently there is a new technological era, utilising polling and computer-driven mail more extensively, with the prime minister a source of short-lived images on television. Polling and marketing professionals have taken over the conduct of the campaign from party administrators and politicians, images matter more than issues, and the prime minister and the alternative prime minister simultaneously matter more because the campaign has been 'presidentialised' to call attention to them and matter less because of the trivialisation of such political content as remains.

There are other things which prime ministers do that have not yet been mentioned. For example, they are the supreme economic manager, and though some of the odium for error or mischance may be off-loaded onto the treasurer as one of the few ministers electors have heard of — as happened to Fadden and Holt, and more recently to Howard and, at first, Keating — the growing sophistication of the electorate and the improved quality of the media in informing electors make this an especially demanding role. In sharp contrast, the prime minister is the central figure for decisions about the federal bureaucracy but electors outside Canberra know and care nothing about that side of the job. In any democracy the relationship between the head of government and the electorate is central to that country's political process. Australia's constitutional arrangements and political history underline that importance.

7

PRIME MINISTERS AND FOREIGN POLICY

Russell Trood

In September 1900, as Edmund Barton was preparing to take office as Australia's first prime minister, he was advised by his friend, future prime minister Alfred Deakin, that external affairs ought always to be the preserve of the premier of the day.[1] Successive prime ministers have tended to accept this advice. Since the Commonwealth of Australia was founded in 1901, most prime ministers have played at the very least a prominent and often a dominant role in the conduct of the nation's external affairs. That they have done so is due less to the historic resonances of Deakin's advice than the considerable discretion they enjoy in the exercise of their authority as head of government. For the power over foreign policy derives from the historic conventions of executive pre-eminence and prime ministerial prerogative that are an elementary part of Australia's modified system of Westminster government. Prime ministers have been able to secure and maintain a degree of control over foreign policy that is unique in government and ensures that they occupy a pre-eminent role in the policy-making process.

This chapter focuses on the prime minister's role in the conduct of Australian foreign policy in the post-war era. In the main it is concerned with the formulation of foreign policy rather than with its implementation, though to some extent the distinction is an artificial one. After considering the changing context of policy-making, the paper examines the prime minister's changing role in several institutional settings, the political executive, cabinet, the bureaucracy, the party and parliament, and offers a brief conclusion.

Context: The Changing Policy Environment

In Australia, the parameters for the exercise of power over foreign affairs are established by the federal constitution and the political conventions that surround the conduct of government within the Westminster system. Section 51(xxix) of the constitution gives power over external affairs to

1. J.A. La Nauze, *Alfred Deakin: A Biography*, vol. 1, Melbourne University Press, 1965, p. 262.

the parliament of the commonwealth, but in political terms it has largely not exercised the power.[2] Since federation, the power over foreign policy has been overwhelmingly the preserve of the executive arm of government. This reflects an historic mandate passed on from the crown during the nineteenth century and the unique properties of foreign affairs compared to other areas of public policy. The often expressed desire, if not always the need, to conduct dealings with foreign governments on a confidential basis, the rapidly changing nature of the international environment, the special expertise demanded by international diplomacy and the tendency for the general public and their legislators to display little interest in foreign affairs, have traditionally all contributed to executive pre-eminence.[3] In Australia, the powerful effect of this combination of forces in securing the virtual dominance of the executive was underscored by a former prime minister, Gough Whitlam. Recalling that foreign policy was one area of administration in which his government was not frustrated in pursuing its policies, Whitlam remarked:

> The vast array of entrenched pressure groups and vested interests and the enormous machinery of obstruction at their disposal — anti Labor states, recalcitrant premiers, constitutional restraints, antagonistic business interests, litigation in the courts, the Senate itself — none could hinder, except in marginal ways, our foreign policy.[4]

Nor was the experience of the Whitlam government an exceptional one. Since federation, all Australian federal governments have enjoyed a similar degree of autonomy over foreign affairs. Prime ministers, as leaders of the government, have consequently had a firm foundation from which to exercise a significant degree of personal power over foreign policy, should they wish to do so.

In the period following World War II the central roles played by both the executive and prime ministers in the conduct of foreign policy have been further shaped by several important changes in the policy environment. There has been a steady growth in executive power across the breadth of government responsibilities. Because the foreign affairs power has always been the privilege of the executive within the Westminster system, the impact of this trend has not been as marked in relation to foreign affairs as in other areas of public policy.

2. Section 51 of the constitution also gives the Commonwealth parliament power over trade and commerce with other countries (i); the naval and military defence of the Commonwealth (vi); naturalisation and aliens (xix); immigration and emigration (xxvii); the relations of the Commonwealth with the islands of the Pacific (xxx).
3. For a discussion, see John Knight and W.J. Hudson, 'Parliament and Foreign Policy', *Canberra Studies in World Affairs*, No. 13, Department of International Relations, Australian National University, 1983, ch. 3.
4. *Ibid.*, p. 27.

Nevertheless, the growing power of the executive has enhanced the role of the prime minister, and to a lesser extent the foreign minister, in the policy-making process. With more power flowing to the executive, the positions of both have become more influential relative to other institutions and agencies of government. Ministers now undertake a wider range of public diplomatic activities, often at the expense of the authority of Australia's foreign diplomatic representatives.

A second trend has been the rapid development of Australia's international personality since the end of World War II. Prior to the war Australians were largely content to define their place in world affairs by reference to their status as a dominion within the British Empire rather than an autonomous independent actor within the wider international community. The growing prospect of war in Asia and the Pacific in the 1930s and its eventual advent brought profound change to Australian foreign policy. After 1945, Australia sought new foundations for the conduct of its foreign relations based on a set of national interests more independent of and separable from those of other countries. Against the background of the Cold War, Australia steadily extended its bilateral diplomatic relations with countries in Asia, the Pacific, Europe, and the Americas, became an active participant in global and regional multilateral political, economic and cultural organisations and joined security alliances such as the South-East Asia Treaty Organisation (SEATO) and the Australia, New Zealand and United States security pact (ANZUS). The post-war expansion of Australia's international personality not only resulted in the rapid development of the nation's diplomatic service, it led to the growth of a large foreign affairs bureaucracy within the federal government, the increasing intrusion of foreign policy issues onto the national political agenda and a growing role for prime ministers and their department in the management of policy issues.[5]

Finally, the post-war role of prime ministers in the conduct of foreign policy has been affected by the changing nature of international diplomacy. Since World War II there has been a marked tendency for national political leaders to play an increasingly active and public part in the implementation of their country's foreign policy. Historically this has been a natural role for political leaders, but in the post-war era, revolutionary changes in international transport and communications have greatly enhanced the opportunities for more direct and more frequent involvement. The speed and ease of international air travel and the instantaneousness of modern telephone and facsimile communications allow political leaders and their advisers to be in touch with their counterparts anywhere around the world at extremely short notice. At one level, this has done no more than improve substantially the ease of

5. For a general account, see T.B. Millar, *Australia in Peace and War: External Relations 1788-1977*, Canberra: Australian National University Press, 1978.

communications between the governments of different countries and between home governments and their representatives abroad. At another, however, it has tended to encourage the direct involvement of more senior political figures, including prime ministers and presidents, in the conduct of policy. Periodic summits, international conferences and official visits, as well as frequent telephone contacts with other world leaders, are now an integral part of the political activities and responsibilities of most political leaders. Recent Australian prime ministers have been as enthusiastic as any world leaders in seeking to take advantage of the diplomatic and political opportunities offered by regular international adventure. Every new diplomatic encounter ineluctably draws prime ministers into the policy process. This not only affects policy outcomes; it focuses attention on prime ministers' performances as leaders, feeding directly into domestic political processes and shaping perceptions of their abilities both at home and abroad.

The Political Executive

In Australia, the executive's power over foreign policy is jealously guarded. William McMahon underscored the point when addressing parliament in 1970:

> The conduct of foreign policy is essentially a function of the executive. It is the government which must be responsible for formulating policy and for carrying it through on a day to day basis. This is a responsibility which the executive cannot and should not abdicate. To have an erosion of the executive's responsibility for foreign policy would be to abandon the approach which has been accepted in the past by the governments of all parties and which is a tried and tested part of our constitutional practice.[6]

All post-war Australian governments have adopted this approach and been reticent to concede any diminution of their authority.

As head of government prime ministers must assume ultimate responsibility for their administration's foreign policy. Even Chifley, who among all post-war prime ministers probably had the least natural interest in the field, found that as leader of the government he had, in Crisp's words, 'an inescapable responsibility to take a hand in tackling the problems thrown up by the fundamental changes in Australia's international position'.[7] The prerogative to decide on the administrative organisation of their governments allows prime ministers considerable scope to decide how they will exercise their responsibilities, and the

6. Quoted in Henry S. Albinski, *Australian External Policy Under Labor: Content, Process and the National Debate,* St Lucia: University of Queensland Press, 1977, p. 278.
7. L.F. Crisp, *Australian National Government,* Croydon, Vic: Longman, 1965, p. 276.

impressive extent of their power invariably means that in style and conduct the cast of their policies sets the tone of their governments' approach to international affairs. This continues to be a notable feature of Australian foreign policy. While Menzies presented generally an image of conviction and assured direction against a background of Western alignment, his conservative successors often appeared confused in an environment of change. Whitlam brought innovation and a perception of greater independence, but also of incoherence in decision-making. Fraser returned security to a central place on the policy agenda and asserted prime ministerial dominance. Hawke made Asia a central motif of his government's policy, encouraged international activism and made consensus an element of his approach to decision-making.

Prime ministers exercise their power in conjunction with their ministerial colleagues. In relation to foreign policy, the prime ministers' natural colleagues are of course their foreign ministers. Tradition and the range of their responsibilities generally dictate that the foreign ministers be senior members of the government, though it is important to note that the minister's power to conduct foreign policy is far from comprehensive. As Millar has pointed out,[8] Australia's foreign policy often includes issues and subjects that fall outside the ministers' portfolio. Trade, defence and immigration have long impinged on Australia's diplomatic relations with other states and the agenda continues to expand. The effect is that particular aspects of policy are often outside the foreign ministers' direct area of control, a situation that often creates ministerial and departmental rivalry. Yet only foreign affairs holds a broad mandate for the conduct of Australia's external relations and this underpins the ministers' senior position in government.

The selection of a foreign minister is approached with some care. Prior to the creation of the modern foreign service it was not unusual for prime ministers to take the portfolio and act as their own foreign ministers. This has now become rare, though premiers continue to serve as acting ministers while their colleagues are engaged on duties abroad. Since 1945 it has only occurred (briefly) on two occasions. In 1960–1, Menzies took over the then external affairs portfolio on an interim basis following the elevation of Richard Casey to governor-general, while in 1972–3 Whitlam assumed the post for nearly ten months, partly because of his own strong interest in the area and also for administrative and party considerations.[9] The growing demands placed on all ministers, not least prime ministers, make it highly unlikely that the pre-1935 practice will ever be resurrected permanently.

In the appointment of a foreign minister the prime minister is bound constitutionally to select from among the ranks of his parliamentary

8. Millar, *op. cit.*, p. 26.
9. Whitlam's decision is discussed in Albinski, *op. cit.*, p. 283.

colleagues. Yet the task of appointment is never a simple or predictable one. Few members of parliament are ever elected with, or still less because of, any experience they may have in the area of foreign policy; prime ministers are almost always forced (and inclined) to select a foreign minister on the basis of criteria other than expertise. On only one occasion in the post-war period did a minister force his selection upon a prime minister, when Bill Hayden was made foreign minister in the first Hawke government. Hayden's removal from the party leadership just prior to the 1983 election was accompanied by an agreement in which the new prime minister allowed his disappointed colleague to select the portfolio of his choice.

Most prime ministers make ministerial selections, perhaps in conjunction with respected party colleagues, for other reasons. Considerable mystery surrounds this process, since few prime ministers have ever been willing to discuss the basis of their decisions. One who has done so is Malcolm Fraser and it is likely that his approach is not too dissimilar to that of others.[10] Fraser has emphasised the importance of parliamentary and administrative competence, an ability to withstand the pressures of office and a capacity for 'team' loyalty in his selections. For the foreign minister's post leaders have often seemed to look for other additional qualities: stamina, for the travel that is generally involved, and political experience, presumably for seasoned advice and in an attempt to avoid unwelcome political misadventure. Periodically, it has been suggested that prime ministers will be inclined to choose colleagues known to have leadership ambitions, on the assumption that the duties of office will demand frequent absences overseas and limit the aspirants' ability to lobby party support for their cause. While it is certainly true that potential leaders have often held the foreign affairs portfolio — Casey and Barwick under Menzies, Hasluck under Holt, Peacock under Fraser, for example — there has only ever been one occasion on which a foreign minister has moved directly into the prime ministership: that was McMahon in 1971.

Once appointed, a foreign minister holds office at the pleasure of the prime minister. In Australia, the foreign minister's post has been a relatively stable position within government. Evatt, Casey, Hasluck, Peacock, Street, Hayden and now Evans all spent lengthy periods in office. Where the terms have been shorter it has often been because of appointment elsewhere or electoral misadventure. Spender left for an ambassadorship in Washington and Barwick to become chief justice of the High Court, while Bowen, Willesee and Freeth all lost office as a result of either personal electoral defeat or rejection of their parties at the polls.

10. Patrick Weller, *Malcolm Fraser PM: A Study in Prime Ministerial Power in Australia*, Ringwood: Penguin, 1989, pp. 61-7.

In the opinion of Australia's longest serving foreign minister, Richard Casey, it is 'essential that the prime minister and the minister for external affairs should be on terms of easy confidence with one another'.[11] In practice there have been few administrations where ministers have enjoyed such equable relations. While Menzies periodically worked well with Spender and Barwick, his relations with Casey were often difficult and, from the minister's perspective at least, constantly unsatisfactory. Gorton's relations with McMahon were characterised by contempt and suspicion, those between McMahon and Bury were distant; Fraser and Peacock lived in a state of mutually repressed tension, while together Hawke and Hayden were often wary and awkward. Only rarely have a prime minister and a foreign minister shared something approaching a close personal relationship: Freeth and Gorton and perhaps Hawke and Evans came close. The differences are often matters of personality rather than disputes over issues of policy. Indeed, the longevity in office of many who have served in the foreign affairs portfolio underscores the extent to which prime ministers have shared their ministers' policy assumptions.

In so far as a satisfactory working relationship depends on appropriate administrative arrangements, this is almost completely in the hands of prime ministers. In the foreign affairs portfolio these are broadly stated and include the provision of advice and support to protect and promote Australia's external interests, the management of foreign political and trade relations and the delivery of Australia's overseas aid program. While easily stated, the broad and general nature of this mandate often results in clear lines of authority being difficult to establish. Moreover, as the policy agenda can often change quickly and unpredictablity the boundaries of responsibility sometimes need to be shifted in ways not originally envisaged. In the end, administrative orders never quite capture the arrangements established in practice.

The key variable in establishing satisfactory working relations may often be the extent to which prime ministers intend exercising their prerogative to become involved in the policy process. Since this is largely a matter of personal discretion, the practices of Australia's post-war prime ministers have varied widely. Chifley, for instance, showed relatively little interest in the day-to-day conduct of foreign policy and was content to leave it to his irrepressible foreign minister, H.V. Evatt. In contrast, prime ministers Whitlam and Fraser took a comprehensive interest in the subject and were inclined to dominate, asserting their authority throughout the full extent of the portfolio. But these examples tend to be at the extremes of the spectrum. In most post-war governments the asymmetries in power and responsibility between the prime ministerial role in the regular conduct of foreign affairs and that of

11. Quoted in W.J. Hudson, *Casey*, Melbourne: Oxford University Press, 1986, p. 265.

the foreign ministers have been less marked. While crises and important policy issues have always commanded prime ministerial attention, regular participation in the day-to-day administration of policy is something that most prime ministers have been too busy to contemplate.

Yet within this arrangement prime ministers have been inclined to mark out one or two areas of policy as being of special personal interest. Menzies, for instance, showed a special concern for Commonwealth relations and defence co-operation with the United Kingdom, Harold Holt for Australia's relations with Asia, Whitlam for China, Fraser for South Africa and human rights issues, and Hawke for relations with Israel and the United States. The reasons for these choices have varied considerably, but they all have the effect of identifying the prime minister with a particular area of policy, both publicly and within government, and isolating that area, except for the unwary or incautious, from concerted ministerial or bureaucratic interference.

Yet there is nothing in the division of responsibilities that guarantee ministers or even prime ministers that their positions will prevail. The balance of political forces within a government may mean that policy proposals emanating from the foreign ministry and opposed by prime ministers are unlikely, at least in the short term, to succeed, while conversely, the ministers' ability to forestall prime ministerial initiatives is likely to be decidedly limited. Controversial measures may require considerable force of argument and perhaps on occasion not a little politicking to ensure their acceptance. Nor can there be much doubt that tough and resilient ministers, like Evatt, Spender and Barwick, will often succeed where less assertive individuals will not. Thus, in summing up Casey's career as foreign minister, Hudson has argued that 'he was not given his head because he was not tough enough, cunning enough or politician enough to carry cabinets with him'.[12]

However successful a relationship between prime ministers and their foreign ministers, conflicts occur almost inevitably. The causes vary: shared approaches to policy may be usual but they are not necessarily enduring, as the celebrated differences between Menzies and Casey over Suez in 1956, Whitlam and Willesee over recognition of the Baltic states in 1974 and Fraser and Peacock over recognition of Cambodia in 1980-1 testify.[13] Similarly, issues of style and approach can be disruptive, whether it be Gorton's *ad hocery*, Whitlam's independence or Fraser's domination. In cases of conflict, the personal and political authority of prime ministers often ensures that they will prevail, but contests can sap the energy of governments, weakening them perhaps irretrievably. Avoiding clashes is clearly to be preferrred, but in an environment where

12. *Ibid.*, p. 288.
13. For accounts see, respectively, *Ibid.*, ch. 12; Albinski, *op. cit.*, ch. 5 and Alan Renouf, *Malcolm Fraser and Australian Foreign Policy*, Sydney: Australian Professional Publications, 1986, ch. 5.

policy options rarely present clear-cut choices for action and where there may often be an array of political, bureaucratic and societal interests marshalled on the various sides of the debate, this is not always possible. The point underscores the need for governments to have effective machinery for making policy and resolving the differences that may arise over it. In the arena of foreign policy as elsewhere, the role of cabinet is important to both.

The Cabinet

All governments face the challenge of developing effective machinery for policy-making. The pre-eminence accorded to cabinet within the Westminster system gives it a natural authority as a decision-making forum, one that is reinforced in relation to foreign policy by the tendency towards executive dominance. Yet in Australia, the patterns of cabinet decision-making in general, and in relation to foreign policy in particular, have been very uneven. This has largely been a reflection of the commitment of prime ministers to the cabinet process itself and the extent of their involvement in the conduct of foreign policy.

The rules and procedures of cabinet often vary from government to government and are invariably a matter for prime ministers to decide. The style of their decision-making will generally determine the extent of cabinet's role in foreign policy and this can, on occasions, be very limited indeed. John Gorton's penchant for making policy pronouncements on the run, without the benefit of consultations with colleagues and often it seemed without having fully thought through the implications, reduced cabinet to a trivial part of the policy process over issues such as the further commitment of Australian troops to South Vietnam and the effects of Britain's withdrawal east of Suez. McMahon came to office better prepared by long experience in senior office to provide greater coherence in cabinet policy-making, but failed to do so. Referring to cabinet's attention to Andrew Peacock's 1972 initiatives over Papua New Guinea as a motif of McMahon's approach, Albinski has noted that the 'prime minister's role was essentially one of concurrence. Cabinet was hardly consulted in advance, and it only in a general, sporadic and after the fact fashion acknowledged the policy.'[14] Nor was Whitlam an improvement. In being determined to place his stamp on foreign policy, he generally avoided taking issues to cabinet, even when forced by dissent to establish a committee to consider policy. By contrast, Malcolm Fraser gave cabinet a central role in the policy process, though with his concern for constitutional form it was often overburdened. Again, these administrations tend to be at the extremes of

14. Albinski, *op. cit.*, p. 24.

the spectrum. In other governments cabinet has played a less predictable role in the policy process, being called into action as issues and circumstances have dictated.

Some foreign policy matters are routinely placed before cabinet (decisions over the use of military force, the ratification of treaties and appointments to senior diplomatic posts, for example), but the criteria for inclusion on the agenda are often difficult to define. Issues of national security or of particular complexity, or those that are especially controversial, will all probably appear, but opinions as to whether an issue fits one of these categories will differ. Thus there can often be inconsistent treatment of similar issues within a government and across governments. Eventually governments develop a culture as to which matters count and should be placed before cabinet and which do not and can be dealt with elsewhere. This will usually reflect the preferences and prejudices of the prime minister.

For most governments the notion of cabinet is a flexible one, embracing both cabinet and its often numerous committees. As part of a process of reforming cabinet procedures after Labor left office in 1949, Menzies established an extensive system of cabinet committees which, while not including one specifically responsible for foreign affairs, nevertheless included the Defence Preparedness Committee. This subsequently became Foreign Affairs and Defence, and later International and Defence with an additional Security committee. The latter is now the only cabinet committee in the foreign policy area. Deciding on the membership of these committees is a prerogative of the prime minister, but over time there has been some consistency. Typically the members include the prime ministers themselves, the foreign, defence and trade ministers, the attorney-general and perhaps one or two others from portfolios with external interests such as industry or immigration.

Originally conceived as a clearing house for issues prior to consideration by the full cabinet, these committees have had a checkered history. During the early years of the Menzies government the whole committee system came near to collapse under its own weight, though Defence Preparedness continued to operate in a rather irregular fashion. During the Gorton, McMahon and Whitlam governments they were largely ignored. During Fraser's administration Foreign Affairs and Defence was among the most active of all cabinet committees and often served as a place where issues received their final executive consideration before a decision was taken and implemented. The Hawke government continued to make extensive use of cabinet committtees, though the frequency of their meetings declined from the historically high levels of the Fraser period.

Allowing for the situation in the Hawke government, in the post-war period there has been a clear trend towards greater use of cabinet committees in relation to foreign policy issues. In the Fraser government their frequent, if not over use, was part of the prime minister's method of preserving the forms of cabinet decision-making for his policies, while in the Hawke government the Security Committee serve as a vehicle for developing the prime minister's desire for policy consensus. In neither case has their agenda been restricted to dealing with low level or relatively unimportant issues. On occasions they have offered the last opportunity for collective ministerial discussion and decision on matters of the highest national importance, as the Hawke government's decision in August 1990 to commit an Australian naval force to the Gulf war demonstrates. At short notice, the prime minister contacted members of cabinet's Security Committee, who were dispersed throughout Australia and in at least one case (the foreign minister) well beyond, and secured agreement for the deployment after what was, by all accounts, a relatively brief period of deliberation.[15]

The Hawke government was certainly not the first to elevate form over substance in an effort to secure cabinet endorsement of its policies. In 1979, Fraser adopted much the same technique to secure a decision on the appointment of an Australian high commissioner to Zambia.[16] These events focus attention on the inner workings of cabinet and the way in which decisions are reached. It illustrates that in foreign policy, governments frequently have to make important policy decisions at short notice and sometimes with a minimum of information. For a country like Australia that is at best a middle power in international affairs and thus often a reactor to rather than an initiator of, foreign policy, the problem can at times be acute. Faced with the twin pressures of limited time and restricted access to information it is doubtful whether any group of decision-makers, let alone a cabinet of relative untutored politicians, will be able to reach the wisest decision. Indeed, in these circumstances there is clearly a case, as many prime ministers have realised, for by-passing cabinet, at least initially, and seeking to respond on the basis of more expert advice.

These constraints aside, the way debate is handled within cabinet will invariably shape the outcome of decisions. How often the prime minister intervenes, at what point in the debate, whether all ministers are given an opportunity to participate, the length of time permitted for discussion, whether votes are taken or are not, and generally the atmosphere of the deliberations, may all be important factors. An example from the Menzies government will serve to illustrate this. Contrary to common belief, prime minister Menzies did not bully his cabinet colleagues, though he was short with contributions which were

15. For a discussion of the decision, see Peter Jennings, 'Australia's Response and Role in the War' in Viberto Selochan (ed.), *The Gulf War Issues and Implications for Australia and Asia*, Bathurst: Crawford House, forthcoming, and 'Hawke takes charge over sending ships to the Gulf', *The Age*, 11 August 1990, p. 2.

16. Weller, *op. cit.*, p. 315.

undisciplined. He sought to be persuaded and to this end liked to hear from at least one or two trusted colleagues. As foreign minister, Casey was not among this select group. In presenting his arguments to cabinet he was consistently disadvantaged by the Menzies style and his own limited capacity for forceful advocacy. Had he been more adept, Australian policy towards Asia or over the Suez crisis or a number of other important matters where he was unable to carry his colleagues might well have been different.[17]

Every prime minister wishes not only to reach a decision, but to do so in a way that will command the widest possible support of cabinet colleagues. The way prime ministers handle foreign policy issues is as integral a part of maintaining the loyalty and support of colleagues as any other policy area and the failure to develop adequate consultative procedures can have a disastrous impact on their authority within their party and the cabinet. Gorton's *ad hoc*, non-consultative approach to the making of foreign policy was one of the factors that served to undermine his standing within cabinet and ultimately forced him from office.[18] On the other hand, the domineering styles of Whitlam, Fraser (and some have said Menzies) regarding foreign policy tended to generate resentment among some colleagues. But these were never so serious as fatally to weaken their cabinet authority. The reason, perhaps, was that unlike Gorton they all enjoyed a strong base of cabinet support and in the end their decisions, however personal they may have been, were acceptable to party and cabinet opinion, something of which Gorton could never be certain.

The Bureaucracy

Of course it is misleading to suggest that post-war Australian prime ministers have made foreign policy on their own. Even if they have been inclined towards independence they have usually received the benefit of considerable advice from an array of specialist foreign policy advisers from within the public service and elsewhere. In Australia, prime ministers can rely for this advice on officials from several different departments and agencies. Indeed, as Australia's contemporary foreign policy agenda has steadily expanded, the number of government agencies involved in policy formulation and implementation has increased appreciably, generating greater demands for more effective methods of policy management. This in turn has drawn prime ministers into a more

17. For a sense of Casey's limitations, see Hudson, op. cit. and T.B. Millar (ed.), *Australian Foreign Minister: The Diaries of R.G. Casey, 1951-60*, London: Collins, 1972.
18. Gorton's methods are discussed in Alan Reid, *The Gorton Experiment*, Sydney: Shakespeare Head Press, 1971.

significant role in policy co-ordination, effectively increasing their authority over the foreign policy agenda.

Australia was slow to develop a foreign policy bureaucracy. For most of the period prior to World War II, bureaucratic authority over foreign policy resided with a small group of officials within the prime minister's own department. Even when a separate Department of External Affairs was finally permanently established in 1935 it struggled to assert its administrative authority against the power of other more established departments such as Trade and Defence.[19] Only with the coming of war, the advent of a Labor government in 1941 and the subsequent installation of Dr Evatt as foreign minister, did the new department begin to develop some administrative clout. When the war ended it profited from Chifley's inclination to allow Evatt considerable latitude in the conduct of foreign policy, steadily expanding both its domestic policy responsibilities and its overseas activities through the post-war expansion of Australian missions. Since then, bureaucratic responsibility for Australian foreign interests, defined to include economic as well as security and diplomatic issues, has been divided largely between four departments, Prime Minister's, Foreign Affairs, Defence and Trade,[20] with the role and importance of each varying across different policy issues and with several other departments being more peripherally involved.

To meet the growing demand for policy advice within this fragmented system of administration, prime ministers have periodically forced considerable change on the structure of government and the methods by which policy information reaches them. Central to this process has always been the prime minister's own department. The Department of Prime Minister and Cabinet has never altogether lost the power it began to exercise over foreign policy when federation was achieved. In the years immediately after the war there was always a group of senior officials within the department on whom the prime minister could call for policy advice. The group lacked a clear identity within the departmental structure until a specific Defence Section was created in 1961. In 1963 an External Relations and Defence Section within a separate Cabinet and External Relations Division was established and in 1970 External Relations and Defence became a division in its own right. By 1991 the International Division, as it is now called, had three branches — Foreign Affairs, North America and Defence, and the Office of Security and Intelligence Co-operation — and a staff establishment of 31.

19. For an account see Peter Edwards, *Prime Ministers and Diplomats: The Making of Australian Foreign Policy 1901-1949*, Melbourne University Press, 1978.
20. In August 1987, the Department of Foreign Affairs was amalgamated with the Department of Trade to form the Department of Foreign Affairs and Trade.

Although a core of foreign and defence expertise has always existed within the department, the extent to which prime ministers have relied on this advice either exclusively or in conjunction with that tendered by other departments and officials has varied considerably. In the Menzies era the minister was required to represent the views of his department.[21] Thus in foreign policy as in other areas of administration, policy advice generally reached the prime minister via departmental briefs and submissions presented by ministers. In these situations Menzies often relied on officials within his own department to provide additional analysis and commentary. But beyond the formalities of this process, the relatively small size of the Canberra bureaucracy and the club-like atmosphere which existed among senior public servants and ministers opened avenues for informal consultation and debate which now no longer exist. Menzies, and to some degree his successor Harold Holt, maintained a circle of public service friendships and relationships that provided a constant source of opinion on foreign policy issues. Senior officials within the Department of External Affairs, such as Alan Watt, James Plimsoll, Laurence McIntyre and Keith Shann, were all at various stages part of the Menzies circle in Canberra and at times accompanied him on trips abroad as expert advisers. Their views were not always decisive. Like most prime ministers Menzies held clear views on certain policy issues, such as Australia's relations with the Commonwealth, which were not easily changed. Typically, he would sift through the advice he received for the material he judged important and would often discuss it further with trusted cabinet colleagues before reaching a settled decision.

Informal contacts between cabinet ministers and senior public servants have always been an element of the policy process in Canberra. In the foreign policy arena, relationships can be reinforced (or equally be damaged) by the demands of international diplomacy which often place ministers, including prime ministers, and official advisers in close contact with each other for several weeks at a time.[22] However, the informal contacts which were such an integral part of the policy process in the Menzies and Holt eras have been steadily breaking down. The causes include changes in the political and official personalities involved, a rapid growth in (and the increasing bureaucratisation of) the public service, and the increasingly crowded nature of the political agenda. By the late 1960s, when Gorton became prime minister, the system was

21. Menzies's approach to governance discussed most fully in Sir John Bunting, *R.G. Menzies: A Portrait*, Sydney: Allen & Unwin, 1988.
22. The literature in this area is essentially anecdotal. See, *inter alia*, Alan Renouf, *The Champagne Trail: Experiences of a Diplomat*, Melbourne: Sun Books, 1980; J.W.C. Cumes, *A Bunch of Amateurs: The Tragedy of Government and Administration in Australia*, Melbourne: Sun Books, 1988; and Peter Henderson, *Privilege and Pleasure*, Sydney: Methuen Haynes, 1986.

clearly in decline, particularly in the area of foreign affairs. Gorton, indeed, had little regard for the Foreign Affairs Department or for its senior officials, a point clearly emphasised by an incident in 1971 when it was suggested that he should take a senior Foreign Affairs official with him on an visit to the United States. '(W)hen it was suggested he metaphorically bit the carpet.' Rejecting all entreaties on the subject, Gorton is reported to have said that ' he did not want any External Affairs types with him. They are all the same. Hopeless.' In the end he undertook the travel with an official party of four which did not include a departmental official.[23] Of course, Gorton could not completely avoid contact with Foreign Affairs officials during his prime ministership, but relations were often strained by his free-wheeling style of leadership and reluctance to consult. Clearly the esteem in which many senior officers had been held during earlier periods of conservative rule had declined, a situation that necessarily resulted in their exclusion from a position of influencing the prime minister.

Yet this did not last. When Whitlam became prime minister he not only brought change to the substance of Australian foreign policy, but also change to its decision-making processes. By taking the foreign affairs portfolio himself, Whitlam placed the key foreign policy advisory agency under his own control and ensured that as prime minister he had direct and immediate access to policy advice. In this position the department was often in a position to establish the policy agenda. Under its innovative Whitlam-appointed secretary, Alan Renouf, the department consistently presented the prime minister with policy proposals as well as responding to his own initiatives. The effect was to revitalise Foreign Affairs as an influential agency of government. Between 1973 and 1975 the staff of the department grew 30.7 per cent from 3201 to 4639 as the Whitlam government expanded the agenda of Australian foreign policy.[24] Senior departmental officials had constant access to the prime minister, their position as policy advisers being reinforced by Whitlam's inclination not to consult widely with cabinet colleagues on foreign issues.

Access, however, did not always guarantee influence. Whitlam had strong views about Australia's role and place in world affairs and was not easily deflected on matters of conviction. At the same time he was suspicious that there were conservatives in the department who would act to obstruct his reforms. These interests and concerns led to clashes with officials who had been encouraged to think in well-established patterns by 23 years of conservative government. Whitlam indicated the changes that were about to disturb their settled existence in his first meeting with officials on becoming prime minister; he rejected advice from the

23. Reid, *op. cit.*, p. 55.
24. Figures drawn from *Annual Report*, Department of Foreign Affairs, 1973, 1974, 1975.

secretary of the department, Sir Keith Waller, on the way Australia should vote on a forthcoming United Nations General Assembly motion on Southern Africa. Canberra would not abstain, as the secretary advised, but would signal a change in policy by supporting the opposition, Afro-Asian position.[25] Yet the clashes between Whitlam and his department were of a different character to those which had taken place between departmental officials and Whitlam's two immediate predecessors. Neither Gorton nor McMahon held the Department of Foreign Affairs in high regard, seeing its officials as distant from the real world of the Canberra bureaucracy and inclined to arrogance in attempting to identify and act in the national interest. By way of contrast, Whitlam respected the department for its professionalism. He did not always welcome the policy advice it tendered, but during the nine months that he was minister and later after he passed the portfolio on to Willesee, the department showed itself capable of responding to the new challenges his foreign policy placed before it. This provided a basis for a largely co-operative partnership throughout his premiership.

For all the co-operation between prime minister and department, however, Australian foreign policy during the Whitlam era lacked both formulatory and implementory coherence.[26] The primary cause was a lack of effective administrative mechanisms to settle the numerous policy disputes that developed between members of his government and their various bureaucratic allies. With the prime minister determined to dominate the foreign policy agenda, but at times facing strong opposition from some ambitious cabinet colleagues, cabinet was unable to play an effective mediating role. The contested areas of policy were usually the preserve of interdepartmental committees which in practice lacked the resolve and authority to act. A particular example was the issue of resources diplomacy. Developed and pushed by the ambitious minister for minerals and energy, R.F.X. Connor, the policy sought to extract greater export value from Australia's trade in natural resources. It met strong opposition within Foreign Affairs and elsewhere in the government and became the basis of a long and bitter bureaucratic battle which was not finally settled until the head of Connor's department was removed and a cabinet committee was established to examine the issue.

In the end, however, the greater part of the responsibility for the character and effectiveness of the policy process comes back to the particular style of the prime minister. In this respect, Malcolm Fraser's commitment to greater ministerial discipline and a reassertion of

25. Gough Whitlam, *The Whitlam Government 1972-1975*, Ringwood: Penguin, 1985, p. 14. For further details of relations with the department during the Whitlam era, see Keith Waller, 'A Diplomatic Life: Some Memories', No. 6, Centre for the Study of Australia-Asia Relations, Griffith University, Brisbane, 1990.
26. See Albinski, *op. cit.*, ch. 8.

cabinet's role as the central decision-making forum of government helped to limit and contain the type of policy disputes that were so destructive of the Whitlam government's unity. Further, Peacock's appointment to the foreign affairs portfolio immediately changed the character of its relations with the prime minister's office. The rapport and confident working relationship that Whitlam had established with senior departmental officials early in his administration was never replicated in the Fraser government. The department was restored to a more traditional place in Canberra's bureauratic firmament — distant and outside the mainstream of power and influence. This meant a decline in the department's access to the prime minister and, predictably, a resultant reduction in influence.

The department was kept at a distance by Fraser's desire for more direct access to policy advice. This resulted in two notable administrative innovations, and a third which he did not instigate but which nevertheless suited his particular style of policy formulation. The first was the revitalisation of the Department of Prime Minister and Cabinet as a source of policy advice. Whitlam's links to Foreign Affairs obviated any need for a strong policy advisory section within his own department and left the External Relations and Defence Division largely unchanged and relatively unimportant during his tenure of office. During the Fraser years, change became a way of life for the officials of the division as personnel and the internal branch structure were shuffled on a frequent, if irregular, basis. The result was a substantial increase in the department's role and influence in the policy process. In the words of a former secretary of the Department of Foreign Affairs, Alan Renouf,

> For the first time in history, power over foreign affairs of any great significance was, at the public service level, concentrated in the Department of Prime Minister and Cabinet. This department became a policy-making body instead of an agency designed primarily to co-ordinate policy; indeed it became accustomed to presenting mainly ideas which would be palatable to the prime minister.[27]

Given other views of the same period, Renouf may be overstating the impact of Fraser's style of policy management. Yet it seems clear that Fraser's department was a decided beneficiary of his approach and became, at the very least, a much more influential actor in the conduct of Australian policy.

Fraser increased his control over foreign policy by ensuring that he remained fully informed on all relevant policy issues. Fraser made extensive use of his advisers in the area of foreign policy and developed a close working relationship with the Sydney academic, Owen Harries, who was originally a member of Peacock's staff. The effect was to

27. Renouf (1986) ,*op. cit.*, p. 80.

provide him with a personal and direct source of policy advice but it also tended to narrow and limit the range of alternative opinions he received. Again, this was part of the Fraser style and in the view of one commentator the success of the association with Harries rested on a sound personal relationship, common philosophical commitments and an ability to 'translate insights derived from that philosophy into a comprehensive policy framework'.[28]

The third significant development during Fraser's period of office was the establishment of the Office of National Assessments (ONA). The Royal Commission on Intelligence Services recommended the establishment of the office to provide a central co-ordinating body for the analysis of intelligence information. The Office, established in 1977 and responsible to the prime minister, fitted Fraser's constant desire for information from sources he knew as reliable. Both at his direction and on its own intitiative, ONA prepared assessments on long- as well as short-term international policy issues, serving as something akin to a personal think-tank for policy development.

Fraser's conduct of Australian foreign policy between 1975 and 1983 did much to institutionalise the prime minister's place at the centre of the policy process. A change in political leadership might be expected to produce concomitant changes in administration. In fact when the Hawke government came to office in 1983 the Fraser system of foreign policy management was adopted, at least intitally, with little change. It gave the new prime minister the opportunity to exercise the same powerful control over the policy process as his predecessor. That this did not occur serves to underscore the extent to which the prime minister's own style and policy interests can shape the decision-making processes of a government.

Hawke came to office with an interest in foreign policy issues but with other issues, such as tax policy and economic reform, higher on his political agenda. During his early years in office he showed little interest in establishing the same dominance over foreign affairs as his predecessor. As a result, there was a drift in power away from the Prime Minister's Department back towards the traditional Foreign Affairs bureaucracy. This shift in the locus of authority was reinforced by the delicate state of the prime minister's personal relations with Bill Hayden, now installed as foreign minister.[29] Yet it is important to emphasise the limits of this change. First, it was a shift from the extreme levels of central administration established during the Fraser administration: the prime minister remained a key figure in policy-making but was not the dominant influence of the previous few years. Secondly, the prime minister retained a special and therefore controlling power over certain

28. James Walter, *The Minister's Minders: Personal Advisers in National Government*, Melbourne: Oxford University Press, 1986.
29. See John Stubbs, *Hayden*, Melbourne: William Heinemann, 1988, ch. 21.

policy issues such as relations with the United States where Washington's suspicions of the foreign minister tended to encourage prime ministerial intervention. Thirdly, the prime minister's role in the conduct of policy has steadily expanded as Australia has confronted a series of important national policy issues.

This intensively activist phase in Australian foreign policy was especially evident after the appointment of Gareth Evans as foreign minister in 1988. The government initiated a succession of new policy proposals in areas such as Antarctic mining, a Cambodian peace settlement, Asia-Pacific Economic Co-operation (APEC), international trade negotiations and the development of closer relations countries in the Asia-Pacific region, and foreign affairs became one of the most demanding and active portfolios in government Some of these initiatives were a response to developments in the international arenȧ, but for the most part they were a response to domestic imperatives placed on the agenda either by interest groups, the department or, in several cases, the minister himself. More than at any time since the Whitlam government, the department's resources came consistently under pressure as senior officials devoted vast amounts of their time and energy to the conduct of this crowded agenda.

An important consequence of all this activity was the installation of foreign policy at a central place on the Hawke government's policy agenda. In the context of Canberra's bureaucratic politics, the effect of this activism was to return Foreign Affairs to a place of considerable influence in the policy process. Amalgamated with the old Department of Trade in 1987, the new Department of Foreign Affairs and Trade was able to secure this position partly by being able to adapt and respond the government's changing policy agenda. The importance of this agenda to the Hawke government generally and to the personal ambitions of both the prime minister and the minister became an asset to the department and underwrote its authority. In effect, the department was able to recover from the position of weakness in which it found itself at the end of the Fraser administration and to a less severe degree during the early years of the Hawke government.

For his part, Hawke tended towards an issue-oriented style of policy management. He resisted the example of his immediate predecessors to establish policy control throughout the full breadth of the foreign policy arena and tended to focus on specific policy interests. During the early years of his government these included relations with China and with the United States, particularly with regard to ANZUS. But as the agenda expanded, the prime minister's inclination was to become more involved. In part this was an institutional role, played out through membership of key policy-making forums such as cabinet and party committees; at other times the contribution was more personal. On some issues Hawke was especially active, using his authority as head of government to intervene periodically to drive the agenda forward both domestically and within the international arena. In general, he was inclined to search for consensus rather than personal control. Except on special issues, such as the Gulf war and the 1989 break with China where his involvement was direct, comprehensive and passionate, his approach was more selective; it entailed intervening and lending his leadership and authority to policy formulation and implementation where conviction and circumstance demanded. Otherwise he left considerable latitude for active ministers to pursue their own ambitious policy agenda.

The Party

As the leader of their party prime ministers enjoy considerable discretion to set the government's policy agenda. In relation to foreign affairs this freedom is enhanced by the tradition of executive dominance and the unique nature of the policy issues it raises. Yet it is clear that the prime ministerial power is not unfettered. Both before they enter office and during their period of tenure the will of their party is one among the several factors that will determine their response to international events. They may, of course, seek to cajole, persuade and otherwise shape their party's views to control policy outcomes, but their position as leader does not always guarantee success. The key to maintaining their authority within the party is ensuring that they remain abreast of its sometimes capricious moods.

The degree of prime ministerial independence is in part a function of the party to which they belong. Within the Labor Party the decisions of the rank and file as expressed through the resolutions of the party national conference are notionally binding on the party's parliamentary caucus and establish the policy parameters within which a government must act. Thus for a Labor prime minister, party opinion formally expressed can effectively limit policy options. Bob Hawke was forced to withdraw Australian support for American testing of MX missile technology in the South Pacific in 1984 and, more recently, the party refused to allow an expansion of uranium mining. By contrast, the policy positions espoused by rank and file members of the main conservative parties of Australian politics offer no more than guidance to the parliamentary party. The party leadership and prime ministers in particular serve as trustees of the party's philosophy and are relatively free to decide how it should be interpreted and applied. While this offers considerable independence of action, most leaders are aware of the limits to party tolerance and know that should they stray too far from its boundaries they run the risk of alienating support and perhaps jeopardising their own positions.

The differences between the mainstream parties in Australia extend beyond matters of procedure. Historically, parties in Australia have tended to espouse different ideological perspectives on Australian foreign policy. The Liberal and National parties have always tended towards a realist perspective on international politics, one that recognises the central role of the state in international affairs, the importance of power as a determinate of outcomes, the particular place of military power as an instrument of policy and, given Australia's particular situation, the value of alliances. In government, Malcolm Fraser introduced some interesting modifications to this tradition of conservative thinking through his emphasis on issues such as the problems of the third world and human rights in South Africa, but the preoccupation with the orthodox Liberal agenda was evident in his government's abiding concern with the Soviet threat and the stability of the 'central balance.'

In contrast, the Labor Party has always tended towards a more idealist and internationalist conception of the international environment and of Australia's place within it. This tradition goes back to the roots of the party, but was most clearly expressed in the philosophical position espoused by Evatt as foreign minister. The elements of this tradition include an emphasis on the equality of states and thus of the right of all countries, whether they be great, middle or small powers, to participate actively in international affairs, the importance of international law and of multilateralism as an integral part of the process of interstate relations, especially in dispute resolution and the importance of other values aside from security: economic opportunity and human rights, for instance.[30]

Within the context of these differing philosophical traditions, the degree to which membership opinion within the Liberal and National parties deviates from the party's core values has always been limited. This appears to be less a reflection of formal constraints on expressions of dissent within the party as the broadly homogeneous philosophical values and interests that members bring to the party. It may also be a reflection of the party's tendency to place a higher priority on policy issues other than foreign policy. In any event, the consequence for the parties in government is a close consensus on the merits of available policy options and, for prime ministers, an easier task of policy management within their party. Few examples demonstrate this consensus more aptly than the continuity of coalition foreign policy during the 23 years of the Menzies, Holt, Gorton and McMahon governments between 1949 and 1972. During the Gorton administration there was a brief flirtation with a set of policies somewhat inconsistent with the traditional themes of party policy, but the destabilising effect of this deviation on the Gorton premiership was quick to emerge and serves

30. The differing nature of these philosophies emerges early in Robert Clyde Toemessen, 'Analysis of the Changing Basis of Australian Foreign Policy' (Ph.D. dissertation, the American University, 1971)

to underline the party's tightly held ideology and limited tolerance for dissent.[31]

Once again the contrast with the Labor Party is instructive. Membership opinion within that party over foreign policy, as over just about every other issue, encompasses a wider range of positions. Within the modern party this range of opinions is reflected, at least within the caucus, in the ideological prejudices of its various factions: left, centre left, centre right and right. Over issues as widely disparate as the American alliance, participation in the Gulf war, uranium mining and economic internationalism, the Labor prime minister from 1983 to 1991, Bob Hawke, had to navigate through the sometimes tumultuous seas of internal party opinion to implement his policies. Without doubt this was an important factor in shaping his government's response to these particular policy issues. The Gorton government's difficulties with his party over forward defence in the late 1960s, and the dissent within the party over Fraser's stance on a multilateral force for the Sinai and an Olympic boycott, provide examples of similar difficulties on the side of politics, but there have been marked differences in the frequency with which this occurs among conservative parties compared to Labor and often in the intensity of the debate once differences do occur. As Bill Hayden recalled to his biographer, 'the Labor Party is an emotional party . . . it can get carried away with emotion at times.'[32]

The philosophical and procedural traditions of Australia's main political parties have their roots in a period well before World War II, but they have been shaped inevitably by the post-1945 climate of Cold War international politics. This era has passed and brought profound change to the structures and processes of the international system and the agenda of world politics. These changes are already having a marked impact on the way states conduct their foreign policies and in Australia as elsewhere are shaping domestic debates over policy issues. As they affect Australia's political parties two trends are already evident. First there is a movement towards a wider, more 'bipartisan' foreign policy agenda. One effect has been the breakdown of the once stark philosophical differences between parties. Ideology has given way to pragmatism in assessing Australia's national policy interests. In the Labor Party this has tended to free the hand of the prime minister in the conduct of policy as containing ideological prejudices of the disparate groups within the party which have dissipated. In a notable departure from the past, within the conservative parties the opposite appears to have occurred: the prime minister's authority has been weakened as the unifying power of a common party ideology has given way to a more widely articulated set of interests among the party faithful. In effect, bipartisanship has opened

31. For an account, see Reid, *op. cit.*
32. Stubbs, *op. cit.*, p. 27.

up a wider area of policy consensus between the main political parties. This has narrowed the scope of political debate over foreign policy issues (less so in the area of defence) and reinforced the continuity of policies of successive governments of different political persuasions.

The second trend is towards the domestication of foreign policy, that is to say the increasing penetration of foreign policy issues onto the domestic political agenda — American trade policy, degradation of the environment and immigration policy are notable examples. This has tended to widen the range of special community lobby groups in the domestic arena and resulted in a greater plurality of interests now seeking to participate in policy formulation. From the perspective of interest groups, the executive arm of government has become more accountable for its policy decisions, while for governments and prime ministers in particular the process of policy-making has become more exacting as the sometimes powerful interests beyond government and party assert a right to be heard.

The Parliament

By comparison with that of the executive and the bureaucracy the role of parliament in the conduct of foreign policy is extremely modest.[33] Indeed, it is a conventional wisdom of Australian politics that parliament plays an unimportant role in either the formulation or implementation of foreign policy. As Knight and Hudson pointed out several years ago,

> if a Commonwealth government wished to declare war simultaneously on the United States and the Soviet Union and thereby guarantee the spoilation of its territory and the destruction of its people, it would be free to do so; if it wished to add a cent in tax to the cost of a packet of cigarettes, it would have to arrange the preparation of appropriate legislation, survive debate in its own party room, pilot a bill through each of the two houses of Federal Parliament, accommodate publicity and calculate the electoral impact of the ire of nicotine addicts.[34]

Put another way, prime ministers bent on a particular course of foreign policy generally have little to fear from parliament in attempting to secure their objectives.

Parliament's relative insignificance in foreign policy derives from the prerogatives of the executive in this area of policy, the strength of party discipline on the floor of the House and the reality that for members of parliament there is usually little political or electoral advantage to be

33. For a general account see Claire Clark, 'Parliament, Defence and Foreign Policy', in J.R. Nethercote (ed.), *Parliament and Bureaucracy*, Sydney: Hale & Iremonger, 1982, ch. 19.
34. Knight and Hudson, *op. cit.*, p. 27.

gained in taking an active interest in the area. These factors not only discourage parliamentarians from pressing a strong claim to a direct role in the conduct of foreign policy; they allow governments to pursue their foreign policy agendas relatively free of parliamentary interference. As one observer has noted, from a member's perspective, parliament's role in relation to foreign and defence policy has been limited to reviewing, investigating and publicising executive actions.[35] For governments, parliament's importance in relation to foreign policy has been either as a forum to announce policy decisions, once they have been taken, or as an arena in which to provide the community with a periodic and public accounting of recent policy developments.

Parliamentary debates often follow parliamentary statements, but only rarely have they had a substantial impact on policy. It is therefore hardly surprising that the number of parliamentary sitting hours devoted to foreign policy is relatively limited. Assessing the record of the Fraser years, for instance, Alan Renouf has commented favourably on the relative frequency of the prime minister's foreign policy statements, but pointed out that he was invariably reluctant to allow parliament time for a lengthy debate: '[i]n Fraser's seven years in office, there were twelve major foreign-policy statements but only four debates worthy of that description. The most important debate, the first one (in June 1976), lasted less than a day and there were only four speakers.'[36] Among post-war parliaments this is certainly not an exceptional record; indeed, at least with regard to the frequency of statements, it may be among the more impressive.

Fraser's active involvement in foreign policy and his commitment to parliament as an institution of government were no doubt important factors in encouraging the frequency of his appearances in debate. But among Australia's post-war prime ministers this is unusual. Most leaders spend relatively little time in parliament beyond the appearances required by convention or the political exigencies of the moment: question time, budget night and debates touching the standing of their government such as a motion of no confidence. Beyond this, all prime ministers make judgments when issues or statements may be of sufficient importance to demand their attention. In the area of foreign policy most leaders have preferred to allow their foreign ministers to represent government interests in debate and only appeared on occasions which might be characterised as being of immediate national importance: examples are Menzies announcing his government's commitment of troops to South Vietnam in 1965, Gorton on allegations of torture by Australian soldiers in Vietnam in 1968, Whitlam outlining his foreign policy in 1973 and Hawke opening debate on the Gulf war in 1990.

35. Clark, *op. cit.*, p. 292.
36. Renouf (1986), *op. cit.*, p. 81.

When prime ministers submit to a foreign policy debate on the floor of parliament or participate in question time they are engaged in an activity that is both constitutional and political in its implications. Constitutionally, they expose their governments' policies to parliamentary scrutiny, thereby highlighting parliament's importance as a forum for legitimising their actions. Only rarely will a foreign policy issue be of sufficient importance to affect the stability of a government, but the mood of parliamentary debate can shape and influence the way in which a policy issue is managed. In this sense the debate is a political activity. Dissent and opposition, especially from the ranks of the prime minister's own party, may encourage caution or even a change of position; support can provide reassurance or even embolden a government. Moreover, the course of a foreign policy debate may have implications which reach well beyond the specific issues at hand. Prime ministers and their governments can profit from parliamentary encounters, but can also be damaged by them. In this sense foreign policy debates are little different to other parliamentary jousts. The point was made by a former Liberal minister of defence, James Killen, that for former prime minister McMahon 'the floor of parliament was a place of danger'[37] where his often poor performances affected his reputation and authority on both sides of the aisle as well as among the public outside. Conversely, a strong parliamentary performance can enhance a reputation. Thus the parliamentary speeches of prime minister Hawke during Australia's participation in the 1990 Gulf crisis not only helped to garner public support for his policy, but reinforced his position within his own party at a time when it was under challenge.

Tradition notwithstanding, it seems clear that parliament's role in the conduct of Australian foreign policy is beginning to expand through the activities of parliamentary committees. The joint (House and Senate) Foreign Affairs, Defence and Trade Committee and the Senate Foreign Affairs and Defence Committee have now established impressive reputations for the quality of their reports on an array of foreign policy issues. Although governments are now required by legislation to consider and respond to the recommendations of committee reports, they are under no obligation to follow or take account of them when formulating policy. Thus for a government and more particularly for prime ministers the expansion of the committee system has not as yet posed any direct threat to their power and prerogatives. Yet in their capacity to offer a parliamentary perspective on the issues of the day or to provide alternative assessments of Australia's national policy interests from a wide array of community interests and a platform for the articulation of community and pressure group interests not always heard within government, these committees are contributing to the public

37. James Killen, *Inside Australian Politics*, Sydney: Methuen Haynes, 1985, p. 187.

debate over foreign policy issues in Australia. In doing so, they are helping both to set the agenda for Australian foreign policy and to determine the parameters within which policy choices are being made. To this extent at least, prime ministers are having to take account of their deliberations in the pursuit of their own policy objectives.

Conclusion

In Australia, the forms and processes of a modified Westminster style government have traditionally meant a concentration of power over foreign policy in the hands of the executive. There is little doubt that this pre-eminence continues and that despite the considerable influence wielded by public servants either collectively through their departments or in some cases individually, the prime minister's role in policy-making remains immensely influential. The source of this power is both personal, fluctuating with the abilities of individual leaders, and political, deriving from their position at the head of government. But although the constitutional context in which prime ministers exercises their power has not altered in its essentials since federation, the wider political and social environment of policy-making has altered markedly and is continuing to change.

For much of the first half of this century, Australia's limited role in world affairs consigned foreign policy to a place of relative unimportance on the public policy agenda, while the modest size of the federal government made the prime minister's task as a policy-maker relatively uncomplicated. Since then, Australia's expanding post-war role in international affairs, the growing complexity of the international environment and the demands of modern democratic government have all encouraged the bureaucratisation of Australian foreign policy. With an expanding foreign policy agenda the task of policy-making and implementation is more exacting. Domestically, prime ministers now exercise their power over foreign affairs within a web of political, bureaucratic and societal constraints which have made them part of a complicated process of policy management, while internationally they now have a much more active role to play in policy implementation.

The societal influences on policy are increasingly important. Foreign policy no longer begins or ends at the water's edge. As foreign policy issues penetrate the domestic political agenda with increasing force and frequency, a wider array of community influences are shaping policy outcomes. The electorate is helping to set the foreign policy agenda, serving as an important source of foreign policy values and norms and increasingly providing a source of pressure group activity. The media too are becoming more important in shaping the policy debate, acting as a conduit of information, a medium for policy debate, a powerful source of image (in relation to both events and personalities) and finally an instrument of persuasion and propaganda.

Within the context of this changing pattern of influences, prime ministers continue to occupy a place of enduring power and influence. Their role as head of government lends a natural authority to their actions which few either inside or outside of government can hope to emulate. The personal, professional and institutional resources they command all help to reinforce their status and ensure that their office still has a role in the conduct of foreign policy closely akin to Deakin's expectations at the turn of the century.

Authors's note:
***I am grateful for the research assistance provided by Carl Ungerer in the preparation of this chapter.**

8

AN AUSTRALIAN PRESIDENT? A COMPARATIVE PERSPECTIVE

John Hart

The Senate is not the only governmental device that Australia has imported from the United States. The Senior Executive Service, freedom-of-information legislation, public-funding of political parties, zero-based budgeting, and televised election campaign debates are but some of the American exports that have found their way into the Australian system of government in recent years and been adapted to suit the antipodean variant of the Westminster model. Other political practices commonly associated with the United States, such as fixed-term parliaments, citizens' initiative and recall elections, have also been advocated as part of the reform agenda for Australian government. This readiness to look to the United States for improvements to governmental structures and processes in Australia is certainly not of recent origin. During the 1890s, when Australia's fathers of federation proposed and debated their own plan for unification, much was said about the American experience and at least one of the leading players of the federation movement, George Dibbs, had cause to remark that the draft Commonwealth Constitution Bill 'leans too much towards American terms and constructions (whole pages are merely a paraphrase of the American Constitution).'[1]

Aside from the federation years however, the propensity to borrow political institutions and practices from the United States in any significant degree has been confined mainly to the post-1972 period — a period in which students of Australian government also began to challenge conventional wisdom about the relevance of the Westminster model to the Australian system. Collective responsibility, ministerial responsibilty, and cabinet government were some of the concepts that were no longer uncritically accepted as essential elements of Australian constitutionalism, especially after the constitutional crisis of 1975.[2]

1. Quoted in L.F. Crisp, *Federation Fathers*, Melbourne University Press, 1990, p. 84.
2. See, for example, Elaine Thompson, 'The "Washminster" Mutation' in Patrick Weller and Dean Jaensch (eds), *Responsible Government in Australia*, Richmond: Drummond Publishing, 1980.

Traditional notions of cabinet government were particularly weakened during the 1970s by a combination of circumstances: the coming-of-age of Australian television which had sharpened the national focus on the prime minister, the dominant leadership of Gough Whitlam and Malcolm Fraser, and the lively debate in Britain over Richard Crossman's prime-ministerial government thesis — a debate which was gradually picked-up in Australia and applied to the Australian context.

In the 1970s the Australian prime minister was, in the words of L.F. Crisp, 'the leader and pivot — and, in an increasing degree, it would seem, normally the master — of the cabinet.'[3] Crisp's use of 'it would seem' indicates a certain hesitancy. He believed that the office of prime minister afforded successive occupants access to great power and authority, but, ultimately, the extent of prime ministerial power depended on the temperament of the individual himself. Other well-known commentators were equally hesistant about ascribing too much prime ministerial power to the Australian prime minister,[4] but this did not stop the prime-ministerial government thesis taking off in Australia. By the mid-1980s, Patrick Weller, commenting on the state of the Australian literature on prime ministerial power, was able to assert that 'while the discussion is seldom systematic, belief in over-powerful prime ministers has become orthodox.'[5]

One problem with the discovery of the over-powerful prime minister in Westminster systems has been the capacity of some contributors to the debate to turn the concept of 'prime ministerial government' into 'presidential government' with remarkable ease. This development has been a particular feature of the prime-ministerial government literature in Britain and, for reasons explained further on, an unfortunate one. Australia has not been immune to this tendency. In 1980 R.S. Parker was emphatically denying that Australian government was a presidential system,[6] but, nevertheless, the 'presidential' prime minister has now become part of the on-going discourse about the nature of political leadership in Australia,[7] and commentators are implicitly suggesting that the American presidency should be added to that list of political imports from the United States which Australia has found so attractive in recent years.

3. L.F. Crisp, *Australian National Government,* 4th edn., Melbourne: Longman Cheshire, 1978, p. 357.
4. See, for example, David Butler, *The Canberra Model: Essays on Australian Government,* Melbourne: Cheshire, 1973, ch. 5.
5. Patrick Weller, *First Among Equals: Prime Ministers in Westminster Systems,* Sydney: Allen & Unwin, 1985, p. 8.
6. R.S. Parker, 'Responsible Government in Australia' in Weller and Jaensch, *op.cit.*, p. 14.
7. For a recent contribution in this vein see Colin Seymour-Ure, 'TV's Impact on the Office of Prime Minister' in Brian Hocking (ed.), *Australia Towards 2000,* London: Macmillan, 1990, pp. 292-5.

That has not happened. Although there are clearly some similarities between the way American presidents and Australian prime ministers behave, particularly in the context of the media and elections, Australia has not imported American-style presidential government, nor even a watered-down version of it. Notwithstanding the political changes that have taken place in Australia and the United States since the early 1970s, structural differences between the two systems remain vast. The separation of powers in the United States[8] and the existence of disciplined political parties in the Australian legislature preclude any significant convergence between the two systems. Assertions about the presidentialisation of the Australian prime ministership all too often embody notions of presidential power that are far removed from reality and based on concepts of heroic leadership which very few occupants of the White House have ever managed to attain. Furthermore, significant developments since Watergate have dramatically affected and weakened the power of the American presidency, and these are rarely given adequate consideration by those who come at the trans-Pacific comparison from a presidential perspective.

In the first place, however, assertions about the existence of presidential government in Australia are not entirely unrelated to the way in which the prime ministerial government debate in Britain became corrupted through a fundamental misunderstanding of what Richard Crossman and his mentor, John Mackintosh, were saying in the 1960s, and any argument must perforce begin by revisting that debate in its British context.

The Prime-Ministerial Government Thesis Revisited[9]

In essence, the prime ministerial government thesis, as propounded by Mackintosh and Crossman, asserted that British prime ministers have come to dominate the cabinet because of their power to hire and fire ministers, their control over the cabinet structure, agenda and meetings, and their dispensation of patronage. Two important developments in the twentieth century — the growth of the civil service and the growth of modern, disciplined, mass political parties — substantially increased the prime minister's power and, to these, Crossman later added prime ministerial domination of the government publicity machine as a vital

8. I use the term 'separation of powers' here as Neustadt uses it, i.e. separate institutions sharing powers. See Richard E. Neustadt, *Presidential Power: The Politics of Leadership*, New York: John Wiley & Sons, 1960, p. 6.
9. This section draws heavily on my article 'President and Prime Minister: Convergence or Divergence?' *Parliamentary Affairs*, 44 (2), April 1991, pp. 208-25.

weapon in the supremacy of prime minister over cabinet.[10] Mackintosh concluded that it would be misleading to say that British government is cabinet government. 'Now the country is governed by the prime minister who leads, co-ordinates and maintains a series of ministers all of whom are advised and backed by the civil service.'[11] Crossman's conclusion went further: 'The post-war epoch', he wrote, 'has seen the final transformation of cabinet government into prime ministerial government. Under this system the "hyphen which joins, the buckle which fastens, the legislative part of the state to the executive part" becomes one single man'.[12] Using Bagehot's terminology, Crossman maintained that the cabinet had joined the 'dignified' elements of the constitution.

Although Mackintosh and Crossman were quite emphatic that Britain had a form of prime ministerial government, neither actually claimed that this was the same as presidential government, nor did they use the term 'presidential government' as a synonym for 'prime ministerial government'. In fact, both considered the comparison between the two systems and both rejected it. 'This is not presidential government,' wrote Mackintosh, 'because the premier can, in exceptional circumstances, be removed and he will collapse if deserted by all his colleagues or by his party.'[13] Crossman said much the same thing, although with somewhat less conviction. 'A prime minister,' he wrote, 'can be unseated by his colleagues; and it is this fact with which the constitutional purists seek to justify the distinction they still make between presidential and prime ministerial government.' 'The distinction is valid,' Crossman asserted, but he added a qualification: 'provided we observe that a British party leader exerts such power and patronage within the machine that he can never be removed in real life by public constitutional procedure. The method employed must always be that of undercover intrigue and sudden unpredicted *coup d'état*.'[14] Crossman was, however, somewhat more emphatic about the differences between the two systems when he delivered his Godkin Lectures at Harvard in 1970. Speaking of the power of the prime minister, he insisted that 'he has not become in the least presidential, but he is certainly more powerful than he was — if only because government itself is so much more powerful.'[15]

While Crossman and Mackintosh maintained the distinction between prime ministerial and presidential government, some of those who

10. Richard Crossman, *Inside View: Three Lectures on Prime Ministerial Government*, London: Cape, 1972, p. 67.
11. John P. Mackintosh, *The British Cabinet*, London: Stevens, 1962, p. 451.
12. Richard Crossman, 'Introduction' to Walter Bagehot, *The English Constitution*, London: Fontana, 1963, p. 51.
13. Mackintosh, *op. cit.*, p. 452.
14. Crossman (1963), *op. cit.*.
15. Crossman (1972), *op.cit.*

subsequently joined the debate did not. The essence of the prime ministerial government thesis was that power in the British system had become concentrated around a single individual and it was this focus on a single individual that made comparison with the American presidency so tempting, however erroneous. The all too casual substitution of 'presidential' for 'prime ministerial' was unfortunate for it did a disservice to the Mackintosh-Crossman thesis, especially to the subtlety of Mackintosh's writings.

The transformation from cabinet to prime ministerial government, as described by Mackintosh, was one that had taken place *within* the cabinet system — a system that obviously had a great deal of latitude and flexibility to be manipulated by prime ministers should they choose to do so. What Mackintosh argued was that the locus of power within the cabinet system had shifted to the prime minister, not that a new system of prime ministerial government had replaced the old system of cabinet government. Indeed, in his original formulation of the argument, Mackintosh did not use the term 'prime ministerial government'. 'There is no single catchphrase that can describe this form of government,' he remarked, 'but it may be pictured as a cone. The prime minister stands at the apex supported by and giving point to a widening series of rings of senior ministers, the cabinet, its committees, non-cabinet ministers and departments.'[16]

Crossman's eagerness to relegate the British cabinet to the dignified elements of the constitution should not obscure the fact that the form of prime ministerial government he identified depended totally on the continued existence of the cabinet system. What Crossman described was a cabinet system in which the institutional mechanisms and constitutional conventions that had previously served a collective body were now being used to serve a single member of that body. Nothing illustrated this better than the doctrine of collective responsibility. As Crossman noted: 'In Bagehot's day, collective cabinet responsibility meant the responsibility of a group of equal colleagues for decisions taken collectively, after full, free and secret discussion in which all could participate. It now means collective obedience by the whole administration — to the will of the man at the apex of power.'[17]

There is nothing in the writings of John Mackintosh or Richard Crossman to justify the substitution of 'presidential' for 'prime ministerial government'. Their analyses can only be read within the context of the cabinet system, otherwise they would not make much sense,[18] but some of those who followed in their footsteps made the

16. Mackintosh, *op. cit.*, p. 452.
17. Crossman (1963), *op. cit.*, p. 53.
18. A similar argument has been made by Bernard Donoughue in his memoir of the Wilson and Callaghan administrations. He wrote: '...it must be conceded that at

transition from 'prime ministerial' to 'presidential' government quite effortlessly. In Britain, the most blatant offender in this respect was the former Conservative member of parliament, Humphry Berkeley. 'I accept that we are now operating a presidential system;' he wrote, 'to do otherwise would be unrealistic. Let us concede the prime minister presidential powers and equip ourselves with the necessary safeguards.'[19] The grounds on which he merges presidential and prime ministerial forms of government are unconvincing and, although he became one of a number of writers to join the debate started by Mackintosh and Crossman, his version of prime ministerial government was a much exaggerated extension of theirs.

Perhaps the ease with which 'prime ministerial government' became 'presidential government' in the more popular forms of the debate in Britain had something to do with the latter being a more convenient phrase and a useful shorthand description of a relatively complex idea. If the term must be used, it is certainly less grating to talk about the 'presidentialisation' of a particular political system than its 'prime ministerialisation', and, if the essence of this shorthand form is to get across the idea that government revolves around a single person, then it is quite likely that the message will be grasped more easily, at a popular level, by focusing on the archetype of one-person leadership in democratic systems — the American presidency. But there is always a danger that, when relatively complex terminology is popularised and debased, the popularisation will feed back into the scholarly debate. Scholars are forced to take note of it merely because it is popular, and that gives the popular form a certain credence even when those scholars may spend a great deal of time demonstrating how unacceptable the debased terminolgy is. Without doubt, some of the theories about the 'presidentialisation' of British government emerged from British commentators in large measure as an unintended by-product of the Mackintosh-Crossman thesis — a consequence of misunderstandings and tendencies to simplify and popularise.

---

times the British people have effectively a "prime-ministerial" form of government within the continuing and evolving cabinet system.' Bernard Donoughue, *Prime Minister: The Conduct of Policy Under Harold Wilson and James Callaghan*, London: Cape, 1987, p. 192.

19. Humphry Berkeley, *The Power of the Prime Minister*, London: Allen & Unwin, 1968, p. 87. This came at the end of a chapter comparing the offices of prime minister and president in which Berkeley reveals some serious misunderstandings of the American system. He writes, for example, that 'members of the cabinet are members of his [i.e. the President's] staff with no formal accountability to Congress' and he also says that 'in the American cabinet members...are responsible to the president and, although their actions can be reviewed by congressional committees, they cannot be restricted in the exercise of their executive functions' (p. 83). The inaccuracy of statements like these undermine the point Berkeley was attempting to make.

Presidential and Prime Ministerial Systems: The American Perspective

From the other side of the Atlantic, the comparison between the British and American systems of government has a very different emphasis. A long tradition, going back to Woodrow Wilson in the late nineteenth century, looks with admiration on parliamentary systems as a solution to the problems caused by the separation of powers and the consequent lack of co-operation between the executive and legislative branches of government. Waves of reformist writing, advocating some adaptation of the Westminster model of parliamentary and cabinet government, have occurred in the United States when the governmental system there has been perceived to be under threat. Woodrow Wilson was only one of a number of political scientists during the progressive era who wanted to change the American system to make it more like the Westminster model.[20] In the late 1930s and early 1940s there was another surge of reformism in reaction to the apparent popularity of efficient totalitarian systems in Europe and the threat they may have posed for the inefficient American system.[21] The same criticism and the same sort of reform proposals reappeared in the 1960s as a response to the problems President Kennedy was having with Congress.[22] Another wave of writers in this tradition was prompted by the Watergate crisis in the early 1970s,[23] and the most recent surge has been triggered by the bicentennial of the drafting of the American Constitution.[24]

This literature abounds with innumerable schemes for selecting the cabinet from among party leaders in Congress, creating a joint executive-legislative council, establishing a more responsible party system, making the losing presidential candidate the official leader of the opposition, and even introducing a parliamentary question-time. Such reforms would involve significant constitutional change and a major

20. See M.J.C. Vile, *Constitutionalism and the Separation of Powers*, Oxford: Clarendon Press, 1967, ch. X.
21. See, for example, Thomas K. Finletter, *Can Representative Government Do the Job?* New York: Reynal & Hitchcock, 1945 and Henry Hazlitt, *A New Constitution Now*, New York: McGraw-Hill, 1942.
22. See, for example, James Macgregor Burns, *The Deadlock of Democracy*, Englewood Cliffs: Prentice-Hall, 1963 and Clinton Rossiter, 'President and Congress in the 1960s' in M.D. Irish (ed.), *Continuing Crisis in American Politics*, Englewood Cliffs: Prentice-Hall, 1963.
23. The post-Watergate literature is vast and not all of it is in this mould, but, of those works that are, the best example is Charles Hardin's *Presidential Power and Accountability: Toward a New Constitution*, Chicago University Press, 1974.
24. See, for example, James L. Sunquist, *Constitutional Reform and Effective Government*, Washington, D.C.: The Brookings Institution, 1986; Donald L. Robinson, *Reforming American Government: The Bicentennial Papers of the Committee on the Constitutional System*, Boulder: Westview Press, 1985; and Lloyd N. Cutler, 'To Form a Government,' *Foreign Affairs*, 59 (1), Fall 1980.

upheaval in presidential-congressional relations in the United States. None has ever got very far from the drawing-board, but the long history and persistence of this mode of reformist writing illustrates one basic point: that the institutional structures of the American and parliamentary systems of government are perceived as quite different by a significant body of opinion in the United States, — hence the desire to change the American system to make it more like the Westminster parliamentary model. If British and Australian commentators want to suggest that these systems are moving towards the presidential model, their counterparts in the United States rarely support those claims.

One notable exception to this tradition was the American political scientist Richard Neustadt who did see some convergence between parliamentary sytems of government, like the British, and the American presidential system. His perspective was rather different from those writers in Britain who erroneously equated 'prime ministerial' with 'presidential' government and, although he was comparing the American president to the British prime minister, his unique approach is just as relevant to the case of the Australian prime ministership and helpful for our present purposes. Using the same analytical framework he developed in his classic study, *Presidential Power,* and, seeking what he called 'functional equivalents' in the British and American systems, he came to the conclusion that 'British government may not be presidential, but our government is more prime ministerial than we incline to think.' If the prime ministerial government debate revolved around the nature of the relationship between the prime minister and cabinet, then, Neustadt argued, the equivalent functional relationship in the United States was not president and 'that pallid institution' called a cabinet, but rather the relationship between 'an informal, shifting aggregation of key individuals, the influentials at both ends of Pennsylvania Avenue.' Neustadt's view was that the work done by the British cabinet was done in the United States by 'our congressional committees, our floor leaderships, and our front-offices downtown, all combined.'[25] Thus the critical relationship in the United States was the one between president and Congress in which the persuasive task of the president was akin to the persuasion that British prime ministers try to exercise over the cabinet, and it was that relationship which made the American system more prime ministerial than the British system was presidential.

In this chapter the comparison of the Australian prime minister and the American president will be based on the two perspectives considered above. Without getting into the finer points of the prime ministerial government thesis as it applies to Australia, it will consider the similiarities between the behaviour of Australian prime ministers and

25. Richard E. Neustadt, 'White House and Whitehall' in Anthony King (ed.), *The British Prime Minister,* 2nd edn., London: Macmillan, 1985, pp. 155-74.

American presidents in recent years whilst emphasising that the differences in the constitutional structure of each office mean that the Australian prime minister can never be presidential in the strict sense of the term. Then, taking Neustadt's starting point, it will describe not only how the post-Watergate American presidency is located far away from the idealised image of strong presidential government, but also how the president's parliamentary task is now considerably more difficult than it was at the time when Neustadt discovered prime ministerial government in the United States.

The Presidential Australian Prime Minister?

While one might want to argue about the degree of prime ministerial power in Australia, there can be little doubt that prime ministers are now much more than *primus inter pares* (to use John Morley's terminology),[26] and these days it would be quite difficult to imagine a future prime minister who would be content to head a cabinet as merely the 'first amongst equals'. Indeed, leaving aside the prime minister, it is even becoming more and more difficult to describe the Australian cabinet as a body of equals. There is clearly a pecking-order among the prime minister's colleagues in the cabinet which is determined in part by the minister's political standing in the party, length of service in the cabinet, and the particular portfolio held. The Australian media will routinely use the term 'senior ministers' to refer to the more exalted members of the cabinet and, even amongst senior ministers, there can be subtle differences in status between those who are coming to the end of their political careers and those who are earmarked as a possible future party leader. Morley's description of the prime minister as *primus inter pares* is misleading in that it both understates the position of modern prime ministers and describes an egalitarian cabinet which simply does not exist in Australia today, if it ever did.

Much of what John Mackintosh and Richard Crossman had to say about the development of the British cabinet system and the shift to prime ministerial government applies equally to Australia,[27] and Australia, no less than Britain, is living in an age of prime ministerial government. The prominence of the prime minister in contemporary

26. See King, *op. cit.*, p. 10–11.
27. There are some important differences between the Australian and British systems in respect of Crossman's prime ministerial government thesis. Australian Labor Party prime ministers do not have the same power of hiring and firing ministers as a British prime minister does. In the case of an Australian Labor government, the choice of ministers is made by the Labor Party's parliamentary caucus, although the prime minister does have the power to determine which of those ministers will be included in the cabinet and can remove ministers from the cabinet to the 'outer-ministry'.

Australian government, as in Britain, is attributable to two major factors: the growth of government itself and the development of the mass media. The scope of government activity requires, at the very least, political and administrative co-ordination and, more usually, political and administrative leadership and direction. Even in modern democracies, the expectation is that co-ordination and leadership is better done by one person than by a collectivity and certainly most recent Australian prime ministers have seen their role as one of leadership rather than chairman of the board. When the new prime minister, Paul Keating, controversially criticised the leadership style of his predecessor on a nationwide televison program in January 1992 and said 'I think the essence of leadership is for the leader to strike out and make the decisions, the directions and take the responsibility',[28] he was implicitly defining prime ministerial government as he envisaged it and not some conception of the *primus inter pares* doctrine.

The development of the mass media, particularly the intrusion of television into Australian politics, has enhanced enormously the prominence of the prime minister. As Clem Lloyd points out in his contribution to this book, television, more than any other factor, has shaped the conduct of the contemporary Australian prime ministership. It has replaced parliament as the main medium through which prime ministers communicate to the people and is also a critical factor in determining the sort of person who gets chosen as party leader and potential prime minister. These days, any political party that chooses a non-telegenic politician as its leader is handicapping itself, given the focus that television places on the leader, particularly at election time. Television partly explains how Bob Hawke and John Hewson, both telegenic politicians, took over their respective party's leadership after unusually short apprenticeships in parliament. In both cases, the potential to perform on television seemed to be more important than their potential to perform in the House of Representatives.

Television has projected prime ministers as national leaders and given the prime minister easy access to a nation-wide constituency. The prime minister now personifies the government of the day through television, and perhaps that is why Bob Hawke so often spoke of 'my government' — a term more appropriately used by the Queen rather than the prime minister, at least constitutionally. Television has also changed what prime ministers do. Summarizing the impact of television on the British prime ministership, Colin Seymour-Ure identified three major changes to the job-description of the modern prime minister: the amount of time they devote to media work has increased, the prime minister's role as an opinion leader or mobiliser has increased, and the importance of

28. Quoted in Michelle Grattan and Greg Roberts, 'PM Spurns Cosmetics and Two MPs Spurn PM,' *The Age*, 21 January 1992, p. 5.

parliament to the job of the prime minister has decreased.[29] Again, the same holds true for Australia and the impact of television in Australia has had a profound effect on the standing of the prime minister in the constitutional system. If television portrays prime ministers as the personification of government and generates the impression that government is led by one person, then we ought not to be surprised if commentators start to talk about presidential government in Australia.

Television forces certain types of behaviour on politicians and in behavioural terms there has undoubtedly been some convergence between prime ministerial government and the American version of presidential government. If the American presidency is the archetype of one-person leadership in democratic systems, that archetype has been strengthened considerably by the development of American television and particularly by the way in which television dominates the conduct of presidential election campaigns in the United States. Australian prime ministers now do a lot of things that American presidents do because the consequences of television's intrusion into politics are almost universal. Australian election campaigns are now firmly built around the personalities of prime ministers and their opponents, the leaders of the opposition. Elections in Australia are increasingly becoming contests between alternative leaders rather than alternative parties, and this is heavily reflected in the content of campaign advertising. Since 1983, the American practice of 'presidential debates' between the two major party leaders has been part of the election campaign agenda in Australia, and throughout campaigns opinion polls in Australia regularly ask questions about the performance of the prime minister, almost as though that performance is analytically distinct from the performance of the cabinet and the government in general. Prime ministerial popularity is rapidly becoming as important a measure of prime ministerial success as presidential popularity is in the United States.

In government, Australian prime ministers have been surrounding themselves with the trappings of American-style presidential leadership. The growth of prime ministers' personal staff and the Department of Prime Minister and Cabinet parallels in kind, although not in degree, the growth of the White House staff and the Executive Office of the President in the United States.[30] Furthermore, like the American presidency, the personal staff in Australian prime ministers' office have been used in a significant degree to expand the prime ministers' capacity to 'go public' and deal with the national electorate that televison has created and exposes

29. Colin Seymour-Ure, *The British Press and Broadcasting Since 1945*, Oxford: Basil Blackwell, 1991, p. 182.
30. On the development of the presidential staff in the USA see John Hart, 'The President and His Staff' in Malcolm Shaw (ed.), *Roosevelt to Reagan: The Development of the Modern Presidency*, London: Hurst, 1987.

them to so readily.[31] Contemporary Australian prime ministers now find that the speechwriters, public opinion pollsters, press secretaries and media experts become an indispensable part of their personal staff simply because that aspect of their job has become so much more significant in the televison age.

The staffing resources now available to Australian prime ministers also strengthens their capacity to second-guess ministers and control the policy initiatives emanating from the departments. That too makes prime ministers more like American presidents, although most American presidents would be quite envious of the relative degree of control that Australian prime ministers have over the government bureaucracy. The policy staff at prime ministers' disposal is particularly significant in one policy arena, that of foreign affairs, and gives prime ministers the ability to be their own minister for foreign affairs in practice if not in name. That also parallels the American situation, although no Australian prime minister is going to emulate the world role that is part of the job description of the post-World War II American president.

Outwardly Australian prime ministers are behaving like American presidents, especially at election time and in the presentation of their public image. Moreover, as chief executives, both Australian prime ministers and the American presidents perform similar executive tasks in the broad sense of giving direction to how government institutions respond to political and policy problems. But what prime ministers do and what American presidents do is done in such different structural contexts that it would be quite misleading to describe the Australian system as 'presidential'. There are fundamental differences between the constraints on American presidents acting under a separation-of-powers system and Australian prime ministers operating in a system where the executive and legislative powers are fused rather than separated.

The main difference between 'prime ministerial' and 'presidential' government is still the fact that sitting prime ministers can be removed from office during their term if they lose the support of their party in parliament. As mentioned earlier, Richard Crossman had thought this was a distinction that only 'purists' made, but recent events in Britain and Australia have shown that prime ministers who lose the support of their party can and do lose their job. Crossman believed that the power of the prime minister as party leader meant that leaders could only be deposed through an undercover *coup d'état*, but both Margaret Thatcher in Britain and Bob Hawke in Australia lost their leadership positions in 1990 and 1991 respectively by means of a formal vote in their party

31. The term 'going public' was coined by Samuel Kernell to describe the importance of public relations strategies to American presidential leadership during the Reagan years. See Samuel Kernell, *Going Public: New Strategies of Presidential Leadership*, Washington, DC: Congressional Quarterly Press, 1986.

caucus conducted under established party rules.[32] What Crossman saw, at least in his earlier writings, as merely a textbook difference between the prime minister and the American president has now proved to be a real difference, and the experience of Margaret Thatcher and Bob Hawke reinforces the fundamental fact that a prime minister who loses the support of party colleagues in parliament is vulnerable. That, of course, is not the case in respect of the American president. The only way in which a president of the United States can be removed from office permanently is through the impeachment process, which is laid out in the Constitution and requires that the president be found guilty of 'treason, bribery, and other high crimes and misdemeanors' — a fate that has yet to befall any American president.[33]

The necessity to maintain the support of party colleagues does constrain what prime ministers can do, and prevents them being presidential. Australian prime ministers cannot ignore the wishes of their party colleagues, at least not for long. By contrast, American presidents can ignore the demands of their party in Congress and can do so for two reasons. First, there is no way that the loss of party support in Congress can directly bring about the removal of presidents during their term of office since tenure in the White House is for a fixed term and quite deliberately independent of Congress. Second, political parties in the United States Congress are weak and are badly structured either to support presidents or to defeat them. The worst that can happen to American presidents is that their party denies them re-nomination for election after their first term, although that decision is made not by the party in Congress but by an amorphous mass of party supporters who participate in the primaries and have, by Australian standards, a very loose attachment to the party.

While the backing of their own party in the Congress can be helpful to American presidents, the usual task of presidents is to build coalitions of support in Congress which invariably have to cut across party lines. Indeed, in the present condition of divided government in the United States (one party controlling the presidency and the opposing party controlling the Congress), presidents cannot gain any victories without the support of some members of the opposition. And that is an essential difference between American presidents and Australian prime ministers. Australian prime ministers may be much more vulnerable to losing their positions than American presidents, but while they hold power they have

32. Technically Mrs Thatcher was not defeated in the 1990 Conservative Party leadership contest. She simply failed to secure enough votes on the first ballot to gain an outright victory and decided to withdraw from the contest rather than face a second ballot.

33. American presidents can be removed from office temporarily under the disability provisions in the 25th Amendment. Attempts have been made to impeach two presidents, Andrew Johnson and Richard Nixon, but neither succeeded.

a much easier time turning their policy initiatives into law because they do not usually have to come to terms with the opposition party in parliament or seek votes from members on the other side of the house. In normal circumstances prime ministers lead a party that holds a majority of seats in the House of Representatives and, given the strength of party discipline, that ensures that the initiatives of the government are carried.[34] In terms of Neustadt's functional equivalents, if the presidential task of wnning support in Congress is equated with the prime ministerial task of winning support in the cabinet, then here again the difference is vital. Australian prime ministers do not have to negotiate with leading members of the opposition party to secure the support of their cabinet.

The cabinet is also an important point of difference between prime ministerial and presidential government. Neustadt is right to call the American cabinet 'a pallid institution'. It has no constitutional status, it has no power independent of the president, its members do not have seats in the legislature, it cannot remove the president from office, cabinet approval is not necessary for any presidential initiatives, and, if members of the cabinet find they cannot support the president, their only option is to resign. The cabinet may serve as a sounding-board for American presidents and could help them co-ordinate government activity, but few recent presidents have shown any interest in giving their cabinets a purposeful function, and much of what cabinets might do for presidents is done, more effectively from the presidents' point of view, by the presidential staff. However, to Australian prime ministers the cabinet is a vital institution; even if the age of 'cabinet government' has passed, that body is the mechanism through which prime ministers exercise prime ministerial government. The cabinet is, as it always has been in the age of mass political parties, the link between the executive and the legislature, and, so long as the Australian cabinet reflects and represents the major strands of opinion within the parliamentary party, then cabinet gives prime ministers a political tool that would be the envy of any American president and one for which there is no functional equivalent in the United States.[35]

34. The situation in the Senate can complicate matters for an Australian prime minister when the governing party does not have an overall majority of Senate seats, but this situation does not compare to the task that American presidents face. It does not usually result in the government negotiating with the opposition, but rather accommodating the wishes of minor parties or accepting defeat'

35. What Neustadt does in his 'functional equivalent' approach to comparing presidents and prime ministers is substitute a *relationship* (i.e.'between an informal, shifting aggregation of key individuals, the influentials at both ends of Pennsylvania Avenue') for a *structure* (i.e. the cabinet). The *relationship* does not give the American president the equivalent political tools that the *structure* gives to a prime minister.

The third crucial difference between prime ministerial and presidential government is the political party itself. Australian prime ministers are party leaders in a system where partisan attachment among the electorate remains very strong, with party still the best cue to voting behaviour, and where party discipline in government ensures that prime ministers who have the support of their party can exercise prime ministerial government reasonably efficiently. By contrast, American presidents enjoy no such benefits from their role as party leader. American political parties are not organised to help presidents in power. American voters are much less inclined to vote on the basis of partisan identification or on the basis of the party platform, especially in congressional elections. Parties lack discipline in Congress. The incentives that drive the behaviour of members of the Congress are not party incentives, but constituency-related and, so long as members of Congress retain the support of their constitutents, they need not worry about party. Political parties in the United States are not effective instruments of governing, as they are in Australia, and that makes a fundamental difference to the nature of executive leadership in both systems.

Finally, one crucial difference that has become increasingly apparent in recent years is that Australian prime ministers operate within a political culture that tolerates, and is not unduly disturbed by, executive power. By and large, Australians do not worry too much that the executive dominates the legislature and that the Australian parliament has little real power to restrain the government and hold it accountable. In all democracies, an equilibrium has to be reached between efficiency of government on the one hand and the accountability of government on the other: in Australia its balance is tilted towards the side of efficiency. That is most definitely not so in the United States.

The Prime Ministerial President?

The Mackintosh-Crossman prime ministerial government thesis was launched at roughly the same time as Neustadt published his *Presidential Power*. The theme of that book was that the American presidency was an office of inherent weakness rather than strength, where powers were no guarantee of power and in which leadership could only be exercised successfully by presidents of extraordinary temperament and experience.[36] If the American presidency was weak when the prime ministerial government debate was first launched in Britain, then it has been weakened even more in the post-Watergate era and particularly in terms of the presidential-congressional relationship that Neustadt thought so central to any comparison with parliamentary models. Numerous changes took place in the wake of Nixon's departure from the White

36. Neustadt (1960), *op. cit.*, p. 195.

House that have increased the constraints on American presidents and made their persuasive task with Congress much more difficult than in was in the mid-1960s.

The first of these changes relates to the way American presidents are selected. The road to the White House has become considerably more arduous in the post-Watergate period. The rules of the nomination game were changed after 1968 by a Democratic Party eager to satisfy the demand for fairer representation at party nominating conventions and for more direct participation in the selection of the party's nominee for the presidency. Those changes in the rules changed the strategic imperatives for the candidates in both major political parties. As Nelson Polsby has explained it, the imperative lies not in forming a broad coalition within the party, as used to be the case, 'but in mobilising a faction by emerging first in rank-order among the numerous presidential candidates who put themselves forward.'[37] Faction-fighting requires different sorts of skills from coalition-building. Yet, although the process of getting to the White House has been transformed dramatically in the 1970s and 1980s, what it takes to be a successful president has not; when in government, there is still every incentive to compromise and seek supporting coalitions for presidential initiatives. The changes in the presidential nomination process have changed the relationship between the presidents and their party in Congress. Presidential candidates in the post-Watergate era can reach the White House without the help of the party organisation because the nomination is now decided by a mass of amorphous voters, with a loose attachment to the party, who participate in an ever-increasing number of primaries, and not by party leaders or elected officials who have been virtually excluded from the nomination process since 1972.[38]

The gulf between candidate and party has also been widened by other changes in the way that American presidents are nominated and elected in the post-Watergate era. The partial public-funding of the nomination contest and full public-funding of the election campaign since 1974 have released presidential candidates from the principal area of dependency upon party. The party is no longer the channel to that most vital resource in presidential election campaigns — money. Nor is the party any longer the intermediary between the candidate and voter. That function has been clearly usurped by the mass media.[39] These developments have weakened the crucial link between presidents and party in the American system and

37. Nelson W. Polsby, *Consequences of Party Reform*, New York: Oxford University Press, 1983, p. 129.
38. Attempts have been made by the Democratic Party to restore a voice in the nomination process for party leaders and elected officials. For a fuller explanation see John Hart, 'The End of Party Reform,' in D.K. Adams (ed.), *Studies in US Politics*, Manchester University Press, 1989.
39. See Polsby, *op. cit.*, ch. IV.

widened the gap between presidents and their base of support in Congress. They have also been part of a much broader decline in the relevance of political parties, particularly the relevance of parties as governing entities, and even if the anti-party consequences of the changes in the nomination process and the conduct of presidential elections could be reversed, American presidents would be still be left with a much weaker base of support than they had in the pre-Watergate period.

With one exception, post-Watergate presidents have also had to contend with a divided government — the presidency in the hands of one party and Congress controlled by the other. At presidential level, the break-up of the New Deal electoral coalition, which had sustained the Democratic Party for thirty years, has left the Republican Party with a lock on the Electoral College. At congressional level, the decline of partisan identification and the increasing attractiveness of incumbency as a cue to voting behaviour has made it as difficult for the Republicans to win control of Congress as it is for the Democrats to win the White House. While Democratic presidential candidates suffered major defeats during the 1980s, the Democratic majority in the House of Representatives was easily able to insulate itself from national trends and comfortably resisted what some commentators believed to be a realignment of voting behaviour away from the Democratic Party. And even though the Senate was won by the Republicans in 1980, and held by them until the 1986 mid-term election, that is now beginning to look like an aberration as senators learned to behave like their counterparts in the House and became more adept at protecting their own incumbency. Eisenhower was the last Republican president to serve with a Congress controlled by his own party, and there is not much evidence to suggest that he will be losing that distinction in the near future.

Changes in the organisation and distribution of power in Congress since the mid-1970s have drastically altered the way Congress does it business. The revolt against seniority in the House in 1975 successfully broke the dominance of a handful of committee chairmen, and the subsequent reforms had the effect of substantially dispersing power in Congress through the sub-committee system and the revived party caucuses. While presidents always encountered difficulties in dealing with the self-perpetuating old guard that ran Congress before its democratisation in the mid-1970s, the president's bargaining task was considerably easier then than it is under the highly fragmented power structure of today. Furthermore, as there is less and less relationship between what American voters express in presidential elections and what they express in congressional elections, and as members of Congress find incumbency-protection behaviour more and more satisfying, so there is today a much smaller incentive for Congress to go along with the president than there was thirty years ago.

That lack of incentive to go along with the president is manifested daily in the way that Congress now routinely involves itself in matters that used to be regarded as the prerogative of the president. The congressional deference that characterised the 'imperial presidency' has now all but disappeared except when the Congress finds it a strategically useful weapon to use in order to avoid those issues that might risk electoral support back home. Today, for example, Congress plays a major role in both budgetary and foreign policy, two policy areas where, before the Nixon administration, the president could be reasonably certain of either support or inertia on the part of Congress. During the Reagan years it became the usual practice of Congress to pronounce the president's budget 'dead-on-arrival' and President Bush has fared little better. In the field of foreign affairs, Congress now regularly involves itself in intelligence matters, arms control policy, foreign trade, diplomacy and the commitment of United States armed forces to hostilities abroad. As one commentator has recently argued, foreign policy is losing its distinctiveness as a domain of presidential responsibility, and the trend toward congressional involvement in foreign policy is irreversible.[40]

The post-Watergate resurgence of congressional independence and assertiveness was also responsible for a series of statutory restrictions on the president's capacity to give direction to government in critical policy areas — areas in which pre-Watergate presidents had had more discretionary authority or met with more predictable congressional deference. The best known of these restrictions are the War Powers Resolution of 1973 and the Congressional Budget and Impoundment Control Act of 1974, but there are also post-Watergate statutory constraints on presidential power relating to arms sales, executive agreements, intelligence operations and foreign assistance, to name but a few.[41] Sometimes the limitations on presidential action have been written into new laws, but more often they are attached to appropriations legislation like the Boland amendment which attempted to prevent the Reagan administration from overthrowing the Sandinista government of Nicaragua. Not all of these post-Watergate statutory restrictions have worked well, especially the War Powers Resolution, but all, including the War Powers Resolution, have constrained post-Watergate presidents to a greater or lesser degree.

The changed relationship between president and Congress in the post-Watergate era has come about because of the institutional uniqueness of American government. The immediate causes, of course, stemmed from the Watergate experience and the realisation by Congress that it had

40. See Thomas. E. Mann (ed.), *A Question of Balance: The President, the Congress and Foreign Policy,* Washington, DC: The Brookings Institution, 1990.
41. For a useful survey of the post-Watergate restrictions on presidential authority in the field of foreign and national security policy, see *ibid.*

abdicated its authority and helped create an imperial presidency. However it was ultimately the institutional structure of American government that allowed the legislature to assert itself against executive power and authority. If Neustadt's 'White House and Whitehall' hinted at a convergence between prime ministers and presidents, the post-Watergate era would tend to suggest divergence. There is no parallel in Australia to the attack on executive power mounted in America since Nixon's resignation.

9

THE DEVELOPMENT OF THE AUSTRALIAN PRIME MINISTERSHIP

Patrick Weller

This book set out to ask to what degree the position of prime ministers has changed, to ask whether prime ministers are now more powerful than fifty years ago and, if so, how that change occurred. Each chapter has, in its own way, sought to identify and trace the changes, asking whether these have had a substantial impact on prime ministerial power or whether the fundamental arrangements are still untouched.

One conclusion is obvious. The position of prime minister has not been transformed in the same way as the American presidency. It is possible to draw distinctions between the traditional and modern presidency, and to nominate stages through which the modern presidency has moved. Shaw identifies the formative stage (Roosevelt, Truman, Eisenhower), the strong (Kennedy, Johnson), the imperial (Johnson and Nixon) and the post-imperial (Ford, Carter, Reagan).[1] There are clearly identifiable characteristics about the way that the presidents in each stage related to Congress, developed their staff and used their powers.

No such clear distinctions can be drawn in an examination of the Australian prime ministers; nor indeed should they be sought. As John Hart has noted, the discussion of the 'presidential' prime minister is useful for media consumption, but does not stand sustained analysis. The relationship between presidents and the other parts of the political system reflects a balance between distinct powers; presidents must negotiate, cajole and persuade in order to persuade others to adopt their policies. The position and the authority they wield is different from that of prime ministers; power is dispersed and individual, rather than concentrated and collective. A comparison of the *differences* between presidents and prime ministers is instructive because it illustrates how the institutions of a political system have an impact on the power of individual office-holders within that system. Presidents have some capacities that prime ministers might covet: personal mandates and the certainty of fixed terms. In other instances prime ministers have the ability to push their wishes through cabinet and parliament with an ease

1. Malcolm Shaw, 'The Traditional and Modern Presidents', in M. Shaw (ed.), *Roosevelt to Reagan: The Development of the Modern Presidency*, London: C. Hurst, 1987, p. 295.

and rapidity that presidents would dearly like to emulate. Presidents and prime ministers wield power by the use of different weapons, but because the president's authority is more specific and individual it has been possible to see more distinct and identifiable stages through which the position has moved.

The Australian prime ministership is far more closely integrated into the political institutions within which its incumbents work: prime ministers are part of the cabinet, the party and the parliament. It is as a consequence harder to identify with any precision an increase in the power of prime ministers and a decline in the power of cabinet or the party. For the Australian prime ministership the question then needs to be asked: have the levers by which power can be manipulated changed over the last fifty years, so that prime ministers have a greater impact on government decisions in 1991 than they did in 1941?

There is of course a need to emphasise the levers of power, as something distinct from the personalities who chose to pull them. Both before and after 1941, those who held the position of prime minister have shown distinctly different propensities to maximise the opportunities of their position. The dominating, eccentric and manipulative Billy Hughes was very different in his approach to the position than the quiet and homely Joe Lyons, who never quite adjusted from the slow, comparatively gentle pace of Tasmanian politics to the rough federal world of the Depression but who still managed to win three elections. Similarly Menzies in the 1960s, experienced, superior, unchallenged and unchallengeable, was able to exert an influence to which McMahon, leading a divided, directionless crew and never certain of his own position, could never aspire. Even within the term of a single prime minister, the position of the leader will change. After the 1987 election, Hawke was able to direct caucus to elect a more balanced selection of ministers and to reorganise the federal bureaucracy with little consultation of his ministers; by 1991, when his hold on the position became tenuous, and with an heir apparent sniping from the backbench, every policy issue became contaminated by the weakness of the leadership and the need to translate the government's intentions into its impact on caucus votes.

The influence of particular prime ministers is not permanent or given; rather it rises and falls as electoral success, polling data, the ambitions of other ministers and economic circumstance change the climate in which that influence must be wielded. These changing personal characteristics and political situations provide constant static that makes the analysis of the prime ministership as an institution difficult. It cannot be entirely isolated from the people who hold the position. Can its career as an institution nevertheless be traced over the past fifty years?

The Nature of the Prime Ministerial Job

These questions of how the position of prime ministers has changed lead to broader questions. What is the job that prime ministers are required to do? Can it be given a succinct job description that allows observers to determine how adequately any one person has performed? The chapters have discussed what prime ministers do in relation to particular institutions. They have explored the links of prime ministers with party or parliament. But there has been no attempt to ask how those parts fit together. The nature of the job is, if anything, deduced from those descriptions. It may be useful to consolidate those ideas, if only to show how illusory or fickle such a concept as a distinct job description is.[2]

The Australian prime minister is not recognised in the constitution; there is no formal position thus created. Prime ministers usually have direct responsibility for the implementation of very few acts of parliament. Whereas it is possible to say their ministers are required by Section 65 of the constitution 'to administer departments of state', there is no equivalent job description for prime ministers. Rather their activities are based on practice, convention and choice.

By convention prime ministers chair cabinet and select ministers. By parliamentary practice, they answer for the general performance of their government and their personal behaviour to the House of Representatives. By choice they may dominate the party's electoral campaigning, respond to the media and play a significant role in foreign affairs. How much time they spend on the different activities depends on their own priorities and on the political circumstances. They must decide what is most important and where their energies are best spent. When they have fulfilled the duties they must do — in cabinet and parliament (and even there how much time they spend is in their hands) — the remainder of the job is a matter of priorities.

It is not that there are no roles that prime ministers must play; just that there is no way of determining how those roles will be balanced. The job is thus a consequence of those choices, of deciding how much time will be spent in each activity. Since prime ministers' time is said to be the most valuable commodity in Canberra, a decision to emphasise one activity means others must receive less or no attention. Often their choices are not appreciated by others who feel, for instance, that more time should be spent on explaining government policy to the electorate and less in cabinet (to note one criticism of Fraser). But no one can see

2. For a fuller discussion, see Patrick Weller, *Malcolm Fraser PM*, Ringwood: Penguin, 1989, Ch. 1. For the wider debate on prime ministeral power, see also Patrick Weller, *First Among Equals*, Sydney: Allen & Unwin, 1985, and P. Dunleavy and R. Rhodes, 'Core Executive Studies in Britain', *Public Administration*, 68 (1), 1990.

the landscape from the same position as prime ministers or really appreciate their problems.

Often prime ministers are forced to respond to external demands. Economic circumstances, media demands or foreign crises may force themselves on the agenda. Prime ministers do what they must as often as they do what they want. They react as often as they initiate. Their choices are made in a political context that limits and shapes their options. One indicator of success is the degree to which they shape those options, change the debate or reinterpret external pressures in a direction they regard as more desirable.

Much of the time they work through others — through ministers who have formal legislative authority, through bureaucrats who will shape and implement their wishes. The collectivity of the governmental process means that prime ministers, like the American president, must persuade and manipulate where they cannot command. They will cajole, anticipate, consult or terrify — different tactics for different people and circumstances, each developed for its own case.

The consequence is that Australian prime ministers do not have a distinct job in either a constitutional or a political sense; they sit at the centre of the political maelstrom, blown by forces they cannot entirely control, and calculate how best to use their limited capacities and resources. What works once may not be suitable the next time. Nevertheless the options, institutions and levers of power remain constant, even if their application will depend on the choices individuals make. The question this book has asked is, given these variations, do prime ministers have greater potential or opportunity to make choices or to get their way?

The Continuities

The continuities of the prime ministership are the most obvious findings. The institutions of Australian government have remained substantially unchanged and the position of prime ministers within them is thus apparently little different.

Cabinet and collective government remains the normal method of policy-making. All prime ministers have chosen to — or, more likely, have been obliged to — work through cabinet. Cabinet decisions are the currency of government, giving clear authority to act. There have been occasions when prime ministers have made important individual decisions and then expected cabinet to fall into line. But they are rare occasions when prime ministers use their stock of political capital. Goodwill may be there — but it is not inexhaustible. Rather the evidence suggests that prime ministers work with or through cabinet far more often than they ignore it. Cabinet government, taken here to indicate the use of cabinet or its committees to make, legitimise, confirm or otherwise process decisions of government, remains a reality in Australia.

Party government too has not changed. As Glyn Davis concludes, the basic contract between the leaders and the led remains the same. Prime ministers must provide electoral victory, with the consequent access to power, patronage, position and authority, in exchange for continued support. Prime ministers hold their position exclusively by virtue of their party leadership; they are the creatures of their parties, liable to removal if they do not deliver their part of the bargain: office.

Indeed this contract seems to be made explicit more often in recent years. Menzies resigned when he could not maintain the support of his party for his future plans in 1941; he was not actually defeated in a party ballot. There was no internal party challenge to an incumbent prime minister between 1941 and 1969; since then, challenges have been rather more frequent. Gorton was forced to a ballot in 1969 and lost in another in 1971. Fraser was challenged by Peacock in 1981, Hawke was challenged by Keating in June 1991; he won that first ballot but, unwilling to accept the decay of his support, was defeated in December 1991 and replaced by Keating. Those challenges now represent only the tip of the iceberg. Speculation about leadership has become endemic (it makes good press and does not need to be based in fact), whenever the fortunes of the prime minister seem low.[3] Prime ministers in Australia have always been vulnerable; it takes only a party meeting and a 'spill' motion to declare the leadership vacant to remove a prime minister. In few other places is the contract between leader and led so distinct and so easy to call to account.

In the parliament the position of prime ministers may even have deteriorated, though not in the House of Representatives, where party discipline remains absolute and independent members are rare. No government has been brought down by a vote in the House of Representatives since 1941, when two independents who held the balance of power switched sides. However the Senate has, as a consequence of the introduction of proportional representation, ceased to be dominated by the major parties. At different times the Democratic Labor Party and the Australian Democrats have been able to force the government to negotiate on major items of legislation, or use the sanction of a double dissolution to threaten their positions. Prime ministers no longer

3. Opposition leaders are even more vulnerable; since 1969 Snedden, Whitlam (in 1977), Hayden, Peacock and Howard have all been challenged successfully or unsuccessfully. It is notable that, whether victor or victim, none of them became prime minister after the challenge. Whitlam's defeat of Cairns's challenge in 1967 is the only time a leader of the opposition held the position and then won an election. The challenge itself is usually a symbol of a terminal illness for any leader.

control the Senate by proxy — although not all senators would readily have ever conceded their right to do so; they still need to rely on their ministerial lieutenants in the Senate to negotiate on their behalf.

Gaining the Edge

If the institutions have not changed, what variations in their working have developed to allow prime ministers better access to the levers of power? In each institution there are some changes that might assist them.

In cabinet the development of cabinet committees and the increasing sophistication of the cabinet procedures give more sustained capacity to prime ministers to influence the way that cabinet receives and considers its submissions. By directing which committee is to consider an issue and by determining its membership and its authority to make final decisions, prime ministers can direct, even manipulate, the processes of government. In Britain it has been argued that the development of cabinet committees has been the principal new power developed by prime ministers.[4]

Improved briefing procedures have ensured that, as the business of cabinet became more extensive and complex, prime ministers have remained the best informed members on all issues. While other ministers may have a full understanding of their own portfolios, and the treasurer may appreciate the financial implications of all the submissions, prime ministers are given notes on all the political and financial implications. If they mastered their briefs — and the more effective prime ministers assuredly did — they were able to direct discussion towards one of the conclusions they regarded as acceptable, if not their preferred option. Where information is a source of power, the briefing becomes an important weapon.

In party management, the growing centralisation of party business, particularly in the development of party secretariats, has given the prime ministers a considerable influence. Consider the need of John Curtin to court and cajole the semi-independent Labor Party state branches in 1943 to change party policy in order to allow the government the freedom to employ militia troops in war. And compare it with the arrogance with which the Hawke government used the Labor federal conference to bring the party's policy into line with the policy of the government. The transference to top-down policy development, whereby the Labor leader was the origin of most ideas, was started by Whitlam; the control by the government through the faction system was later brought to a new level of skill by Hawke.

4. A.G. Jordan and J.J. Richardson, *British Politics and the Policy Process*, London: Allen & Unwin, 1987, p. 152.

Of course Labor prime ministers have only since 1967 been a member of the federal conference and federal executive. A direct voice assists the case. Further, the federal executive of the Labor Party has gradually extended its powers; now it can and will intervene even in the selection of candidates, once the jealously guarded prerogative of state branches. As members of that executive, Labor prime ministers have greater access to the party levers of power.

The development of the position of federal secretary in the past 20 years has given both Labor and Liberal prime ministers direct access to party thinking. Tony Eggleton had a close working relationship with Fraser; Bob McMullen and Bob Hogg had regular access to Hawke. The federal party machine can work more directly with the prime minister, providing data on polls, feeding back party opinions, and giving a party perspective to debates.

The bureaucracy of the parties has therefore assisted the prime minister, giving the capacity to influence the use of party sanctions and direct access to party forums. Its support has become more sophisticated and continual. The fiefdoms that characterised the state branches of both major parties have been to a degree better integrated into a system of management that is at the disposal of prime ministers, if they know how to use it to best effect. But only to a degree; it is still possible for a state branch and a prime minister to be at loggerheads, as Fraser's frigid relations with the Queensland division of the Liberal Party illustrates.

Parliament too may be easier to manage by means other than the use of sheer numbers. If the Senate has been less amenable to control as minor parties hold the balance of power, the House of Representative is now controlled by a series of standing orders which have one common feature: they assist the executive in its dominance of parliamentary timetables. The gag, the guillotine, the requirement for ministers to introduce financial measures — all, as Uhr makes clear, assist the executive. Management of parliamentary business is now easier and, with the growth in the legislative agenda, probably regarded as more necessary. The Senate, with its committees and demands for special treatment, may be different, but that is primarily because the government lacks control. The history of parliament is dominated by the desire of governments to control proceedings as a means of passing their legislative programs. Such changes as governments have been able to introduce since 1940 have followed that trend.

The Changes

There have been some substantial changes in the position of prime ministers in other areas of governing too. The bureaucracy that supports them is more sophisticated, larger and capable of providing support over a wider range of issues. So too is the prime minister's private office. Whereas once the Department of the Prime Minister and Cabinet acted primarly as a post-box and the private office as a means of sorting paper and making appointments, both have now become more ambitious in their support. The department has developed a capacity for providing policy advice on any issues in which prime ministers develop an interest. The private office has included a selection of high-powered staff who can act as policy advisers, political fixers, press officers or in any other role that prime ministers wish. The interests of the private staff are effectively the same as that of their boss's; they are an extension of the leader's personality. Combined, the official and partisan wings have provided a powerhouse available to be tapped.

So too have the changes to the media and to the nature of electoral campaigns made prime ministers more obviously the heads and mouthpieces of government. Lloyd emphasises the growing impact of the electronic media on the presentation of prime ministers and the need for them to react rapidly to requests for detail. Media that will ask questions on any topic and intrude constantly on the activities of a leader give little scope for uninformed comment by prime ministers. Wide briefing is necessary; the pressure to perform is constant.

That immediate access to the electorate through the media provides opportunities for media manipulation, without the opportunity for intervening analysis by journalists. The lack of privacy has been counterbalanced by frequent opportunities for prime ministers to get the message across, even though a message conveyed by photo opportunities and 20-second grabs must lack any of the substance that might once be conveyed in more leisured days. One consequence is that the media have often replaced parliament as the forum for announcing government decisions.

Never is this more so that in election campaigns. The electorate may see the prime minister in many guises. During campaigns the position appears at its most important, for the packaging of the leaders has been intensified to the extent that few other ministers receive much attention, unless they commit some *faux pas* that can hit the headlines. The development of opinion polls and the packaging of leaders into suitable electoral images has indeed heightened the tension of the party contract: leaders must provide victory to retain support.

In some areas of policy development prime ministers too have increased their potential authority. As leaders of a federal government, prime ministers must deal with the state premiers who in their turn regard themselves as heads of government. The increase in federal authority — through the increased federal control of finances and the broadening interpretation by the High Court of the federal powers enumerated in the constitution, particularly in its application of the external affairs power — has meant that prime ministers have a much greater capacity to dictate to the states in 1991 than fifty years ago. But there remain political costs in failing to negotiate the demands of premiers, particularly those from the same party. Eventually the potential power is less crucial than the political consequences; prime ministers must decide what compromises they can live with, rather than insisting on winning at all costs.

A further consequence of the changes in advice and the improved technology is a capacity for prime ministers to become deeply involved in specific policy affairs. Economic policy was always a matter of decision between treasurers and prime ministers, when prime ministers were interested. Not all were, although none has tried to emulate Chifley's decision to be both prime minister and treasurer. The task now would simply be too big. But the general involvement of cabinet in economic decisions has grown, thus strengthening the prime minister's opportunities to question Treasury's advice. Modern technology has also allowed prime ministers to play a far more active role in foreign policy, as Trood shows. The ability to attend summits and yet only be away for a week is tempting for all prime ministers. The feeling of mixing with the world's leaders must be intoxicating; the pleasure of getting away from the routine of domestic politicking must be marked. Whereas once a prime minister had to spend months abroad to have a substantial international impact, by 1991 several quick trips by comfortable jet were easier and politically safer. Hence all the recent prime ministers have played an active and peripatetic role on the international scene.

The Impact

At first sight it seems likely that the capacity of prime ministers has increased as a consequence of the changes. Better advice, more media access, greater attention, better control over party policy, a more distinct and regular international presence: all these have assisted. But their impact on the security and power of prime ministers can easily be exaggerated. Media manipulation, for instance, has not made prime ministers immune from electoral defeat, or even from party revolt.

The environment has changed too. More rapid reactions are needed, media attention is more sustained, expectations of government are greater. As Hughes has illustrated, a changing, larger, better-educated electorate may make greater demands on prime ministers. Indeed all the changes may be required for prime ministers merely to stand still, to maintain the same control that they had before circumstances began to make their lives more complicated. Without the changes they would have been unable to control events at all.

It is necessary therefore to distinguish between the control of the internal procedures, over which prime ministers have some influence, and those that are external to the machinery of government. Internally the additional briefing, the power over committees, the influence over party policy, the greater opportunities in foreign and economic affairs have all added to the potential for the exercise of power, although that power may not be exercised individually but through the mechanics of collective cabinet government. Collective discussion of issues need not be a sign of prime ministerial weakness; it is how that discussion is conducted, by what rules and in what terms that matters. The procedures that have been adopted give prime ministers the potential to control those outcomes more systematically. But that influence is only a matter of potential; to apply it too regularly may be eventually to upset too many powerful ministers. Prime ministers' political capital may be exhausted. It is preferable to take ministers along, not to fight; persuade, not to command; achieve agreement, or at least acquiesience, not sullen resentment. Cabinets still need to be managed; they require the political skill and constant attention of prime ministers if they are to be effective.

The external environment has made prime ministers even more public figures than they were before, with their face beamed directly into the living rooms of the electorate. That gives them the ability to woo their supporters, to become so popular individually that they are regarded as indispensable (for as long as that popularity lasts). They can make policy announcements on the airwaves, and then seek cabinet approval. Parliament, even party, can be bypassed — occasionally.

But that very publicity has its problems. Those who are elected by opinion polls may find their position undermined when the polls show declining support. If the parties now have more precise evidence of their electoral prospects, they may be more inclined to change leaders than they were when that evidence was more instinctive and anecdotal. The concentration of electorate and media on the leader may give prime ministers more immediate scope for decision; yet it also makes them more vulnerable.

There is then no trend that has inescapably shifted power from ministers or cabinet to prime ministers; nor any massive institutional restructuring that allows notions of prime ministerial government to be presented as a given. The potential for greater control may have been achieved, but the circumstances have made those changes necessary merely to keep up. And they have been achieved at a cost. If prime ministers are now seen as primarily responsible for their governments' actions, they are also held more directly accountable — in the polls and by their parties. The most distinct consequence is that they must now deliver office or face party defeat. It is constant success or symbolic sacrifice.

SELECTED BIBLIOGRAPHY

Aitkin, D. (1982), *Stability and Change in Australian Politics*, 2nd ed., Canberra: Australian National University Press.

Aitkin, D., B. Jinks and J. Warhurst (1989), *Australian Political Institutions*, 4th edn, Melbourne: Longman.

Albinski, H.S. (1977), *Australian External Policy Under Labor: Content, Process and the National Debate*, St. Lucia: University of Queensland Press.

Ayres, P.J. (1987), *Malcolm Fraser: A Biography*, Melbourne: William Heinemann Australia.

Bagehot, W. (1963), *The English Constitution*, London: Fontana.

Bean, C. and A. Mughan, (1989), 'Leadership Effects in Parliamentary Elections in Australia and Britain', *American Political Science Review* 31(4).

Bean, C. (1988), 'Politics and the Public: Mass Attitudes towards the Australian Political System', in J. Kelly and C. Bean (eds), *Australian Attitudes: Social and Political Analyses from the National Social Science Survey*, Sydney: Allen & Unwin.

Beed, T.W. (1977), 'Opinion Polling and the Elections', in H.R. Penniman (ed.), *Australia at the Polls: The National Elections of 1975*, Washington: American Enterprise Institute.

Berkeley, H. (1968), *The Power of the Prime Minister*, London: Allen & Unwin.

Blau, P.M. (1964), *Exchange and Power in Social Life*, New York: John Wiley & Sons.

Blondel, J. (1973), *Comparative Legislatures*, New Jersey: Prentice-Hall.

Briot, G.T. and C. Lloyd (1976), 'Ministerial Staff Members', Submission No. 466, *Royal Commission on Australian Government Administration*, Canberra: RCAGA.

Brodie, S. (1984), *Statesmen, Leaders and Losers: The Twenty-three Prime Ministers of Australia*, Sydney: Dreamweaver Books.

Bunting, Sir John (1988), *R.G. Menzies: A Portrait*, Sydney: Allen & Unwin.

Butler, D. (1973), *The Canberra Model: Essays on Australian Government*, Melbourne: Cheshire.

Cameron, C. (1990), *The Cameron Diaries*, Sydney: Allen & Unwin.

Carroll, B. (1978), *From Barton to Fraser: Every Australian Prime Minister*, Sydney: Cassell.

Clark, C. (1982), 'Parliament Defence and Foreign Policy', in J.R. Nethercote (ed.), *Parliament and Bureaucracy*, Sydney: Hale and Iremonger.

Clarke, J. and K. White (1983), *Women in Australian Politics*, Sydney: Fontana.

Cockerill, M., P. Hennessy and D. Walker (1984), *Sources close to the Prime Minister*, London: Macmillan.

Codd, M. (1988), 'Inside the Government Changes', *GO: Government Officers Magazine of Administration and Purchasing*, March.

--- (1990), 'Cabinet Operations of the Australian Government', in B. Galligan, J. Nethercote and C. Walsh (eds), *The Cabinet and Budget Processes*, Canberra: The Federalism Research Centre.

--- (1990), 'The Role of Secretaries of Departments in the Australian Public Service', *Public Service Commission Executive Staffing Unit, Occasional Papers No. 8*, Canberra.

--- (1991), 'Federal Public Sector Management Reform: Recent History and Current Priorities', *Public Service Commission Executive Staffing Unit, Occasional Paper No. 11*, Canberra.

Costar, B. and D.F. Woodward (eds) (1985), *Country to National: Australian Rural Politics and Beyond*, Sydney: Allen & Unwin.

Costar, B. and S. Prasser (eds) (1990), *Amalgamate or Perish: The Future of Non-Labor Parties in Australia*, School of Management, University College of Southern Queensland, Toowoomba.

Cramer, J. (1989), *Pioneers, Politics and People: A Political Memoir*, Sydney: Allen & Unwin.

Crisp, L.F. (1961), *Ben Chifley: A Political Biography*, Sydney: Angus & Robertson.

--- (1965), *Australian National Government*, Melbourne: Longmans.

--- (1967), 'Central Coordination of Commonwealth Policy-Making: Roles and Dilemmas of the Prime Minister's Department', *Public Administration*, 26 (1).

--- (1978), *Australian National Government* 4th edn, Melbourne: Longman Cheshire.

--- (1990), *Federation Fathers*, Melbourne University Press.

Crossman, R.H.S. (1963), 'Introduction' to Walter Bagehot's, *The English Constitution*, London: Fontana.

--- (1972), *Inside View: Three Lectures on Prime Ministerial Government*, London: Cape.

Cumes, J.W.C. (1988), *A Bunch of Amateurs: the Tradegy of Government and Administration in Australia*, Melbourne: Sun Books.

Curnow, R. and H. Mayer (1968), 'Hunting the P.M. – Country Style', *Australian Quarterly*, 40 (4) March.

Cutler, L.N. (1980), 'To Form a Government', *Foreign Affairs*, 59 (1).

D'Alpuget, B. (1984), *Robert J. Hawke*, Ringwood: Penguin.

Daly, F. (1977), *From Curtin to Kerr*, Melbourne: Sun Books.

Donoughue, B. (1987), *Prime Minister: The Conduct of Policy Under Harold Wilson and James Callaghan*, London: Cape.

Dunleavy, P. and R. Rhodes (1990), 'Core Executive Studies in Britain', *Public Administration*, 68 (1).

Dunleavy, P., G.W. Jones and B. O'Leary (1990), 'Prime Ministers and the Commons: Patterns of Behaviour, 1868-1987' *Public Administration*, 68 (1).
Duthie, G. (1984), *I had 50,000 Bosses: Memoirs of a Labor Backbencher 1946-1975*, Sydney: Angus & Robertson.
Easthope, G. (1974), *A History of Social Research Methods*, London: Longman.
Eden, R. (1983), *Political Leadership and Nihilism*, Tampa: University Press of Florida.
Edwards, J. (1973), 'Political Scientists in Politics', Paper delivered at the Australasian Political Studies Association Conference.
Edwards, P. (1978), *Prime Ministers and Diplomats: The Making of Australian Foreign Policy 1901-1949*, Melbourne University Press.
Encel, S.(1974), *Cabinet Government in Australia*, 2nd ed., Melbourne University Press.
Finletter, T.K. (1945), *Can Representative Government Do the Job?*, New York: Reynal & Hitchcock.
Forward, F. (1977), 'Ministerial Staff Under Whitlam and Fraser', *Australian Journal of Public Administration*, 36 (2).
Freudenberg, G. (1977), *A Certain Grandeur: Gough Whitlam in Politics,* Melbourne: Macmillan.
Galligan, B. and J.R. Nethercote (eds) (1989), *The Constitutional Commission and the 1989 Referendum*, Canberra: Federalism Research Centre.
Halligan, J. (1987), 'Reorganizing Australian Government Departments', *Canberra Bulletin of Public Administration*, 52.
Hamer, D. (1979), 'Some Proposals for Senate Reform', in G. Hawker *et al., Working Papers on Parliament*, Canberra: Canberra CAE.
--- (1989), 'Australia's Commonwealth Parliament', *Legislative Studies*, 4 (2).
Hardin, C. (1974), *Presidential Power and Accountability: Towards a New Constitution*, Chicago University Press.
Hart, J. (1987), 'The President and His Staff', in Malcolm Shaw (ed.), *Roosevelt to Reagan: The Development of the Modern Presidency*, London: C. Hurst.
--- (1989), 'The End of Party Reform', in D.K. Adams (ed.), *Studies in U.S. Politics*, Manchester University Press.
--- (1991), 'President and Prime Minister: Convergence or Divergence?' *Parliamentary Affairs*, 44 (2).
Hasluck, P. (1980), *Sir Robert Menzies*, Melbourne University Press.
Hawker, G., R.F.I. Smith and P. Weller (1979), *Politics and Policy in Australia,* St. Lucia: University of Queensland Press.
Hazlitt, H. (1942), *A New Constitution Now*, New York: McGraw Hill.

Head, B.W. and A. Patience (eds) (1989), *From Fraser to Hawke: Australian Public Policy in the 1980s*, Melbourne: Longman Cheshire.

Henderson, P. (1986), *Privilege and Pleasure*, Sydney: Methuen Haynes.

Hertsgaard, M. (1989), *On Bended Knee: the Press and the Reagan Presidency*, New York: Schocken Books.

Horne, D. (1964), *The Lucky Country: Australia in the Sixties*, Ringwood: Penguin.

Howard, J. (1990), 'Reflections on the Cabinet Process', in B. Galligan, J.R. Nethercote and C. Walsh (eds), *The Cabinet and Budget Processes*, Canberra: Federalism Research Centre.

Howson, P. (1984), *The Life of Politics*, edited by D. Aitkin, Melbourne: Viking Press.

Hudson, W.J. (1986), *Casey*, Melbourne: Oxford University Press.

Hughes, C.A. (1976), *Mr Prime Minister: Australian Prime Ministers 1901-1972*, Melbourne: Oxford University Press.

Hughes, C.A. and J.S. Western (1972), 'Hunting the P.M.: The Sequel', *Australian Quarterly*, 44 (1).

Ingham, B. (1991), *Kill the Messenger*, London: Harper Collins.

Jaensch, D. (1989), *Power Politics: Australia's Party System*, Sydney: Allen & Unwin.

--- (1989), *The Hawke-Keating Hijack*, Sydney: Allen & Unwin.

Jennett, C. and R.G. Stewart (eds) (1990), *Hawke and Australian Public Policy*, Melbourne: Macmillan.

Jennings, P. (1991), 'Australia's Response and Role in the War', in Viberto Selochan (ed.), *The Gulf War Issues and Implications for Australia and Asia*, Bathurst: Crawford House.

Jordan, A.G. and J.J. Richardson (1987), *British Politics and the Policy Process*, London: Allen & Unwin.

Jupp, J. (ed.) (1984), *Ethnic Politics in Australia*, Sydney: Allen & Unwin.

--- (1988), 'The Defused Issues: Ethnic and Aboriginal Affairs' in I. McAllister and J. Warhurst (eds), *Australia Votes: The 1987 Federal Election*, Melbourne: Longman Cheshire.

Kelleher, S.R. (1987), 'Scrutinizing a Scrutiny', *Canberra Bulletin of Public Administration*, 52.

--- (1988), 'The Apotheosis of the Department of the Prime Minister and Cabinet', *Canberra Bulletin of Public Administration*, 54.

--- (1989), 'Departmental Secretary Appointments Observed', *Canberra Bulletin of Public Administration*, 58.

Kelly, P. (1984), *The Hawke Ascendancy*, Sydney: Angus & Robertson.

--- (1985), 'Leadership, Factionalism and the Prospects of the Hawke Government', *Canberra Bulletin of Public Administration*, 12 (2).

Kemp, D. (1973), 'A leader and a philosophy', in Mayer, H. (ed.) *Labour to Power*, Sydney: Angus & Robertson.

Kernell, S. (1986), *Going Public: New Strategies of Presidential Leadership*, Washington, DC: Congressional Quarterly Press.

Knight, J. and W.J. Hudson (1983), 'Parliament and Foreign Policy', *Canberra Studies in World Affairs*, No. 13 Department of International Relations, Australian National University.

La Nauze, J.A. (1965), *Alfred Deakin: A Biography*, Melbourne University Press.

Little, G. (1982), 'Fraser and Fraserism', *Meanjin*, 41 (3).

--- (1989), 'Leadership Styles: Fraser and Hawke', in B. Head and A. Patience (eds), *From Fraser to Hawke*, Melbourne: Longman Cheshire.

Lloyd, C.J. (1988), *Press and Parliament*, Melbourne University Press.

Lloyd, C.J. and G.S. Reid (1974), *Out of the Wilderness: the Return of Labor*, Melbourne: Cassell.

Macgregor Burns, J. (1963), *The Deadlock of Democracy*, Englewood Cliffs: Prentice Hall.

Mackintosh, J.P. (1962), *The British Cabinet*, London: Stevens.

Maddox, G. (1985), *Australian Democracy in Theory and Practice*, Melbourne: Longman Cheshire.

--- (1989), *The Hawke Government and Labor Tradition*, Ringwood: Penguin.

Mann, T.E. (ed.) (1990), *A Question of Balance: The President, the Congress and Foreign Policy*, Washington DC : The Brookings Institution.

Marsfield, H.J. (1989), *Taming the Prince: The Ambivalence of Modern Executive Power*, New York: Free Press.

Mayer, H. and R. Curnow (1968), 'Hunting the P.M.', *Australian Quarterly*, 40 (1).

McInnes, M. (1990), 'Public Sector Reform Under the Hawke Government: Reconstruction or Deconstruction?' *Australian Quarterly*, 62 (2).

Mediansky, F.A. and J.A. Nockels (1975), 'The Prime Minister's Bureaucracy', *Public Administration*, 34 (3).

--- (1981), 'Malcolm Fraser's Bureaucracy', *Australian Quarterly*, 53 (4).

Menzies, R.G. (1967), *Afternoon Light*, Melbourne: Cassell.

--- (1970), *The Measure of the Years*, London: Cassell.

Millar, T.B. (ed.) (1972), *Australian Foreign Minister: The Diaries of R.G. Casey 1951–60*, London: Collins.

--- (1978), *Australia in Peace and War: External Relations 1788-1977*, Canberra: Australian National University Press.

Mills, S. (1986), *The New Machine Men*, Ringwood: Penguin.

Nance, L. (1989), *Prime Ministers of Australia*, London: Bison Books.

Neustadt, R.E. (1960), *Presidential Power: The Politics of Leadership*, New York: John Wiley.

--- (1985), 'White House and Whitehall' in Anthony King (ed.), *The British Prime Minister*, 2nd ed., London: Macmillan.

Papadakis, E. (1990), 'Minor Parties, the Environment and the New Politics', in C. Bean, I. McAllister and J. Warhurst (eds), *The Greening of Australian Politics: The 1990 Federal Election*, Melbourne: Longman Cheshire.

Parker, D. (1990), *The Courtesans: The Press Gallery in the Hawke Era*, Sydney: Allen & Unwin.

Parker, R.S. (1980), 'Responsible Government in Australia', in P. Weller & D. Jaensch (eds), *Responsible Government in Australia*, Melbourne: Drummond.

Parkin, A. (1983), 'Party Organization and Machine Politics: the ALP in Perspective', in A. Parkin and J. Warhurst (eds), *Machine Politics in the Australian Labor Party* , Sydney: Allen & Unwin.

Pettifer, J.A. (1981), *House of Representatives Practice*, Canberra: AGPS.

Polsby, N.W. (1983), *Consequences of Party Reform*, New York: Oxford University Press.

Reid, A. (1971), *The Gorton Experiment*, Sydney: Shakespeare Head Press.

Reid, G.S. and M. Forrest (1989), *Australia's Commonwealth Parliament, 1901-88*, Melbourne University Press.

Renouf, A. (1980), *The Champagne Trail: Experiences of a Diplomat*, Melbourne: Sun Books.

--- (1986), *Malcolm Fraser and Australian Foreign Policy*, Sydney: Australian Professional Publications.

Roberts, M. (1976), 'Ministerial Advisors: A Background Paper', *Research Paper No. 6*, Canberra: RCAGA.

Robinson, D. (1985), *Reforming American Government: The Bicentennial Papers of the Committee on the Constitutional System*, Boulder Colorado: Westview Press.

Rossiter, C. (1963), 'President and Congress in the 1960s', in M.D. Irish (ed.), *Continuing Crisis in American Politics*, Englewood Cliffs: Prentice-Hall.

Sawer, G. (1963), *Australian Federal Politics and Law, 1929-1949*, Melbourne University Press.

Sawer, M. and M. Simms (1984), *A Women's Place: Women and Politics in Australia*, Sydney: Allen & Unwin.

Schneider, R. (1980), *War Without Blood: Malcolm Fraser in Power*, London: Angus & Robertson.

Scott, A. (1991), *Fading Loyalties*, Sydney: Pluto Press.

Seymour-Ure, C. (1990), 'TVs Impact on the Office of Prime Minister', in B. Hocking (ed.), *Australia Towards 2000*, London: Macmillan.

--- (1991), *The British Press and Broadcasting since 1945*, Oxford: Basil Blackwell.

Shaw, M. (1987), 'The Traditional and Modern Presidents', in M. Shaw (ed.) *Roosevelt to Reagan: The Development of the Modern Presidency,* London: C. Hurst.

--- (ed.) (1987), *Roosevelt to Reagan,* London: C. Hurst.

Simms, M. (1982), *A Liberal Nation,* Sydney: Hale & Iremonger.

--- (ed.) (1984), *Australian Women and the Political System,* Melbourne: Longman Cheshire.

Sinclair, I. (1982), 'Government, Parliament and Administration', in J.E. Nethercote (ed.), *Parliament and Bureaucracy,* Sydney: Hale & Iremonger.

Smith, C. (1990), *Presidential Press Conferences: A Critical Appraisal,* New York: Praeger.

Smith, H. (1988), *The Power Game,* London: Collins.

Smith, R.F.I. (1977), 'Ministerial Advisors: The Experience of the Whitlam Government', *Australian Journal of Public Administration,* 36 (2).

Souter, G. (1988), *Acts of Parliament,* Melbourne University Press.

Speakes, L. (1988), *Speaking out: Inside the Reagan White House,* New York: Charles Scribner.

St. John, E. (1969), *A Time to Speak,* Melbourne: Sun Books.

Stubbs, J. (1988), *Hayden,* Melbourne: William Heinemann.

Sundquist, J.L. (1986), *Constitutional Reform and Effective Government,* Washington, DC: The Brookings Institution.

Thompson, E. (1980), 'The "Washminister" Mutation', in P. Weller and D. Jaensch (eds), *Responsible Government in Australia,* Melbourne: Drummond.

Thrasher, F.M. (1927), *The Gang,* University of Chicago Press.

Toemesssen, R.C. (1971), Analysis of the Changing Basis of Australian Foreign Policy, Ph.D. dissertation, The American University.

Uhr, J. (1982), *Questions Without Answers,* Canberra: Australasian Political Studies Association.

--- (1984), '*Parliament and Administration in Australian Commonwealth Administration,* Canberra College of Advanced Education.

--- (forthcoming), 'Parliamentary Measures: Evaluating Parliaments' Policy Role' in I. Marsh (ed.), *Governing in the 90s,* Sydney: CEDA.

Vile, M.J.C. (1967), *Constitutionalism and the Separation of Powers,* Oxford: Clarendon Press.

Waller, K. (1990), '*A Diplomatic Life: Some Memories*', no. 6, Centre for the Study of Australia - Asia Relations, Brisbane: Griffith University.

Walter, J. (1980), *The Leader: A Political Biography of Gough Whitlam,* St. Lucia: University of Queensland Press.

--- (1986), *The Minister's Minders: Personal Advisors in National Government,* Melbourne: Oxford University Press.

--- (1988), 'Intellectuals and the Political Culture' in B. Head and J. Walter (eds), *Intellectual Movements and Australian Society*, Melbourne: Oxford University Press.

Weber, M. (1947), 'Politics as a Vocation', in H. Gerth and C.W. Mills (eds), *From Max Weber*, London: Routledge Kegan and Paul.

--- (1968), 'Parliament and Government in a Reconstructed Germany', Appendix 2 in G. Roth and C. Wittich (eds), *Economy and Society*, New York: Bedminster.

Weller, P. (1983), 'Do Prime Minister's Departments Really Create Problems?' *Public Administration*, 61 (1).

--- (1983), 'Transition: Taking over Power in 1983', *Australian Journal of Public Administration*, 42 (3).

--- (1985), *First Among Equals: Prime Ministers in Westminister Systems*, Sydney: Allen & Unwin.

--- (1989), 'Politicisation and the Australian Public Service', *Australian Journal of Public Administration*, 48 (4).

--- (1989), *Malcolm Fraser PM: A Study in Prime Ministerial Power in Australia*, Ringwood: Penguin.

Weller, P. and M. Grattan (1981), *Can Ministers Cope? Australian Ministers at Work*, Melbourne: Hutchinson.

Western, J.S. and C.A. Hughes (1983), *The Mass Media in Australia*, 2nd ed., St. Lucia: University of Queensland Press.

Whitlam, G. (1985), *The Whitlam Government 1972-1975*, Melbourne: Viking.

Whyte, W.F. (1943), *Street Corner Society*, University of Chicago Press.

Wilenski, P. (1979), 'Ministers, Public Servants and Public Policy', *Australian Quarterly*, 51 (2).

Winterton, G. (1986), *Monarchy to Republic: Australian Republican Government*, Melbourne: Oxford University Press.

Yeend, G.J. (1979), 'The Department of Prime Minister and Cabinet in Perspective' *Australian Journal of Public Administration*, 38 (2).

--- (1989), 'The Coordinating Role of the Department of Prime Minister and Cabinet', in M. Wood, C. Williams and C. Sharman (eds), *Governing Federations: Constitution, Politics, Resources*, Sydney: Hale and Iremonger.

INDEX

academic consultants, 52–3, 56, 62
Administrative Arrangements Act (1987), 41
Albinski, Henry, 164
Anthony, Doug, 16, 141
Asia-Pacific Economic Co-operation (APEC), 174
Attlee, Clement, 112, 126
Australia Party, 88
Australian Council of Trade Unions (ACTU), 3, 72, 73, 121–2
Australian Democrats, 101, 146, 206
Australian Labor Party (ALP): 3, 22, 35, 40, 44, 46, 47, 48, 66, 74, 75, 87, 90, 120, 122, 146, 147, 207, 208; caucus, 66, 72; economic policies, 142; federal executive, 73; foreign affairs, 175–8; President, 73
Australian Public Service Management Advisory Board, 41
Australian Security and Intelligence Organisation (ASIO), 104
Australian, New Zealand and United States Security Pact (ANZUS), 158, 174
Ayres, Phillip, 130

backbenchers, 68, 69, 70, 71, 72, 76, 195, 103, 104, 108, 146
Bagehot, Walter, 187
Barnard, Lance, 89
Barnett, David, 50, 51, 55
Barron, Peter, 56, 57
Barton, Edmund, 139, 156
Barwick, Garfield, 94, 105, 161, 162, 163
Beasley, Kim, 96
Berkeley, Humphrey, 188
Berry, Graham, 115
Block, David, 40–1
Blackburn, Doris, 143
Bowen, Lionel, 161
Britain: government, 29, 42, 44, 185–6, 207, 189; media and politics, 109, 112–13, 126, 132, 133–5; relations with Australia, 163
Brown, Allen, 30–3, 61
Bruce, Stanley, 18, 139, 141
Budd, Dale, 50, 51, 52, 55
budgets, 23–4, 145
Bunting, Sir John, 9, 14, 15–16, 17, 25, 31–5, 36, 44, 61
bureaucracy: academics' influence, 52–3; foreign policy role, 156, 167–75; politicisation, 41, 51; reform of, 39–42, 85, 173; staff, 44–6; values, 53;
Bury, Leslie, 162
Bush, George, 135, 200
Button, John, 90

cabinet: 5–27, 57, 80, 205–6; agenda of, 14, 15, 16, 18; department of Prime Minister and Cabinet, 34; bureaucratisation, 8, 43; committees of 11, 12–13, 14, 25, 165; foreign policy role, 156, 164–7, 171, 172; impact of media on, 110; ministers of, 8, 71, 191; procedures, 9, 10, 18, 23, 24, 25, 164; prime minister, 5, 205–6, 207; review of, 10; role of, 5, 26, 191; workload of, 5, 6–8, 43
cabinet committees: prime minister's, 11, vice-president's, 11, Expenditure Review, 12, 13; Monetary Policy, 12, 13, 16, 26; Wages Policy, 12; Co-ordination, 12, 16; Foreign Affairs and Defence, 16, 165; Security, 166
Cabinet Handbook, 9, 10
Cabinet Office, 8, 9, 10, 14, 16, 19
Cairns, Jim, 48

Calwell, Arthur, 138, 153
Callaghan, James, 133
Cameron, Clyde, 48, 78, 92, 94
Canada, government, 42
Carmody, Alan, 38
Carter, Jimmy, 131, 202
Casey, Richard, 160, 161, 162, 163, 167
caucus, role of, 78, 79
Charlton, Matthew, 139
Chifley, Ben: 1, 3, 31, 43–4, 61, 138, 210; cabinet of, 11, 13, 21, 24; foreign policy, 159, 162, 168; ministers, 23; parliament, 81, 86, 87–8, 92–3, 98–9, 102, 105–6; parties, 69, 79; the electorate, 138, 140, 144, 148, 150, 151, 152, 153; the media, 111, 116, 118, 123, 128–9, 136; Prime Minister's department, 29–30, 62–3; Treasury, 42;
Child, Joan, 95
Chipp, Don, 101, 147
Churchill, Sir Winston, 96, 112, 117–18, 126
Codd, Mike, 40–1, 58, 62
Cold War, 158, 177
Combe, David, 72
Commonwealth relations, 68, 163, 169
Connor, Rex, 48, 171
Constitution, Australia, 1, 82, 83, 84, 99, 100, 101, 204, 205, 156–7, 180, 204, 205; crisis, 183, 184; reform of, 105, 106, 107;
Conybeare, Chris, 58
Cook, Michael, 51–2, 139
Coolidge, Calvin, 153
Coombs Royal Commission, Report of, 104
Coombs, H.C., 44, 61
Cope, Jim, 94
Cormack, Magnus, 88
Cornwell, Elmer, 128
Cramer, John, 69, 70
Crean, Simon, 48
Crisp, L.F., 13, 68, 116, 159, 184
Crossman, Richard, 184, 185, 186, 187, 191, 194, 195, 197
Curtin, John, 3, 86, 87, 92, 115, 116, 139, 150, 153, 207

D'Alpuget, Blanche, 73, 122
Daly, Fred, 69
Deakin, Alfred, 115, 139, 156, 182
Dedman, John, 30, 60
Defence, department of, 168
Democratic Labor Party (DLP), 87, 88, 101, 146, 147, 206
Dibbs, George, 183
diplomacy, 158
Dorfman, Ron, 128
Douglas-Home, Sir Alec, 120
Drysdale, Alastair, 49, 51
Dumas, Lloyd, 43
Dunleavy, Patrick, 24

Economic Policy Advisory Council (EPAC), 40, 42–3
Edwards, John, 49
Efficiency Scrutiny Review, 41
Eggleton, Tony, 51, 74, 77, 126, 208
Eisenhower, Dwight, 202
elections: 44, 51, 73, 138–155; and the media, 110, 155, 192, 193
Electoral Commission, 91
electorate: safe seats, 139; structure of, 139, 141–43; voting patterns, 140; history of, 140, 142; issues and opinions, 147–8; gender differences, 143; demography, 143–45; political actors 145
Elliot, John, 73
Evans, Gareth, 23, 101, 161, 162, 174
Evans, Graham, 56, 58
Evatt, Dr H.V., 23, 103, 138, 161, 162, 163, 168, 176
External Affairs, department of, 168, 169

Fadden, Arthur, 2, 16, 32, 102, 139
federalism, 156, 209–10
Fisher, Andrew, 28, 139
Ford, Gerald, 131, 202
Forde, Frank, 2, 139
Foreign Affairs, department of: 35–6, 42, 158, 168, 170–1, 172; and Trade, 174
foreign ministers, 160–4
foreign policy: characteristics, 156, 157, 166, 171, 180–1; community and pressure groups, 180–1; domestication of, 178, 181; ideology, 175–7; pragmatism, 177–8; role of executive, 156, 157–8, 159–64, 181; role of parliamentary committees, 180; role of prime minister, 156, 158–9, 162, 166, 167–8, 181; the media, 181–1
Forrest, Martin, 82
France, government, 44
Fraser, Malcolm: 3, 22, 42, 67, 184; cabinet, 8, 10, 12, 13, 14, 15–16, 17, 19, 25; department of Prime Minister and Cabinet, 37–9, 51, 61, 62; development of prime ministership, 204, 206; foreign policy, 160, 161, 162, 163, 164, 165–6, 167, 171–3, 174, 176, 177, 179; parliament, 81, 89–90, 95; parties, 69, 71, 74, 75, 76, 77, 81, 89, 90, 95 208; the electorate, 138, 141, 143, 145, 147, 151, 153; the media, 111–12, 117, 119, 121, 122, 124–5, 127, 129–30, 134, 136; ministers, 16, 23; private office, 49–56, 58, 60, 62
Freeth, Gordon, 161, 162
Freudenberg, Graham, 68, 73,119, 120, 121, 126

Georgiou, Petro, 51
Gilmour, Sir Ian, 133
Gorton, John: 3, 44, 61; cabinet, 13–14, 19; development of prime ministership, 206; foreign policy, 162, 163, 164, 165, 167, 169–70, 171, 176–7, 179; parliament, 88, 104; parties, 70, 71, 75; Prime Minister's department, 34–5; the electorate, 144, 153; the media, 110–11, 119–20, 122, 124, 126, 130, 136
Government Information Unit (GIU), 127
Gulf war, 166, 175, 177, 179, 180

Haldeman, H.R., 131
Harries, Professor Owen, 53, 55, 172
Hart, John, 202
Harvey, Ron, 55
Hasluck, Sir Paul, 19, 161
Haupt, Robert, 47
Hawke, Robert: 1, 2–3, 40, 48, 56, 62, 67, 192, 194; cabinet, 12, 15, 17, 19, 25; foreign policy, 160, 161, 162, 163, 165–6, 173–5, 177, 179, 180; ministers, 22–3; parliament, 81, 90–92, 95, 101; parties, 67, 73, 74, 75, 78, 79, 207, 208; PMC, 39–42, 58, 61; private office, 56–60, 127; the development of the prime ministership, 203, 206; the electorate, 138, 143, 145, 147, 148, 151, 152–4; the media, 111–12, 122, 125, 127, 129, 131, 134, 135–6
Hayden, Bill, 90, 95, 138, 152, 161, 162, 173, 177
Heath, Edward, 112
Hewitt, Lennox, 31–34, 44, 61
Hewson, Dr John, 1, 73, 74, 52, 55–6, 138, 192
Higinbotham, George, 115
Hogg, Bob, 56, 57, 74, 208
Holloway, Sandy, 58
Holt, Edgar, 44
Holt, Harold: 3, 34, 44, 87, 97, 99; the electorate, 151, 153, 154, 155; foreign policy, 163, 169, 176; parliament, 87, 97, 99; the media, 111, 119, 121–2, 124, 125, 126, 130, 136

House of Representatives, 1, 89, 140, 143, 144, 192, 196
Howard, John, 44, 52, 73, 89, 138, 148, 155
Howson, Peter, 70
Hudson, W.J., 163, 178
Hughes, Billy: 43, 138, 139, 203; cabinet, 18, 24; the media, 126
Hyde, John, 95

Ingham, Bernard, 126, 127, 132, 134–5

Jones, Alan, 55
Johnson, Lyndon, 121, 135, 202
Janka, Leslie, 131

Keating, Paul: 8, 22, 111, 127–8, 136, 155, 192, 206
Kemp, Dr David, 49–50, 51, 52, 55, 56, 62
Kennedy, John F., 121, 202
Kerr, Sir John, 94, 105
Killen, James, 104, 180
Kissinger, Henry, 131
Knight, John, 178

Latham, Sir John, 139
leadership: 64–73, 76, 79, 81, 86, 87, 108, 192, 194, 197; accountability, 85, 98; executive, 83, 84, 85, 92; parliamentary, 84, 85, 88, 92, 107
Liberal Party: 20, 22, 33, 50, 54, 69, 71, 74, 76, 87, 95, 148, 208; foreign policy, 176–8; leaders, 78, 142
Little, Graham, 77
Lloyd, Clem, 192
Lynch, Phillip, 12
Lyons, Enid, 143
Lyons, Joe, 139, 203

Mackintosh, John, 185, 186, 187, 191, 197
McBride, Philip, 16
McEwen, John: 2, 16, 11, 141
McIntyre, Laurence, 169
McKell, William, 93
McMahon, William: 3, 13, 44; cabinet, 8; development of prime ministership, 203; foreign policy, 159, 162, 164, 165, 171, 176, 180; parliament, 88, 104; parties, 70; PMC, 35; the electorate, 141, 144; the media, 111, 120, 124, 129, 130, 136;
McMullen, Bob, 74, 208
media: 'door-stopping', 125, 129, 133; accountability, 109; elections, 110, 120, 132, 135, 137; effect on policy, 115, 181–2; freedom of, 116; impact of, 109–10, 111, 120, 132, 135–6; leaks to, 133–4; lobby system, 113; regulation of, 118, 125
Menadue, John, 36–8, 62
Menzies, Robert: 1, 2–3, 34, 44, 61; cabinet, 8, 11, 13, 15–16, 17, 19, 31; development of prime ministership, 203, 206; foreign policy, 160, 162, 163, 165, 166–7, 169, 176, 179; ministers, 16, 23; parliament, 81, 86–7, 92, 96, 97–100, 102, 103, 105–7; parties, 69–70, 74; Prime Minister's department, 31–3, 62; the electorate, 138, 140, 141, 143–5, 147, 150–4; the media, 111, 116–9, 123, 124, 125, 126, 129–30, 135, 136; Treasury, 42
Millar, T.B., 160
ministerial staff: 47–8; conflict with ministers, 48
ministers: 8, 16, 21, 22–3, 25, 71, 158
Missen, Alan, 95, 104
monarchy, opinions of, 148
Morley, John, 191, 192

Murdoch, Rupert, 120, 121, 133
Murdoch, Sir Keith, 117
Murphy, Lionel, 89, 94, 101

National Country Party: 11, 22, 141, 176;
National Crimes Authority (NCA), 104
National Economic Summit, 40
National Media Liaison Service (aNiMaLS), 127
Neustadt, Richard, 190, 191, 196, 197
Nixon, Peter, 16, 141
Nixon, Richard, 121, 124, 131, 197, 201, 202

Office of National Assessment (ONA), 42, 173

Packer, Kerry, 134
Page, Earle, 141
Paltridge, Shane, 16
Parker, Derek, 136
Parker, R., 184
Packer, Sir Frank, 119, 120
Parkes, Sir Henry, 115
Parliament: 67, 78, 85, 87; committees, 85, 88, 89, 96, 97, 103, 104, 180; conflict, 91, 94; executive and legislative powers, 82, 86, 92; foreign policy role, 156–7, 178–81; leaders, 76; question time, 110; reform of, 89, 90–2, 95, 96, 97, 98, 103, 104, 105
Parliament House: 1, 49, 110, 112, 113, 125; networks, 49, 62
parties: 67, 68, 71, 86; leaders, 66; executive, 96, 197; elections, 78, 79; foreign policy role, 156, 175–8; legislative responsibilities, 95; whips, 76, 77, 78
Peacock, Andrew, 22, 53, 74, 127, 138, 148,161, 162, 163, 164, 172, 206
Plimsoll, James, 169
political media, growth of, 109–10
Polsby, Nelson, 198
premiers' departments, 29
presidency: Australia's prospects, 183–201; structural differences, 185, 193, 195; functional differences, 196
press conferences, 128, 129–31
press gallery, 112, 113, 114, 115, 120, 122–5
press secretaries, 43, 126–7
Prime Minister and Cabinet, department of (PM and C): 21, 28–35, 35–42, 61–3; cabinet, 32, 34; administrative reform, 41; line departments, 37–8, 43; co-ordination of, 29–30, 33; economic policy and research section, 30, 32; foreign policy, 168–9, 172; influence of, 41, 42; internal conflict, 39; Policy Co-ordination Unit, 36–7; relations with private office, 51, 58, 59–60, 62–3; reorganisation of, 30–1, 38, 39–40; role and functions of, 29–30, 31–2, 35–6, 39, 40–2, 43; secretaries of, 29–30, 32, 33, 34, 42
Prime Minister's Department (see Prime Minister and Cabinet, department of)
Prime Minister's Office: changes in, 47, 52, 55; evaluation of, 55–6, 60–3; relations with PM and C, 51, 58, 59–60, 62; role and function, 47, 51, 52, 53, 60–1
prime ministers: accentuated role, 28, 30, 35, 53, 63, 136, 147, 155, 192, 204; as foreign ministers, 160, 170–1; attitudes to, 147; backbenchers, 78, 103, 104; briefing of, 20–1, 24, 43, 58, 207; cabinet, 5–27, 78, 90, 205–6, 207; cabinet committees, 11, 13, 90, 207; cabinet decisions, 15, 16; challenges to, 3, 22, 154, 206; compared with U.S. presidents, 186, 187, 188, 190–1, 202–3; control of cabinet, 17–23, 25–6;

department of Foreign Affairs, 170–1; electoral campaigns, 154, 193, 194; electorate, 138–155, 197, 206, 209, 210; executive and legislative responsibilities, 89–90, 92, 106–7, 194; foreign policy, 150, 156–82, 210; impact of media on, 109, 110, 111, 120; incumbents, 2–3; leadership, 64–73, 78, 175, 184, 192, 194; media, 109–37, 209; media manipulation, 121, 131–4, 137; media strategy, 114–15, 118, 136; ministerial responsibility, 105; ministers, 21, 25, 71, 77, 78; opposition leaders, 105, 106; parliament, 81–108, 193, 206–7, 208; parliamentary control, 81, 82, 83, 88, 91, 92; parties, 64–80, 206, 207–8; party presidents, 73; personal support, 43–4; policy co-ordination, 31, 35, 37, 210; political management, 81, 85, 90; political resources, 42–3; popularity, 151, 192, 193; power over foreign policy, 157, 167, 170–1, 173–4, 181, 182; power, 92–4, 100–3, 184, 186, 202–3, 210–1; premiers, 68; press conferences 115, 128–31; press gallery, 122–5; press office, 114, 123, 125, 127; press secretary, 115, 1256–8; pressure groups, 153; Prime Minister's department (see also PM and C), 33, 208–9; private office, 47–60, 62, 209; relations with foreign ministers, 160–4; role in foreign policy, 156, 158–9, 166, 167–8, 173–4; sensitive policy areas, 146; staff, 28–63,193; voter expectations, 145; Westminster system, 184
prime ministership: 2–3, 67, 70, 78, 79, 80, 185; development of, 202–11
Public Service Board, 31–2, 38, 41, 46, 48

Rae, Peter, 82, 104
Randall, Richard, 44
Rankin, Annabelle, 143
Rather, Dan, 121
Reagan, Ronald, 123, 131, 132, 134, 200, 202
Reid, Alan, 20, 68, 71, 139
Reid, George, 82
Renouf, Alan, 170, 172, 179
Reston, James, 133
Rhodes, Rod, 214
Richardson, Dennis, 58
Roosevelt, Franklin D., 202
Roosevelt, Theodore, 128
Rose, Professor John, 52, 55, 56
Rosevear, Sol, 103
Royal Commission on Australian Government Administration, 47

Sawer, Geoffrey, 86
Scullin, James, 115, 139
Senate: 1, 81, 87, 88, 91, 93, 95, 98, 99, 100, 101, 103, 104, 107, 146, 151, 183; elections, 146
Seymour-Ure, Colin, 109, 192
Shann, Keith, 169
Shaw, Malcolm, 202
Shepherd, M., 28
Sinclair, Ian, 96, 104, 141
Sinclair, Keith, 44
Slim, Sir William, 93
Snedden, Sir Billy, 49–50, 90, 95
Sorby, Bob, 57
South-East Asian Treaty Organisation (SEATO), 130, 158
Speakes, Larry, 132, 134
Spender, John, 23, 161, 162, 163
Staley, Tony, 50
state governments, 68
Stephen, Sir Ninian, 94
Strahan, Frank, 29, 30
Street, Tony, 161

Tangay, Dorothy, 143
Thatcher, Margaret, 112, 126, 133, 134–5, 194
Thrasher, Frederic, 64, 68
Townley, Athol, 16, 30
Trade, department of, 168
Treasury, 13, 26, 31–2, 42, 44, 47–8, 56, 210
Tronson, Darcy, 51
Truman, Harry, 202
Tudor, Frank, 139
Turner, Harry, 103

United States: Congress, 195, 196, 197, 198, 199, 200; presidency, 4, 110, 183–201, 189–90, 202, 205; media and politics, 109, 114, 121, 123, 125, 131–2, 133, 134, 136, 198

Vietnam war, 164, 179
Visbord, Ed, 56
voting: preferential, 145–6

Waller, Sir Keith, 36, 171
Walsh, Geoff, 57
Walsh, Professor Cliff, 52, 55–6
Walter, James, 68, 73
Ward, Eddie, 153
Washington, George, 148
Watson, John, 139
Watt, Alan, 169
Weber, Max, 83
Weller, Patrick, 66, 68, 75, 76, 78, 184
Wentworth, W.C., 103
Westminster system: 1, 156, 157, 164, 181, 183, 189; media in, 112–3, 114, 122–3, 136–7
White, Denis, 55
Whitlam, E.Gough: 3, 44, 48, 49, 61, 184; cabinet, 8, 11–12, 13, 17; electorate, 138, 140, 143–45, 147, 149, 151, 153; foreign policy, 35–6, 42, 157, 160, 162, 163, 164, 165, 167, 170–2, 174, 179; media, 111, 119, 120–1, 122, 125, 126, 128–9, 130, 136; ministers, 23; parliament, 81, 88–91, 94, 98–101, 105; parties, 72–3, 78, 207; PM and C, 35–7, 61; private office, 35–6, 47, 54, 55, 56, 58, 62; Wilenski, Peter, 47, 56, 62
Willesee, Don, 161, 163, 171
Willoughby, J.R., 44
Wilson, Roland, 44
Wilson, Harold, 44, 112
Wilson, Woodrow, 189
Withers, Reg, 100
Witney, Keith, 55
Wood, Ian, 88
Wran, Neville, 56
Wright, Reg, 88

Yeend, Geoffrey, 31, 38–40, 51, 58, 62